FLAME FROM AN OXFORD CLOISTER

Above: P.N.W. in 1901
Below: P.N.W. on sick leave, 1915

Above: In the U.S.A., 1924
Below: The Last Days at Cowley, 1933

FLAME FROM
AN OXFORD CLOISTER

The Life and Writings of
Philip Napier Waggett
1862 – 1939
Scientist, Religious
Theologian, Missionary, Philosopher
Diplomat, Author, Orator
Poet

BY JOHN NIAS

'God is powerful on both sides of every
pressure.'　　　P. N. WAGGETT
The Scientific Temper in Religion, p. 76

LONDON – THE FAITH PRESS

In Piam Memoriam

Matris et Patris

Violetae et Haroldi Nias

PRINTED IN GREAT BRITAIN
in 10 point Garamond type
BY THE FAITH PRESS LTD.
LEIGHTON BUZZARD

CURSUS VITAE

Born 27th February 1862

1862–1880 Childhood and youth. Charterhouse 1875

1880–1884 Oxford

    1884 First Class in Natural Sciences

    1885 Second Class in Theology

1885–1887 Christ Church Mission at Poplar

1887–1889 St. Pancras Parish Church

1889–1892 Missioner at Charterhouse in Southwark

    1889 Membership of Aristotelian Society

1892–1895 Novitiate at Cowley

    1895 Life Profession to S.S.J.E. at Cowley

1896–1899 Capetown

    1901 Publication of *The Age of Decision*

1901–1909 St. Edward's House, Westminster

    1902 Publication of *The Heart of Jesus* and *Is There a Religion of Nature?*

    1904 Mission of Help to South Africa

    1904 Publication of *Religion and Science*

    1905 Publication of *The Scientific Temper in Religion*

    1906 Publication of *The Holy Eucharist*

    1907 Publication of *Hope and Strength*

1909–1914 At Cambridge: St. Anselm's House and elsewhere

    1912 Publication of *Our Profession*

    1914 Appointed Hulsean Lecturer.

1914–1918 Army Chaplain in France and at Tidworth

1918–1920 Assistant Political Officer in Palestine

    1921 Hulsean Lectures delivered at Cambridge; Hon. D.D. at Oxford

    1922 Mission of Help to India

    1924 Lectures in the U.S.A.

    1924 Publication of Hulsean Lectures *Knowledge and Virtue*

    1925 Publication of *The Industry of Faith*

1927–1930 Vicar of Great St. Mary's (University Church) Cambridge

1930–1939 Invalid

Died 4th July 1939

CONTENTS

INTRODUCTION   *page* 9

   I. Family and Home Background   15

  II. Oxford 1880–4   20

 III. London 1885–92   25

 IV. Entry upon the Religious Life at
     Cowley 1892–6   47

  V. Capetown 1896–9   57

 VI. Interlude 1899–1901 and Westminster
     1901–9   74

 VII. Cambridge 1909–14   108

VIII. The War 1914–18   127

  IX. Palestine 1918–20   141

   X. In England, India and America 1920–5   165

 XI. A Characteristic Year—1926   191

 XII. The Last Active Years 1927–30;
     Illness 1930–9   201

LIST OF PUBLICATIONS   215

INDEX   218

INTRODUCTION

PHILIP NAPIER WAGGETT is described, in the only official biography of him which has hitherto been published apart from obituary notices in newspapers and periodicals, as 'a priest whom his Church delighted not to honour.' [1] It is not clear what honour this biographer (Sidney Dark) would have considered appropriate for Father Waggett, nor what body in the Church of England he is blaming—if he is blaming any—for not having conferred this honour upon him. These are academic questions, but this study of Waggett's life and writings claims to be nothing more than a filial attempt to redeem, at least in part, another dishonour to its subject: the fact that there has been until now no book about him. I say 'filial' attempt because I feel that is the relationship which has sprung up between myself and Father Waggett during these last two or three years in which I have been examining his words and deeds. I have become, in some small sense, a disciple of a great mind and have incurred a heavy debt, which the present volume does not go very far to discharge, to those who gave me this task which has involved spending happy and exhilarating hours in the presence of a holy man.

The Second World War began only three months after Philip Waggett died, and had it not been for this fact almost certainly his biography would have been written before now by someone who knew him in the flesh and in the spirit better than the present writer. I only met him once, and although I have read all his published writings there must be others still living who know the soul of the man better than I do. However, in these years round about 1960, which have seen the centenary of the publication of Darwin's *Origin of Species* and the tercentenary of the founding of the body which became the Royal Society, it may not be without interest to read the following account of the reasonings and prayers of an eminent member of the second generation of post-Darwinian Christian apologists. But this study has been written in the conviction that Father Waggett claims the attention of spiritual men of the 1960s as a person whose life and

[1] *Dictionary of National Biography*, 1931–40, p. 883.

work ought to be known—quite apart from the interest which his story will arouse in those who are students of the evolution of methods in Christian apologetic or in those who are old enough to remember something of the fame of this most widely known of all the Cowley Fathers.

The definition of the word 'saint' is still far from clear, and probably it is best that it should remain so. Some say that the title is due to all Christian people inasmuch as St. Paul addressed the whole Church in some particular place with the name; others that only those possessing outstanding holiness and sanctity can rightly be thus described. A large number of those who knew Philip Waggett—and I have met many of them and talked with them for many hours—are agreed that they would not instinctively apply the description to him in the second sense. For all his great gifts of mind, expression and personality, including his flashes of the deepest spiritual insight, he remained entirely and delightfully a human being; and those who would recall his memory in a way to do him and his ideals the best service would not allow this fact to be forgotten. He did not suppress what Jungians call his 'shadow side'; and by this is not meant something sinister but the part of our nature which is on the ground.

Waggett's life story reveals that from time to time he experienced quite severe 'trough' periods during which depression, accompanied by considerable physical pain, assailed him. The most pronounced of these low periods were on his return from South Africa in 1899, his time at Cambridge 1909–14 and to a certain extent his second Cambridge period 1927–30. But the tendency to feel under a cloud appears on a number of other occasions. This means that the brilliant Waggett who scintillated at public gatherings and who enjoyed his triumphs was not that dullest of all figures, the subject of a 'success story.' He had congenital defects of temperament which had to be carried about as a burden which might at any time nearly crush him. These episodes provide insights to his nature which should assist those who would judge Philip Waggett to be a really great man.

The 'stories' about a remarkable man, as has been said many times, may often give a truer picture of that man than accurate historical reports of him and his words. Father Waggett was a person around whom story-telling wove a considerable legend.

We hear of his appreciation of the delights of the table. Who was it who overheard a certain padre in a restaurant in Rouen early in 1915 saying: 'Now my dear So-and-So, the present state of things makes it quite clear that it is not merely permissible but obligatory that we should have a bottle of champagne with this meal'? And there are legends—not altogether discredited even at Cowley—of his having a different gold fountain pen for every day of the week. Those who did not understand the soul of this priest were apt to be judicial when they noticed the beautifully cut silk cassock which he occasionally wore, thinking it to be out of accord with the austerities exemplified by Father Benson. Father O'Brien, S.S.J.E., told me, with a chuckle, that he once overheard Father Waggett murmuring to Father Spence Burton (now Bishop of Nassau) as the latter was helping Waggett to get his bag packed in time for the train which was to take him somewhere to carry out a preaching engagement: 'Don't forget this and that because I must live up to the reputation I have of being one of the more *dressy* of the Cowley Fathers.' Some forms of holiness, not only those which call themselves Puritan, do fail to take account of the real humanity of men and forget that we need not

. . . strive to wind ourselves too high
For sinful man beneath the sky.

Not so the holiness of Father Waggett—though in this respect the following pages may be said to reveal some of the defects of his qualities. And who will dare to pronounce that he was not the greater man, and the more holy, for it?

If the reader has the patience to work through these chapters, and will consider Philip Waggett's competence as a scientist, his vision as a philosopher, his gifts as a poet (and that not only in verse), his love of souls, his endurances as an army chaplain and slum priest, his work as a political officer in the Middle East, his social gifts and his inner humility—in short what the Bishop of Nassau has called 'a complex and brilliant personality like an elaborately cut diamond'—he will see that the time is ripe for his memory to be recalled before all his contemporaries have passed with him off the present stage and before his successors have had time to grow up hearing too vague a reputation of him. He will also believe that the Public Orator at Oxford (Dr. A. D. Godley of Magdalen) was not being the rhetorical declaimer he sometimes is when, on presenting Waggett for admission to a doctorate in Divinity in 1921, he read the citation which follows this introduction.

I wish to record my gratitude to the many people who have helped me in the production of this book, especially the following. Miss Joan Shaxby of Oxford did much preliminary work on Father Waggett's life and letters and I am more indebted to her than I like to think for the groundwork of the book. Professor Austin Duncan-Jones gave much help. The present Father Superior at Cowley, Father Dalby, s.s.j.e., and other members of the Society of St. John the Evangelist, notably Fathers O'Brien and Hill, gave me their full support and much personal kindness and hospitality and a great deal of practical help. Members of Father Waggett's family, particularly Mrs. Robert Aitken and Mr. G. Freire-Marreco, have given their consent and encouragement. Many other friends of Father Waggett, among whom I would specially mention Sir Will Spens, c.b.e., the late Revd. Michael Champneys, Bishop John C. H. How, d.d., and the Revd. A. G. Kayll, helped me with reminiscences. For parts of the Palestine period I am indebted to an informant who wishes to be anonymous, to Colonel Sir Archer Cust, k.c.b. (who was with Waggett on Gen. Money's staff at that time) and to the Ven. C. Witton-Davies, Archdeacon of Oxford, for criticisms of that chapter. The Revd. Professor F. L. Cross, d.d., of Christ Church gave me some advice on the parts of the book which deal with the science and religion controversies. The Revd. A. L. M. Arnold, o.g.s., Vicar of Cowley St. John, allowed me the use of a quiet room in his house without which the book could scarcely have been written at all. I am very grateful to the Revd. C. E. Goshawk, Rector of Fifield Merrymouth, Oxon, for preparing the index.

The title of the book has been chosen to suggest that the red hair of Father Waggett, which he shared with his surgeon brother, and which retained its bright hue well beyond middle age— making him easily distinguishable among the more venerable looking grey heads of the other Cowley Fathers—was a symbol of the light and energy which his personality radiated in many parts of the world.

J.C.S.N.

Ramsden Vicarage, Oxford. May 1960

Citation of the Revd. P. N. Waggett on his Admission to the Degree of Doctor in Divinity at Oxford in 1921

Theologia studia cum philosophicis e prima Universitatis nostrae origine semper apud nos arctissime esse conjuncta nemo ignorat; neque nunc minus id fit, sed has disciplinas alteram altera illustrari atque corroborari res ipsa et doctrinae ratio quotidie demonstrat. Est igitur optimo sensu Oxoniensis et Oxoniensibus honorandus qui hanc discendi et docendi viam antiquitus probatam sequitur; id quod hic sedulo facit quem ad vos adduco. Postquam enim prima juventa evolvendis naturalis quam vocant scientiae arcanis vel primarios honores adeptus erat, mox idem ad theologiam conversus quam habet in investigando diligentiam et in praedicando eloquentiam eo semper intendit ut collatis inter se diversissimi generis studiis utrique lucem offunderet. Atque si hoc tantum fecisset, erat jam quem et propter ingenium et propter finem quem sibi proposuerat ornare deberemus; nunc homo versatilis non modo iis rebus insistitur quae ad humanitatem et Musas pertinent, sed cum reipublicae tempora ad militiam et castra ab ecclesiarum cura et scriniis avocavissent, quantum in eo erat, patriae laborantis commodis inserviit. Testatur Gallia, in qua fidei Xtianae veritatem ne inter arma quidem non valere praeceptis et exemplo docebat; testatur Syrorum civitas longo Marte commota, mox ducibus nostris auctoribus ab hoc milite eodem et clerico sapientissime ad pacem reducta. Quid quaeritis? eum habetis, cujus sive mores sive eloquentiam sive rerum difficillimarum administrationem respexeritis, perpetuus vitae tenor numquam non aliquid in se habuit quod alumnum nostrum et jam ante nobis probatum huic Universitati commendare deberet. Itaqe praesento vobis virum reverendum Philippum Napier Waggett, ex Aede Xti, Artium Magistrum, ut admittatur ad gradum Doctoris in Sacra Theologia honoris causa.[1]

[1] 'Theology and Philosophy, as every one knows, have here from the very beginning of our University been intimately connected. At the present time, as much as ever, fact and theory daily show that these

studies derive light and strength from each other. Accordingly he who pursues such a course of learning and instruction, that has stood the test of time, is in the best sense of the word an Oxonian, and to be honoured by Oxonians. The man I now bring before you assiduously performs this task. During his first years here he won outstanding distinction in investigating the mysteries of Natural Science. Next he turned to Theology and, with his characteristic industry in research and eloquence in speech, he sought by the comparison of two contrasted branches of knowledge to illuminate both. This would have been enough to demand our praise for one who displayed such outstanding ability and such laudable aims; but his versatility was not confined to academic pursuits; in the Great War his country called him from church and library to active service; and his service was whole-hearted. In France, by word and example he showed that Christian truth does not lose its validity even amid the clash of arms. In Syria, both as soldier and chaplain, he gave wise help to our generals in restoring to peace a country distracted by years of conflict. In short, when we consider his character, his eloquence, his practical ability in face of difficulties, his whole career, we constantly see good grounds for our University to welcome a son who had years before won her approval. I present the Reverend Philip Napier Waggett, M.A., Christ Church, for admission to the honorary degree of D.D.'

The present Public Orator, Mr. A. N. Bryan-Brown of Worcester College, to whom I am indebted for this translation, remarks 'Of course Natural Science (in embryo) used to be called Natural Philosophy, and perhaps "Science" should be put for "Philosophy" in the first line.'

CHAPTER I

Family and Home Background

DOCTOR JOHN WAGGETT, the father of the subject of this study, was born in 1818 and spent the full forty years of his active working life as a family doctor in the very best old tradition. He was of the type of general practitioner, so very rare at the present time because of the changed conditions under which doctors have to live and work, who was loved and trusted by many of his patients' families to the third generation. Trained at University College Hospital and at the University of Edinburgh he became in 1841 a member of the Royal College of Surgeons of England and in 1842 received the degree of M.D. at Edinburgh. He was also an Edinburgh gold medallist. He was a fellow student and friend of Sir William Jenner and Sir William Ferguson and for a time a pupil of the famous surgeon Robert Liston. As soon as he became qualified Dr. Waggett settled in Kensington and he worked in general practice in that neighbourhood for the whole of his active life until he retired in 1884. There are extant references in periodicals and letters of the period to the great success of his work which was the result of a combination of ability, skill in personal relationships and the gift of inspiring confidence in his patients. It is said that Dr. Waggett distinctly disliked public life, but he was usually ready to help a good cause and he accepted appointment as consultant to one or two institutions in the neighbourhood. In 1855 he was asked by the Government to write a report on the recent epidemic of cholera which was published with the title *Observations on Cholera.*

There is no evidence of any marked party affiliations in the religious life of Philip Waggett's father—only that of a humble-hearted man of God devoted to his family and to the faithful carrying out of the responsibilities of his profession. From the paternal side of his background, though, Philip did no doubt inherit scientific competence, the power of easy dealings with all kinds of people, social gifts valuable in contacts with distinguished persons and the manner of authority.

In 1846 Dr. Waggett married Miss Florence Blechynden Whitchurch. It is recorded that Mrs. Waggett had the appearance of a dark and slender Norman. She was descended from a family of Non-jurors and professed a strong churchmanship, attributed to this fact, which she impressed upon her large family. As a boy it made a great impression on Philip Waggett to receive from his mother the gold cross of one of her Non-juror forbears. The combination of the two inheritances goes a long way towards explaining the general shape of his mind and instincts.

Philip Napier Waggett was born on 27th February 1862 at 4 Stanley Terrace, Kensington. His second name came from his godfather Admiral Napier and perhaps something of the service tradition entered his life at this point. Philip was the second son of his parents to survive infancy, the first boy having died when very young, and he had six sisters and one brother (John Francis who died in 1908) older than himself and one brother only (Ernest Blechynden) younger than himself. There is little to record of the elder brother chiefly because he died at the relatively premature age of 57. He had, however, in that time attained a certain distinction in the legal profession, having been called to the Bar in 1876 and eleven years later he published a treatise on the law relating to letters patent for inventions.

Philip's younger brother, Ernest Blechynden Waggett, who was born in 1866 and died in 1939, only six months before him, however, reached what might be judged as the outstanding eminence of the three. He took a First in the Natural Sciences tripos at Pembroke College, Cambridge, in 1887 and after a brilliant career at St. Bartholomew's Hospital was elected assistant surgeon at the London Throat Hospital in 1896. In 1910 he was appointed surgeon-in-ordinary to T.R.H. Prince and Princess Christian. Brilliant surgical feats in 1912 brought him into great prominence. He had been made President of the United Services Medical Society in 1911, and he took a prominent part about this time in the movement to establish universal military service in this country. Very distinguished war service with the R.A.M.C. from 1914–18 included his being three times mentioned in despatches and the award of the D.S.O. The setting up of the R.A.M.C. memorial window in Westminster Abbey was largely the result of his exertions. He was an amateur artist and a sportsman. Towards the end of his life (1933) he was obliged to have both of his legs amputated and, as a result of the suffering he endured at this time, he contributed to the *British Medical Journal* in 1935 an article entitled *Criteria of Intolerable Pain* which, though intended solely for his professional colleagues, created a considerable stir in the daily press. In 1931 he was made C.B.E.

The marriages of Philip's elder brother and sisters all took place when he was still a schoolboy and so, when his nephews and nieces were born, they were not very far removed from his own age group and he took the keenest interest in their happiness. His great gifts of affection found exercise in this young circle very early in his life and, having grown then, spread themselves later to enfold a vast company of friends far outside his own natural family and what was to become his spiritual family—the Society of St. John the Evangelist.

Dr. Waggett spent the last twenty-five years of his life in retirement at Bournemouth and after his wife's death in 1902 his daughters Marian and Katharine stayed there with him until his own death, at the age of nearly 91, on 2nd November 1909. The picture which forms the reredos in the chapel of the Holy Name in the conventual church at Cowley commemorates Dr. Waggett and his wife.[1] Philip's devotion to his parents is shown by his dedication of his first published work (*The Age of Decision* 1901) to his 'carissimi' father and mother. What has been held to be his best book (*The Scientific Temper in Religion* 1905) bears a dedication to his father; and his spiritual debt to his mother's inner life is expressed in his dedication of his Holy Week addresses at St. Paul's Cathedral in 1901 which were published as *The Heart of Jesus.*

'To my dear and most loving Mother, by whose side I first took part in the Devotion of the Three Hours, and from whose lips I learned the Name which is above every Name, the holy, saving, and ever-blessed Name of JESUS.'

Of the four youngest Waggetts, Marian, Katharine, Philip and

[1] A window in St. Stephen's, Bournemouth commemorates their daughter Florence, who married Dr. E. C. Seaton.

Ernest, only Ernest was married, but they all kept up a remarkably close relationship between each other throughout their long lives. It is noteworthy that when the quartet began to break up it was very quickly all gone. Ernest died in January 1939, Philip in July of the same year and both Marian and Katharine went the next year. Echoes of the family language appear in Philip's letters even in the years when he was most preoccupied. Ernest and Philip were bound together through their interest in, and aptitude for, natural science, and it must not be supposed that Ernest profited any less than Philip from his mother's spiritual guidance. There is record of a happy remark made in later years by Ernest to Mr. Herbert Tilley [2] : 'I teach my brother religion and he teaches me science.'

Surviving correspondence reveals that the gentle, beautiful Marian was more especially devoted to her younger brother, while there was a very strong bond of sympathy between Philip and the fiery Katharine with her keen, cultivated intellect. From the time of Philip's leaving home in early manhood, almost until the end of his active days, he and Katharine kept up a voluminous correspondence exchanging letters several times a week. To his sister he confided as much as could be told of his doings, his hopes and plans and something of his inner spiritual life. Whenever he needed books or anything else for his work it was Katharine who went shopping for him. If papers were to be stored it was she who kept them. In return for all this she received a deep sympathy and understanding from her brother and he gave her much valuable advice in the difficulties which arose in connection with her various good works.

Mr. O. H. Latter, for many years an assistant master at Charterhouse, records recollections of the two 'red-haired brothers' at the school. Besides specializing in natural science they both entered fully into the general life of the school. It was at Charterhouse that Philip laid the foundations of his wide knowledge of English literature and of several modern languages. He entered Charterhouse in the Summer Quarter of 1875 and was first in Daviesites, then in Saunderites (Dr. Haig Brown's house). Athletics do not

[2] President, at one time, of the Laryngological and Otological Sections, Royal College of Medicine.

seem to have interested him much, unlike his brother who excelled in this direction, and he took almost no part in school games. This exposed him to a certain amount of good natured chaff which he accepted in the spirit in which it was given, recalls Mr. Latter, who was contemporary with both the Waggetts as a boy in Saunderites. Philip should have regarded himself as fortunate that the veneration of athleticism in those days did not cause him to be the object of more malicious ragging : but it was probably because of his lack of interest in games that he was not made a monitor until his last Quarter, and that Mr. Latter's impression is that 'he had little influence in his house.' This is an interesting fragment of the early history of one who was to be so magnetic a personality in his later life.

CHAPTER II

Oxford 1880–4

IN 1880 Philip Waggett went up to Christ Church with a school leaving exhibition in Natural Science. He won the Holford Exhibition (a close award for Carthusians) and did excellent work for the schools, taking in 1883 one of the most brilliant Firsts of his year with Biology as his special subject. In after years, when writing and lecturing on the subject of science and religion— work which made a substantial contribution, in those days of open antagonism, to the healing of the breach between the two—he recalled Professor Mosely's insistence, when teaching morphology in the University Museum, that every student should handle the evidence for himself (*The Scientific Temper in Religion*, p. 52). There is an extant photograph of Philip in his undergraduate days doing precisely this—handling the evidence for himself. It is a group of his fellow biologists each holding one of the museum skeletons or other properties in a slightly disrespectful attitude. The photograph is of Professor Mosely's class [1] and Philip stands to one side looking very youthful—as he continued to do well into middle age—contemplating his specimen with fascinated pride and the newly acquired seriousness of the university man.

At Oxford riding seems to have been the form of exercise which he liked most and he became a good horseman. This was an accomplishment which was to prove useful later on when he was an army chaplain in France and as a means of joining in the social and sporting activities of that wide circle of friends whom he came to regard as being part of his 'flock.' He used to say that riding had provided him with his only experience of being consciously very near death—on an occasion when his girths

---

[1] There is a story of an old University Museum servant, who remembered Waggett, being shown this photograph years later and saying ruefully: 'And to think that a gentleman like that should have left us for the Church!'

slipped and he was dragged along the ground with the horse's hooves only just above his head.

The conditions of university life began to provide just the scope which Philip's brilliance and his charming personality needed for him to fulfil himself. He made many friends at the House and a real place for himself in the social life of his contemporaries. In those early days, as later on, he appreciated elegance and enjoyed the luxuries of life and at one time he seems to have moved in a rather expensive set. One of the acquaintances which began in these days and ripened into a lifelong friendship was that with James Adderley who had come up in 1879 to read history. In his reminiscences Adderley says of Waggett, 'I little thought when I used to nod "Good morning" to the young science student as he passed through Peckwater that there went one of the strongest personalities whom I was to reckon as my friend in the near future. "The cleverest man I know," was said of him by one who knows most of the great men of the day . . .'

Scattered remarks in letters to Katharine show that Philip kept in touch with friends of undergraduate days long after he had gone down and in one such letter he refers to a Censor's dinner at the House—probably on the occasion of his taking his M.A.— at which Adderley, Stephen Paget and other 'particular friends' not specified were present.

All this time Philip seems to have been in a good deal of un- certainty about what his future work should be. He clearly had a boyhood attraction to Holy Orders but many changes of experience were going to be necessary before his vocation became established. His father had been keeping a kindly watch on the boy's mind as these questions came up in it, and it seems that he had even allowed him to go up to Oxford preserving the idea of ordination at the back of his mind. In a letter to Katharine dated 24th August 1900 he refers to all this :

'. . . our own dear Father for many years did not encourage any idea of my being ordained—and I think that may be specially right with regard to Holy Orders—and I had quite the idea all the while I was at Charterhouse that it was *quite* impossible for me to be ordained, and the only question was between medicine and civil engineering.

'It was only *after* I had left school that Father (who no doubt had been watching sympathetically) revealed to me *to my immense surprise* that it was *possible* to reopen the subject and we went afterwards to

St. Leonard's to do so—and in the square garden of some square there after immense thinkings the conclusion was arrived at that I might go to Oxford.'

In any case the years spent working in the biological laboratories, in which Philip showed such outstanding ability, were to give him magnificent equipment to prepare him for an important part of his priestly ministry. In his undergraduate days his mind must certainly have been open all the time to the possibility of a call to ordination and this would have kept him alert to religious influences surrounding him at the time. There was no lack of significant development of religious thought in the Oxford of his day.

In 1882, two years after Waggett had matriculated, Dr. Pusey died and brought to an end a long period of retirement during which he had remained the leader of the Oxford Movement, but Canon Liddon had been its mouthpiece. Waggett was soon to know Liddon well. With the death of Pusey a group of younger Oxford dons, who had become heirs to the tradition of the Movement and who were destined to reshape it to meet the needs of the second generation, stepped forward and assumed the leadership and began to have a large following among the young intellectuals of the next few years. From 1875 the 'Holy Party,' led by Gore and including Illingworth, Scott-Holland, Talbot, Francis Paget and Aubrey Moore had been meeting together in country rectories, chiefly at Illingworth's rectory at Longworth, Berks, and conferring together to work out an Anglican theology to meet the demands and intellectual challenges of the day. The early tractarians had undertaken the task of re-exploring first principles and their work had been limited to the renewal of personal religion and the restoration of the ordered beauty of worship. But now a Catholic theology was needed to face the claims of Biblical criticism, Hegelian philosophy and Darwinian biology. Talbot had written in 1873 [3] :

'A Catholic theology utterly fixed in its great central principles and in many of their corollaries, yet ever yielding up new meanings, even from its central depths, in the light of other knowledge and human development. Such a theology, and at the same time a Church system, unchanging in one sense, yet elastic in another—and these two together capable of

[3] From *Edward Stuart Talbot* by Gwendolen Stephenson, 1936, p. 56.

22

laying hold upon the future, its movements, questions, temptations, advantages, discoveries: this is what we want.'

The main outcome of these aspirations was the publication in 1889 of the volume of essays known as *Lux Mundi* : and the principles which were to be enunciated in that book were all being hotly debated in Oxford at just the time when Waggett was an undergraduate. In 1884 Pusey House was opened as a memorial to the old tractarian leader. It had Gore as its first Principal and its objects were the promotion of theological research, securing able teachers of theology and providing clergy who could be friends and advisers of the junior members of the university. In the early days, as frequently since, large numbers of undergraduates flocked to the house and it was a very powerful influence.

The problem of the relation of science to the Christian faith was the great living theological issue of the time and Waggett was to make this subject the chief field of his study so soon as he had finished mastering the technicalities of one branch of knowledge. He may, perhaps, have heard Gore's lectures to undergraduates on the subject in 1881 when the latter was Vice-Principal of Cuddesdon. This exposition was regarded as marking an important stage in the discussion. He may also have heard the Bampton Lectures for 1884 on the same topic by Frederick Temple, then Bishop of Exeter. At the same time as all this academic work there was a growing consciousness among theologians of the need for social action. Scott Holland was the leading champion of this and the formation of the Christian Social Union in 1889 was to mark the definite linking of the Catholic movement with enterprises for social improvement of many kinds. Waggett came strongly under the influence of all these streams of thought.

After taking his First in Natural Sciences in 1884, Waggett stayed up another year reading for the Honours School of Theology as a pupil of Scott Holland. In this school he took a second class in 1885 after only a year's work, having been told in the Viva Voce examination that he only missed being placed in the first class because he did not know his Bible well enough! Scott Holland is said to have remarked that Waggett's brain was the quickest he had ever known. A great and deepening friendship sprang up between pupil and tutor, enduring till Holland's death in 1918. Waggett wrote in 1918:

'There was a certain sternness. You remember, at Christ Church, Holland's white face when some disturbance was forward which we thought innocent enough. There was a fire under that geniality, the geniality which sometimes led people to think that he was tolerant of real mischief.

'No man could be more tender with those who failed and stumbled; no man was more conscious of infirmity and fault in himself. No man could be gentler with the largest possible transgressions in a multitude or in an individual. But speak a word in the sense that failure did not matter, that failure might not be failure, that transgression might do no harm, that we might in some degree unclasp the armour of holiness or put aside a demand of the great law: and there was a new note in Holland's voice.

'He was intolerant of every compromise of the abstract claim of right. He was intolerant also of every compromise of the abstract claim of reason' (*Henry Scott Holland,* ed. Stephen Paget, 1921, p. 135).

It was probably to Holland that Waggett owed his introduction to Gore and F. E. Brightman at Pusey House and to Talbot and Aubrey Moore at Keble. Many years later, in the preface to *Knowledge and Virtue* his Hulsean Lectures published in 1924, he acknowledged the 'unwearied kindness of many years' of Brightman. Aubrey Moore died in 1890; but the friendship with the others deepened as the years went by.

Holland was greatly interested in the Christ Church Mission in Poplar which had been founded in 1881 and was later, in 1914, to become the parish of St. Frideswide's, Poplar. His personal influence over Waggett must have played a large part in the latter's decision, so soon after leaving Oxford, to seek work in the East End of London. He did so with a tremendous conviction about his ministry and with intellectual and personal equipment which was sure to lead him to play an influential part amongst the men and movements of his generation. James Adderley remarked: 'When Aubrey Moore passed away it was instinctively felt that Philip was the only man who could succeed to his position in the Church as its best apologist on the side of science and theology.'

CHAPTER III

London 1885–92

THE Christ Church Mission in Poplar was one of a number in the East End founded in connection with public schools and Oxford and Cambridge colleges about this time. During the episcopate of Bishop Blomfield of London from 1828 to 1868 two hundred churches and nearly as many schools had been built in the East End to provide for the spiritual and educational needs of the rapidly increasing population which had been spreading that way since the beginning of the century. To Bishop Jackson, Blomfield's successor from 1868 to 1885, fell the enormous task of staffing and maintaining these new foundations, and in this work he had the assistance of Walsham How who was consecrated suffragan with the title of Bishop of Bedford. Walsham How vigorously encouraged the 'adopting' of parishes by schools and colleges and the tendency, common among university men of the 'sixties and later, to spend periods during vacations at the missions and to study social services and social conditions in the East End.

Luke Paget was appointed the first head of the Christ Church Mission in 1881 and was given charge of a district carved out of neighbouring parishes which eventually, in 1914, became the new and independent parish of St. Frideswide's, Poplar. It must not be imagined that the surroundings were utterly grim and sordid, as one is apt to suppose when thinking of working class areas in late-Victorian England. Sir James Paget told his son that he did not pity him at all on account of his circumstances. Luke Paget had gone up to Christ Church in 1872, had been curate of St. Andrew's, Wells Street, from 1877–80, and Vice-Principal of the Leeds Clergy School from 1880–1. He was later to become Bishop of Chester; his brother Francis was successively Dean of Christ Church and Bishop of Oxford. Luke's wife describes the scene at Poplar in her biography of her husband (*Henry Luke Paget* by Elma K. Paget, 1939, p. 87):

25

'the splendid width of the East India Dock Road, with dock gates and shipmasts at the end of it: and Poplar Church, and the recreation ground, and the rows of nice houses and . . . tokens of foreign travel and seafaring life, the flying fish in bottles . . . the Oriental curiosities which used to adorn some of our windows.'

The first 'hiving-off' centre which marked the beginning of the Christ Church Mission's progress towards parochial independence was established at 14 Lodore Street. This was nothing more than a four-roomed cottage which provided a meeting place for all the activities of the Mission. The upper floor was occupied by the caretakers and the ground floor rooms were used for services, Sunday School and clubs and meetings of all kinds. The place was always crowded to capacity for the Sunday evening service.

Hither came Waggett as a new member of the staff in December 1885. He, too, had several times spent parts of his vacations at the Mission, so on arrival as a new curate he was not a complete stranger to the place. He was ordained deacon at Advent this year and priest twelve months later, both at the hands of Frederick Temple who had only just become Bishop of London. In 1931 Luke Paget recalled Waggett's arrival upon the scene at Poplar, 'First as a very smart young layman, then as deacon, and in due time as priest. Looking back, I can hardly imagine anything more delightful than his mind, his temper, his spirit in those early days of his wonderful life. The seriousness, the fun, the depth, the lightness of his words and his doings! We recognize them all in his later life and work. But you will easily understand their charm and attractiveness in those early days : and somehow Poplar felt it.'

Waggett was soon drawing the faithful Katharine into his interests at Poplar and there is a letter (27th March 1886) in which he asks for her assistance 'to raise about £2 to place the Band of Hope in a sound financial position. But you *mustn't* give me any yourself.' At Christmas that year he was proposing to spend some funds which she had collected on a Punch and Judy entertainment and tea for the Band of Hope children which would 'really go further than something useful.' How familiar all this sounds to any one who has been told to 'take an interest in the children' at the beginning of a first curacy! There is a letter in which he expresses the hope, very hesitantly put, that Katharine herself might some day come to the Mission to work. In another letter to her, Philip says that he is having difficulty in managing the boys' club, and he attributes this to 'a constitutional dislike of high spirits.'

He had, of course, at this time all the pressing duties of the busy town priest: 'a long succession of sermons, remarks [*sic!*], letters, diplomacy among our fidgety working men, etc.' (1st June 1887). Occasionally he was able to get away from it all to have an afternoon walk with Katharine through the picture galleries of Burlington House, or a breath of fresh air with her in Hyde Park. There were meetings with his father and brothers together and on another occasion he would arrange to meet his barrister brother alone 'in the Palace of Justice.' After the Advent Ordination of 1886 he had a short holiday in Bournemouth after which he remarked to Katharine, 'It's a many years since you saw me without any examination on the carpet.'

On 1st June 1887 he wrote to Katharine about his forthcoming summer holiday. His observations on this topic might be said to constitute his 'philosophy of holidays' and the emergence of a certain obscurity of style which sometimes makes his more formal disquisitions rather difficult to read:

'. . . when I am left alone with the Parish it had better perhaps be after than before a period of change, reading and silence . . . A holiday cannot be made up of ever so many "changes of air": it differs from these by its duration in one stay. Twelve months' change in a year would not make one annual holiday. You must separate one year from the next. The present relations of time and space, if one may respectfully say so, have this defect—a want of intervals. "Nihil per saltum" is said to be a favourite maxim of Nature's. Accordingly no sooner is one minute over than the next begins. With us, instinctive promptings, civilized invention and the instruction of grace, have provided remedies in change of occupation, the alternation of the sleeping and waking states, sabbaths, holidays. If I divide my six weeks, how am I to tell whether I am having a fortnight's change this year or a month's next—or which is the holiday and which the new year?'

Philip was already, apparently, beginning to become known as a preacher. On 14th February 1887 he wrote: 'In spite of good resolutions, and having made a good beginning in refusing, I am going out to preach too much in Lent.' We may assume that Katharine had asked for his advice and see in the following counsel for the keeping of Lent the beginning of Waggett's wisdom as a spiritual director (1st March 1887):

'I dare say that you will have made some simple but special rule . . . for Lent. Nobody would guess from abstract consideration how great is the blessing God gives by means of a rule strictly kept. It prepares for some *emergency* at the end. By the story of the wise and foolish virgins we learn that life is made up mostly of emergencies and the preparation for them. At the end of Lent there may turn up some temptation which will be the Lord's opportunity for cutting some fault away at the roots— if we have been prepared for it. Most bad things go not out but by prayer and fasting . . . I wonder if all. That we might have no speculative difficulties . . . God Himself fasted for us and in the strength of that fast conquered the devil.'

All this varied work at the beginning of his ordained ministry did not prevent Waggett from keeping up with old friends and old interests. He still saw Scott Holland from time to time and attended his lectures in St. Paul's, where he had now become a Canon. Luke Paget had left Poplar in 1886 for St. Ives in Huntingdonshire, to be succeeded by R. E. Adderley. Early in 1887 Paget looked in on Waggett for a brief visit which gave the latter the greatest delight, including hearty amusement at Paget's comments on the organ in the church to which he had gone:

'He . . . has no time to say much except that the Vox Humana in their organ is like a Puritan with a sore throat or a heretical sheep. "It conveys," says Ser Luca (a nickname of P.N.W.'s for Paget), "mild and tasteless private judgment in every slow and timid vibration. I wish," he continues, "it were dead"' (undated letter to K.B.W.).[1]

So long as Waggett was at Poplar he had plenty of opportunity to keep up contacts with Christ Church. Many visitors came from the House to the Mission and Paget used to go to Oxford to enlist help from time to time. One of the most interesting visitors at this period was George Romanes, the eminent disciple of Charles Darwin, writer on biological and other scientific subjects and, later, founder of the Romanes Lecture at Oxford. Romanes was in the first place drawn to visit Poplar by his friendship with the Paget brothers whom he had first met when they were all three at a preparatory school together. It will be obvious at once how there came to be an affinity of soul between Waggett and Romanes. The latter had intended, while a schoolboy and

[1] Here and throughout 'K.B.W.' refers to his sister Katharine Blechynden Waggett.

later, to take holy orders; but while at Cambridge he had abandoned the idea, partly on account of opposition which he met at home, and had turned to the study of biology. In 1873 George Romanes was still in the way of faith, however, and that year he won the Burney Prize at Cambridge for an essay on *Christian Prayer and General Laws*. His biological work brought him into friendship with Darwin and although the latter strenuously repudiated any desire to attack Christianity with his theories, Romanes found that the path along which he now walked led him to a position in which he was intellectually unable to retain Christian beliefs. His change of view was expressed in an anonymous essay entitled *A Candid Examination of Theism* which appeared in 1876. But he did not stop there; and the next few years were spent in groping his way back to Christian belief and must have cost him a very intense interior conflict. It has often been said that Waggett was the chief instrument in the conversion of George Romanes; but the evidence is not nearly sufficient to warrant this statement. It is true, however, that the process of Romanes's return to Christianity was contemporary with his connections with the Christ Church Mission. Maybe he saw there a Christianity in action which appealed to a larger part of his being than the academic theology with which he had been in contact at Oxford and Cambridge.

Whatever may have been the influence of Waggett on Romanes in this connection there can be no doubt that a deep sympathy quickly arose between them from the moment when the latter first visited Poplar with his wife and daughter: it was a personal *rapport* and also an understanding springing from their common interest in biology and religious questions. His wife wrote later that Waggett was one of her husband's 'most intimate friends. Mr. Waggett's scientific attainments made him a most valuable as well as a much loved friend.' [2] Paget recalled Romanes's second visit to the Mission when

'. . . in the guise of Father Christmas he lifted up his hand over the children and said: "God bless you." Father Waggett said to me afterwards: "He would not have said that last year"' (*Henry Luke Paget*, p. 92).

[2] *The Life and Letters of George John Romanes* by his wife (London 1895), 2nd edition, p. 284 footnote.

The friendship was to continue to the end of Romanes's life and Waggett and he certainly had an important influence on each other.

Only just over eighteen months after going to Poplar as a newly ordained deacon, Waggett was invited in July 1887 to join the staff of St. Pancras parish church to which living Luke Paget had just been appointed by the Dean and Chapter of St. Paul's. The moves of Paget no doubt made Waggett feel, as he had every right to feel, that he was not tied to Poplar for the full two years of his 'title,' but he left the place with many a wistful backward glance. Writing six years later, when he was at the Charterhouse Mission, he recalled the happiness of those first eighteen months of his ministry :

'Poplar is still the home of my soul—and I cannot help it in spite of dear Tabard St. . . . The people are on the whole very human and cheerful . . . the seafaring element in Poplar is very interesting . . . Poplar did so much for me, that I cannot think of it as not an immensely happy place. It alone carried me through St. Pancras, and early days at Tabard St. . . .' (Letters of 8th and 13th November 1893 to K.B.W.).

It was an able body of men whom Waggett now joined at St. Pancras—G. H. Vincent, later Rector of St. Martin's, Ludgate Hill; Fred Douglass, later of the Oxford Mission to Calcutta; John Chapman, who was to become Abbot of Downside; Harold Anson, later Master of the Temple; and C. C. Bell, a future Canon of York. The parish church in which he was now to minister, built in 1816 to a classical design by Inwood, is graphically described by John Summerson in *Georgian London* (1945). In 1887 the parish, built on the Bedford Estate, was still what is called 'a good residential neighbourhood.' Until Paget's marriage in 1892 the Vicarage in Gordon Square was used as a clergy house. The daily life of the Vicar and the curates was much what came to be the familiar pattern in parishes like St. Mary's, Portsea and elsewhere. The whole staff was expected to be present at the daily Eucharist and offices; mornings were given (as far as possible) to study; two hours each day on five days in the week were to be spent in visiting; all taught in the day school and had individual oversight of parochial organizations, clubs and so forth.

There is a pleasant story told of Waggett soon after his arrival at St. Pancras. His brother Ernest, then a medical student at

Bart's, had appeared in the parish one day and had made a very favourable impression on an elderly female parishioner, who was heard to remark afterwards : 'We've got a very nice curate now. His brother's a gentleman.'

In due course Katharine was called upon for assistance, and there occurs again the suggestion that she should go there and work with him. 'I wonder if you could collect me, from time to time, a little money. I want to improve my chapel.' It is not quite clear, though, which chapel is referred to. And 'I wish you could come here and work with me. I feel sure we should think alike.' (Letters of May 1889 to K.B.W.)

In other letters to his sister at this time he gives some idea of how tremendously crowded his days were. Early services, teaching for an hour in the girls' school; visitors' meetings, letters; Mr. and Mrs. Romanes to lunch, visits at Orphanage and instruction of Confirmation candidates there; 'wet through' on the way to another group of six boy candidates who were 'more trouble than a whole class'; rushed dinner followed by a meeting with two city missionaries; finally a long but 'delightful visit' from 'a young blood who means to do all sorts of good things'; to bed at 12.30 'without having got into the parish at all.'

In a letter to Katharine dated 19th December 1887 he describes some of the personal rubs which are the lot of every priest in a place like St. Pancras and how he has to restrain himself in dealing with them :

'Most of the people are very kind to us, and of sterling stuff. Some *seem* to me to behave ill and in an old neighbourhood one knocks up against many conflicting interests and so on—some of which conflict with us. Money very much to the fore. I find myself getting very fierce sometimes and not afraid of the people who are baddish. This high heartedness must be eliminated. And the people whom I should be afraid of are as kind as can be and most generous in every way.'

He did not forget his beloved East End and he preached at St. Peter's, London Docks on the Sunday evenings of Advent 1887 and visited Poplar early in the following year. As a result of all this spell of heavy work and his generous response to the ceaseless demands of the first two years of his work as a priest, Father Waggett experienced the first of a number of periods which were to occur in his life when he was overcome with weariness and exhaustion. In the spring and early summer of 1888 he was, apparently, largely incapacitated by physical weakness and mental fatigue. On 9th June that year he wrote :

'I get stronger every day . . . and only to-day got near a sermon—after so long a time I shall be quite frightened again preaching . . . I hope I shall be able to do my work again soon, but I have never been like this before. It is quite astonishing how those few weeks before my change took everything out of me. I see that it will be a matter of many months' care to make me really myself again' (letter to K.B.W.).

And even at the end of March 1889 he was saying : 'I have not been fatiguing myself at all—because I have unfortunately been very tired and beset with neuralgia.' However, whatever break from ordinary work he had to be given, he was still able to maintain his meetings with friends. Scott Holland appears in the letters of this time and there was an arrangement to accompany him and the St. Paul's choirboys to Willesden for cricket. In September 1888 he remarks, 'Scotty has been too delicious; we have had lots of walks and talks'; and in the following spring dinner with Holland became a weekly event.[3] At the same time his friendship with the Romanes was growing closer. They frequently visited him in Gordon Square and he says : 'Mr. and Mrs. Romanes are nearly invading Scotty's place in my heart.' In 1888, the year of his enforced rest, and the following year, Waggett spent an autumn holiday at the Romanes' home at Geanies in Scotland. Although he always appeared on social occasions to be completely at ease, there were, even in him, some unexpected corners of shyness and shrinking from the world. Before the first of these holidays with the Romanes in Scotland he felt almost a terror of the strangers whom he was to meet and a desire to flee into the bosom of his family. In September 1888 he wrote :

'I perfectly dread the journey to Scotland and all the well dressed people. They seem to have a large party and shooting and things, and will all be so vigorous and so kind. I ought never to have engaged myself to weeks among strangers . . . The surroundings will be lovely and healthful—but I have such a very strong preference for my own people and home—that even people I am most familiar with seem to me all but complete strangers. I am down at the bottom of a deep pond of

[3] The regard which Waggett had for H.S.H. comes out in the characteristic remark : 'Holland's men of straw are more formidable than other folks' men-at-arms' (*Henry Scott Holland,* ed. Stephen Paget, 1921, p. 158).

my own, while they lay lines for me and send down ground bait from the surface' (letter to K.B.W.).

However, these social occasions and house-parties were to bring Waggett into contact with people who would lead him into fields where he could find room for new exercises of the soul and mind. In April 1889 he speaks of meeting at the Romanes's house 'poet Gosse and—I fear—some rather fierce infidels.' And, about the same time, 'The Huxley paper made me laugh, too, with its jokes —but oh dear it was dreary . . . Quite apart from the faith there is such a fearful loss in abandoning metaphysic . . . I am to belong to the Aristotelian Society whose meetings are sometimes very interesting.[4] I have been there as a visitor' (letter to K.B.W.).

It was during his St. Pancras' curacy that Waggett was first invited to deliver a sermon in St. Paul's Cathedral. He began to know Liddon there, who soon observed his abilities as a preacher. The growing of ferns became a diversion for him about this time, and he must have had quite a number of seed boxes and fern-cases in his room—

'One Christmas tree doing well, the other not so well. Fern cases depopulated rather. No signs of oranges—no marmalade for me *this* year' (letter to K.B.W.).

Going to concerts was another source of refreshment for him. Although not a great musician Waggett possessed a sensitive and poetic appreciation of music, as is revealed, for instance, in an almost lyrical sermon on plainsong which he delivered years later.[5]

In 1889, through arrangements made by his Vicar's father Sir James Paget, then a member of the Council of the Royal College of Surgeons, Waggett went to Paris with his surgeon brother (Ernest) to meet Louis Pasteur whom he described as 'in my poor judgment the greatest scientist and the greatest Frenchman of the age that has passed.' In his book *The Scientific Temper in Religion* (pp. 78–80) Waggett reveals his own reverence for the processes which were going on in the fields of medical discoveries and other natural sciences. He spoke of Pasteur as a great scientist who 'moved securely in a great range of the most minute facts' and who was 'accessible and very considerate to those who came

[4] He was elected a member on 11th March 1889. It is not known to what paper he refers.
[5] See pp. 194ff. *infra.*

to him to learn and very patient in showing them the way about his wonderful works.' Waggett drew attention to the fact that Pasteur believed sincerely in the Incarnation, and expressed the view that his importance as a Christian had not been sufficiently understood. He quotes Pasteur as saying:

'I see everywhere the inevitable expression of the Infinite in the world: through it the supernatural is at the bottom of every heart.' [6]

Before the end of this year, 1889, there began the last chapter in Waggett's life as a secular priest. This summer he was invited by his old school to become Missioner at Charterhouse in Southwark. It was to be the third change of work in four years and he showed signs of the strain of another uprooting. Of course the request and the acceptance came some time before the parishioners, and some of his colleagues, were informed and he wrote on 29th August to K.B.W.: 'Nobody here knows that I am going away, and I daily relish the joke. And glad I am for the joke, for I am very melancholy about going.'

There is a lively account in the *Church Times* of 14th July 1939 of Waggett's first encounter with the evangelical bishop of the diocese in which his new work was to lie, Dr. Thorold of Rochester. In this episode Waggett begins to show his skilful handling of powerful people of all kinds: 'Mr. Waggett arrived and was shown into the Bishop's study. The Bishop was more than usually frigid. He said: "Mr. Waggett, I am very much surprised to see you," to which came the reply, "I don't know why you should be, my lord, since you invited me to dine and sleep here to-day." The Bishop answered, "I did indeed invite you, but you did not do me the favour of answering my letter," to which Mr. Waggett replied, "Of course I answered your letter by return of post, and I suggest that you make some inquiry of your postal authorities. And as for being surprised, I confess that I was a little surprised to find no one to meet me at the station and to relieve me of my bag." The boot was now on the other leg: Mr. Waggett was shown a room and placed next to the Bishop at dinner, where he entranced him with his brilliant talk. When the guests retired for the night Bishop Thorold handed each his

[6] *The Scientific Temper in Religion*, p. 80, quoting Pasteur, *Discours de reception à l'Académie francaise.*

34

candle, and when he came to Waggett he said, "Mr. Waggett, when you arrived I said that I was surprised to see you. I cannot withdraw my expression for I was indeed very much surprised. But I should like to add that surprise has been changed into delight." '

Waggett took up residence at 40 Tabard Street, Southwark, in October 1889. The neighbourhood in those days was a really poor one and many of the people had to be constantly on the alert to make any kind of living at all. In an article written for a report three years later, Waggett mentioned wood chopping, rough boot making, the manufacture of tin pots and marking and naming them for use in public houses as being characteristic occupations— all poorly paid. The cutting of paper bags, drawing of bristles into brushes, taking in of mangling and other such trivial jobs were the only occupations which many of his new flock could find. One of the first things that had to be established at the Mission was a kitchen where meals could be obtained at a maximum charge of 4d.

Vice and violence of many kinds were rife in Tabard Street and its neighbourhood when Waggett went there. It was to be a very different story from his surroundings in the East End. He could soon see what he was 'up against' and that the work to be done there would make very heavy demands on the new Missioner. Waggett describes some of the almost desperate situations in an article on 'Noisy Minorities' in *Charterhouse in Southwark, 1885–92*:

'If you have once stood, helpless, between two brawlers, surrounded by a mass of men and women, not one of whom will stir a finger to help you to preserve peace, men who knew you but whose eyes are fixed on a beastly expectation, and their minds too full to attend to any call, you will know what the spirit of brother-killing really is, and why the Devil is, before all things, a murderer. Sometimes, as I say, this spirit is rampant, seizes a whole mass. A street like ours at times seems given up to lust, to hatred, to persistent excess of drink. There is no pause, no limit, they "sin as it were with a cart rope," and never is a street like ours free from awful words, and the sight of brutal intemperance : men, women, and little children, alike, repeat the same unspeakable songs.

'Do we blame, do we despair of, those who are thus in bondage? No, but we wish now to recognize the gigantic force of the enemies of truth and peace . . . It is their misery, their wretched unhappiness, and awful future which moves us . . . And what means can we take to meet in any measure such a curse? I do not say, what strength; I say what means? In this conflict a man does not hate, he loves, his adversary. It is mere mystification to separate the sin from the sinner. Sin is *nothing* apart from the sinner, whether that sinner be our brother or an evil spirit. The drunkard also is, in a real sense, our adversary. But we oppose him, we fight against him, we conquer (ah! if so it might be) by love. And if we win, he is no longer our adversary, he is not a conquered foe, but a rescued friend. In the victory, he changes sides. For indeed there is within him still a spirit that strives for good. It is this spirit within him to which we bring our succours, for whom sometimes we raise the siege and who alone can give the decisive stroke.'

The way in which Waggett, as in his attitude towards a great man like Pasteur, reverenced those with whom he came into contact is brought out again in the following description of one of the boys of the Mission, which he wrote in the annual report of 1889 :

'Surely it is not hard to admire the boys for all their faults. How hard they work all day! How hard they play all night! Endurance and spirit like this, supported on scanty meals and scanty kindness, would take a lad to the top of the tree in any generous society of his kind. I was timing my friend Henry Matthew last night, while he fought three rounds of three minutes each with his equally hard-hitting, bullet-headed step-brother. Our gloves are not too soft, the little pit for fighting is rather close and we have but a moderate notion of playing "light." Now Matthew has been working from 6 a.m. to 7 p.m. in a factory of floor-cloth; he is boisterous, and I have known him troublesome. But, upon my word, I felt shamed of ever having checked noisiness when I remembered his strenuous, struggling life, and what I was doing at his age.'

When Waggett came to Tabard Street the Charterhouse Mission had been in existence only five years. During this time, although the premises had been very cramped, it had grown into a solid organization and had become ripe for expansion. Very soon after he arrived the first enlargement took place : the Church was removed from the basement of No. 40 to the basements of Nos. 34 and 36 knocked into one. In the 1889 report Waggett said that the congregation here was 'wonderfully steady in attendance and reverent and thankful and happy in worship.' In the first year of his ministry there were fifty-one babies baptized. Katharine Waggett provided linen and other requirements for the small church and on Easter Eve 1890 a new altar was dedicated. Three years after Father Waggett went there, in May 1891, Dr. David-son, Thorold's successor as Bishop of Rochester, held a Confirma-tion in the mission church.

The men's club began to prosper and it was reported that the men had made it a 'distinctly churchgoing club'; it soon became self-governing and that brought it an increase in vigour. The Women's Help Society was giving much needed relief in the way of holidays for children, factory girls and tired mothers. But all the activities were hampered by the lack of space. The Missioner was very soon launching a number of persuasive appeals for money to buy a piece of land which was available in Crosby Row, on which it was planned to build 'a block, containing Church to hold 450, Meeting Room, and Gymnasium of the same size, and several large classrooms.'

Waggett's ambition for the atmosphere and furnishings of the new church, which he hoped would soon be built, was thus expressed in the above-mentioned article 'Noisy Minorities' :

'In a place like this it was of the utmost importance that the Mission should be homely, should be rough, should be near the ground . . . it is just what we want that in outward things Christ's house should be like the rest . . . it must be like to the poor by being poor in spirit. But it must not be disorderly, or dirty, or confused. It must show, continually, the opposite of all this . . . it *cannot* be attempted in our present premises with any fair opportunity of success. How we heap up difficulties against creating a sense of rest, of trust, of the presence and protection of the unseen, when our Church is exposed to the disturbance of every footstep or word in the house above, when it is shaken by the thunder of every passing cart . . .'

In 1892 an iron chapel was erected in Crosby Row and it was so arranged that this could be used during the whole period of the building of the permanent church. Waggett had organized an Association of old Carthusians for obtaining interest in, and support for, the Mission; and by the generosity of the members of this association enough money was obtained to rent a house near the site of the new buildings in which the boys' club had its room pending the opening of the new establishment.

The necessary funds steadily came in, largely as a result of the energy of Waggett and of the enthusiasm inspired by him, and on 2nd November 1892 the foundation stone of the new building was laid by H.R.H. Princess Christian. Five years later the new Church was dedicated (5th February 1897) and another five years saw the completion of the top storey of the buildings in Crosby Row. Waggett only saw the beginning of the completion of his plans, for in the same month as the foundation stone was laid he announced his departure from the Mission. Nevertheless he had put things well into the way of having a great dream fulfilled.

One of the great problems with which Waggett had to deal when he was in Southwark was the organization of relief work. Those were the days, which now so many are unable to recall, when going to the Infirmary might well mean the breaking of a home. The district was in three different Unions and the working of the Poor Law was by no means standardized and so it was impossible to make a uniform plan for the whole area. Waggett made a point of trying to 'rope in' old Carthusians to sit on the various committees which administered the relief funds which the Mission possessed. Some extravagances were inevitable and the directions he gave to the committees were to deal with the needy 'as a wise and just man would with his blood relations—not fostering faults nor letting misfortune have all its own way,' as he put it in his first annual report.

Waggett, in the short time he was at Southwark, drew in his family and friends to take an interest in the work. His father subscribed generously; his surgeon brother Ernest gave a great deal of practical help. Katharine was at last prevailed upon to become a regular worker in her brother's parish in 1890: but this lasted only a year because she overworked and did some damage to her health. The Romanes, Scott Holland and Luke Paget all showed a keen interest in Waggett's work at the Mission.

In February 1890 Waggett began the publication of a two-monthly parish paper which he found a useful means of communication with his people. The aim of the paper was to give clear and simple teaching on the Church's year, on the problems facing the Mission at the time and to outline plans for future ventures. In the winter of 1890, for instance, as well as the teaching in the parish paper there was a campaign by the Missioner against excessive drinking and the giving of alcoholic liquor to children under 16.

These were almost excessively strenuous days for Waggett and early in 1890 he was deeply affected by the death of his friend Aubrey Moore. On 18th January he wrote about this to Katharine:

'I wonder if I have mentioned to you Mr. Aubrey Moore whose death, from results of the influenza, was reported last night? Just latterly I have known him better and like him too, very much. He was far the most alive of all the Oxford men, very learned, brilliantly clear, fresh, calm, untroubled. It is, as we see things, an immense loss to the Church and to Oxford.'

Henry Parry Liddon, another great luminary of that era, whom Waggett had known since he was first invited to preach in St. Paul's two years earlier, also died in 1890. In 1904 J. O. Johnston published a biography of Liddon in New York and Waggett wrote in *The Churchman* [7] an appreciation of him following the publication of this book. This tribute to Liddon is, in the opinion of the present author, the purest piece of concentrated lyrical prose from Waggett's pen which has survived. For this reason, as much as for what it tells us of Liddon himself or of Waggett's interpretation and understanding of him, this appreciation will be transcribed here in full :

'It is not yet clear that the greatness of Dr. Liddon's self-denial is at all generally understood. His was a high achievement of sacrifice. He went far. It is something, and means a journey, for a really clever man, a brilliant man, of hard, fine intellect and generous warmth, of great gifts held in complete mastery by a flexible management, to give himself up to the official ministry of the Gospel. That is something, but it is little. Other men have done it who, like Liddon, like Manning earlier, had the quality and extent of power which would have given them distinction in letters, or still more in statecraft. It was much, again, that Liddon, being what he was, with the prizes of distinction at his command, should have thought quite nothing of them in comparison with the one great aim of doing the best for the Church. Other men have refused the bishoprics which were never offered, as firmly as Liddon declined a preferment pressed upon him in Arlington House by Salisbury and Gladstone combined. Others have slighted a world which never courted them. Liddon, with a sensitiveness which surely must have felt the charm of refined adulation, never either allowed it to turn or influence him, or allowed himself to come, without surrender, within breathing range of its agreeable incense.

'But these things, sacrifices as they are, beyond the reach of many men who, in the abstract and untried, conceive themselves more than capable of them, were small things compared to Liddon's actual achievement. His great flight was to the suppression of self in all its most fascinating exhibitions. He had the gifts which we sum up as brilliancy in a degree altogether unusual, perhaps unique in the age lately passed. Gladstone, a giant of eloquence, as of other energies on a scale outside this comparison, had not a spark of Liddon's abundant glow of humour. Wilberforce, who to eloquence added a skilful, useful, homely wit, had not a touch, or more than a touch, of his exquisite felicity. Maurice, who could wrap all things, as he pleased, in a luminous cloud of words, did not excel Liddon in the mastery of our language. Do I seem to be using the

[7] *The Churchman* (New York), 10th June 1905.

expressions of exaggeration? I only seem to do so because of Liddon's vast modesty. He had all the capacity for paradox of the most famous of our heretics, and he chose to be straightforward. He could have startled like the most acrobatic of our *poseurs* but he preferred or he subdued himself to be simple. He spent his great gifts, his brilliant insight, his varied learning, his master's silver tongue, in making plain things plainer still to plain people. He pruned away every *mot,* he softened the sting of his wit, and hid the lightning of his scorn, so that the patient, dull eyes might through him catch sight of the solid things, the things which belong unto our peace.

'This was a great triumph of self-restraint, a great sacrifice gladly made, a great proof of the mastery of the highest in him. In no other man of that which we love to call "our time" was there so much of the image of an apostle—"a slave of Jesus Christ"—separated unto the Gospel of Christ, doing all he did, leaving undone all he refrained from, that men in deed and in every thought might be brought into subjection to the Master whom he constantly in every moment loved.

'It is this single eye in Liddon which we would have recorded. It is this absolute devotion which makes him one of those whose lives are built into the one foundation of our hope. It is this deep seriousness which was the open secret of the most radiant personality many of us have ever seen.

'And, on this account, we can accept as a serious and most useful instalment the life which we have all been reading. It gives us such an account as Liddon would have preferred, one which reflects his own modesty, and shows him as a willing learner, a very humble disciple of "the Doctor," Dr. Pusey, and as a bound servant of the Church.

'Recognition was the last thing Liddon wished for. The brilliant wit flashed from him in spite of himself. The book shows this rare person as the serious man he was; gives you the burning earnestness of the workman, if it fails to show the sparks which flew about him as he worked. It suggests, by its solidity, the solid simplicity of Liddon's faith, and the plainness of which I wrote just now. This plainness carries with it, for some minds, the impression that Dr. Liddon was less richly endowed with subtle insight and with the sense of wonder and mystery than he was with the power of utterance and the delight of dogmatic lucidity. It is true that in some respects, or in some departments, he sacrificed to the rigour of verbal consistency the opportunity for a real distinction of value between matters which in value really differ. But this characteristic—part of his system of self-sacrifice—cannot with any measure of truth at all be traced to an absence or a defect in Dr. Liddon, either of the capacity for distinction, or, on the other hand, of the sense of mystery. "Subtilty, dear friend," he would say, "is often of the essence of truth." The distinction, the infinite fineness of the line of truth, was as perpetually impressed upon his delicate faith as the line of truth in art was upon Ruskin's. The silences, the abysses, the unutterable, were as continually present to him as to Carlyle. He knew the depths of experience, he looked out into the vast, encompassing world of utter reality. But the sense of mystery need not be joined with obscurity about that measure of revelation which is given us for clearness. A mystery is one thing and a muddle is another. It is so easy to be muddled and to think one's self profound, to spell "mysticism" with an "i" in the first syllable, as if it were derived from

"misty." A truth which in its total reality infinitely transcends any knowledge gained or given may yet be studied with ceaseless pains and with
continually advancing success.

'During his Embankment walks—those inspiring walks by the river
from Blackfriars to Westminster—Liddon talked of many things. He
noticed the new buildings. He pleaded in melting tones with the children
and hardy boys who hung, as he thought, too near the parapet's edge,
and who looked up with entirely incredulous, and perhaps coldly wonder-
ing, eyes at the "old swell" who assured them so affectionately that "dear
children" they would assuredly be drowned. He wanted to know all one
was doing or thinking. But most of all he returned again and again in
these informal instructions to the mystery of the Gospel. God's truth,
salvation, that in which and by which we live, was a vast, an infinite
world of real existence, mounting far above us, stretching far beneath us,
far beyond, engulfing a life which yet in truth was fed by all its resources.
The thought, the faith, addressed to this reality, were immersed, plunged
into a great deep. And it was good to be aware of this, and yet to
maintain the gaze which was so far transcended by the object. We were
to know a love which passeth knowledge.

'But, on the other hand, it was to be remembered that, in the vast
whole of existence, there was a path for one journey. It had limits,
the limits of clear light vouchsafed. It had barriers, the barriers of
commandments, of dogma. And the preacher's task was to point to this
path, to show these boundary-lines, to insist upon these rules of safety,
just because the mystery encompassed us, and the possibilities could not
be inspected, and the goal was far away. It was, indeed, the sense of
mystery which made Liddon most of all the preacher of a line, a rule:
which made him seem to shallow men like a stream with marble floor and
sides; which made his speech to Philistines "unmystical," which made him
care nothing what men might think of him, if only, by unrelenting self-
discipline, he might do something, "however little," as he would say,
to bring one thought more into obedience to the law and truth of Christ.
"Take infinite pains"—that was his lesson. "Divide your task, divide your
flock, digest your message. Trust nothing to natural warmth, natural
quickness. Seek the right word, the right style, the right tone and time
and place. For the time is short, the judgment sure, the peril infinite, the
possibility a possibility of glory, the grace ready. We walk in a glory
and a mystery. But we walk on a path which need not be mistaken, which
must not—God forbid it—by any word of ours be left encumbered or
confused."

'It was in correspondence with this high sense of the great pilgrimage
that he urged the smaller duties, insisted, for example, upon the classifica-
tion of hearers, so that there might be in every parish a special preparation
for Communion offered every month, by classes, to each section of the
parish, adults and youths and children, men and women. It was in correspondence with this power of wonder in him, and the responsibility
which he so mercilessly accepted for himself, that he would never preach
to the little group of poor girls under the charge of the Clewer Sisters at
Oxford without preparation. From this came the preciseness in talk of
one who was as rich for talk as the most fluent Celt; from this the
beautiful fresh-coined phrases with which he introduced his lectures on
Sunday evenings in Christ Church hall; from this the exquisite urbanity,

the refined dignity which went along with the generous consideration of this most genial man. To be exquisite, and utterly humble; to be entirely liberal and entirely refined, quite unselfish and quite, quite dignified—that was Liddon's strange and brilliant flower of life, and it found its roots in his religious faith.

'Other men have other gifts. The wonder of faith has other and more obvious manifestations. There may be need, in our time, of something to rouse the clergy from a kind of *bourgeois* certainty about something which we hear called "the faith in its fullness." The sense of mystery needs perhaps to be called upon at other times in tones which were not the tones of Liddon's memorable voice. It should not be forgotten that his lessons were his way of fostering the same sense; and that because it was strong in him his tongue was trained and his memory disciplined, and his selection of truth for teaching anxiously definite, and constantly successful.

'Partly his own reluctance, partly at the last the force of circumstances, prevented his becoming a bishop. But his deeply reverent sense of responsibility gave to Liddon's life as a priest much of the apostolical character. We lost in him—let us say, rather, we had in him—what may be more valuable than a great official ruler of the Church. We had a great spiritual leader—a champion in the battle against unbelief and sin.'

His contact with Scott Holland continued to delight and inspire Waggett, and on 17th February 1890 he wrote to his sister what could hardly have been a higher tribute to his friend :

'I have seen a great many more people and more honourable than I had when first I knew him—but I feel more than ever that he is altogether in a different rank to any one in any walk of life I have ever seen. I should think that Gladstone was as fine perhaps but not so charming. It is delightful to see how his people adore him.'

All the while, in the midst of the vast pastoral labours chronicled in the early part of this chapter, he was writing reviews of scientific works for *The Guardian,* reading a paper to the Aristotelian Society and keeping up his reading of important contemporary books. In a letter of 13th May 1890 to his sister he comments on the recent publication of *Lux Mundi* and the excitement which it had caused—which, he thought, was 'very encouraging.' 'I had no notion they (presumably the reading public) cared about the Bible so much.'

Waggett read a paper to the Aristotelian Society during the session 1889–90 (*Proceedings,* Vol. I, p. 129) and it was on the subject of 'Beauty.' Some fairly lengthy quotations must suffice here : anything more is of interest to few but specialists in philosophy and they must be referred to the full text in the published records of the Society. He begins :

'An essay which sets out to ask what Beauty is in itself will not promise much entertainment or discovery to any who have attended to the subject. For those teachers who evidently believe most certainly in the reality of Beauty, who know most about it and love it best, those whom we are most willing to take for guides in the Ethic about beauty, and who have by beautifully speaking added to our stock of it, have refused, more or less steadily, to inquire what beauty is itself. In the chapter called the Lamp of Beauty, in the "Seven Lamps," Ruskin will not ask the question, "Only asserting that to be beauty which I believe will be granted me to be so without dispute, I would endeavour" (he says) "shortly to trace the manner in which the element of delight is to be engrafted upon architectural design, what are the purest sources from which it is to be derived, and what the errors to be avoided in its pursuit." And Jacobi (quoted by Martineau) says, "The beautiful has this feature, in common with all that is original, that there is no mark by which we know it. It exists and is self-manifest; you can show it but not prove it—*es kann gewiesen, aber nicht bewiesen weiden.*" The masters, the amateurs are right.

'My paper then promises little. It will perform even less than it might seem to promise; for it offers no answer; it only attempts, by excluding some methods which are perhaps unfruitful, and by resigning explicitly great fields of interest which lie about the subject, to get the question nearer to being at least asked alone, not overshadowed by those greater questions which it has a singular (I believe singular) power of introducing and connecting. If what I can find to say is thrown to some extent into the form of criticism, this does not spring, I believe, from peevish ingratitude to those seers of beauty to whom we owe, if not a quite clear question, at least most that we have towards an answer.

'Let me add to this disheartening commencement that it may well prove worth while to have put the name of Beauty at the head of to-night's discussion, because we have in it a text upon which every one has a discourse. We live by admiration. In beauty, all of us are specialists. Other qualities of things interest many or few; this one attracts all. The beauty sense lies close to the speculative faculty itself—it is illuminative, thought-carrying—and in many persons has been the path of least resistance along which theory has begun to run its course.

'I have begun by saying that those who practically know most of beauty, decline to deal with it by way of special inquiry. I mean by these, the artists and men of the artistic temper. They take beauty, generally speaking, to be a real thing, an absolute, a concrete ideal. Taste is the genuine apprehension of this real existence; there is a true standard of judgment about it, and it is the one thing with which art should properly concern itself. If its discovery and enjoyment is the work of a faculty of the soul, if it is in itself an absolute, a spirit rather than a quality, they are content to leave alone the attempt to analyse either the thing or the enjoyment; they will concern themselves with the rules of art, with the perfecting of taste by practice in its native air, and with the jealous guarding for beauty of the sovereign dignity which belongs to it in nature and in art.

'. . . the treasure found is not to be dissected or even roughly handled; it is to be delicately framed and thankfully enjoyed. This is the artist's right way.

'. . . We learn more of moral excellence (do we not?) from the saints than from the casuists.

43

'The artists, painters, poets, music makers, will not stop to tell us what Beauty is—but they will show it to us.

'On the other hand, the writers who, for short, may be called the inartistic, rather explain away beauty than take it for granted. It is with them, the good, the useful, as with Hume; Order, as with St. Augustine; Relation, as with Diderot; or simply confused with all that is pleasant or amiable; or it is analysed more or less crudely as association . . .

'. . . The great German teachers of classical æsthetics take beauty in general for granted. The Abbé Winckelman (whom I know only at second hand), Lessing of course conspicuously, and Goethe, have written on *art*. Goethe exalts art above beauty. Burke is so far of the artist mind that he believes in the reality of beauty and the fixity of taste—only he explains beauty as if it were amiableness, or loveliness, or facility.

'Sir Joshua Reynolds is an artist who writes like one of the inartistics. He scoffs at genius if it pretends to be more than skill.'

Waggett then runs through a large field of attempts to produce a definition of beauty and of different expressions of the indefinability of beauty; and he ends thus :

'Look round your room. It is hard not to remain in the belief that the little statuette, the portrait, the book-backs, have each a real several quasi-personality in itself. And yet each is a perfectly indifferent lump of clay, or leather, except in so far as a human mind observes it now, and once dealt with it. They are like the wire in a low-tension current—only the poles give them quality. They are missiles from one mind to another—otherwise most certainly, positively, experimentally, they are nothing but a lump of clay, a collection of black marks. But lying between two minds they are real, individual, significant . . .

'. . . The statuette is such because it lies between two minds, as a wire between poles. All its difference depends on that—cut it off from the two minds and it is as other clay. Is not the clay *clay* because it lies between two minds? And the flower a flower, and the flashing sea all that it is, and the multitude of living things because they lie between two minds, or all in mind, the mind of the universe, which in the exuberance of creation at last makes possible an answering mind of men . . .

'. . . What I have said amounts to this little; that we must in the first place, have a beauty inquiry which shall be apart from art criticism, apart from ethics and the illustration of its uses. That Beauty is not association . . . That we ought to have a psychological and physiological analysis of its separate effect—a physical ætiology of its origin in things. And these need not prevent us here, unless they do in other kinds of phenomena, from seeking to know the meanings of the world, secrets that come in joy rather than in argument; nor should a high regard for such speculations make any one despise the physics of the matter. These several disciplines are necessary to each other, but they may work without interference; no one of them need exclude or displace the others in the general field of discussion, or in the mind of a single disciple.'

There is much in the full text of this paper for the philosopher to enjoy and profit from, but there is also much in these extracts— and in others which could be made—for the lay mind to understand and appreciate : not least the way in which this newly elected member addresses this learned society with a subtle mixture of deference and confidence which is effective and masterly.

It is not surprising that with all this multifarious activity outlined in this chapter Waggett had a partial recurrence of the disabling weariness which he had experienced two years before. Headaches, catarrh and rheumatism beset him in the spring of that year and he gave vent to some of his jaded feelings :

'I am so busy and so lazy, tortured with the slackness within and the bustle without. I cannot get these review things written—and, worse still, I don't care to. I hate the name of evolution and criticism and don't care whether people think lightly or wrongly about it' (letter of 13th May 1890 to K.B.W.).

During this Southwark period he preached a sermon, long to be remembered, in the school chapel at Charterhouse. The sermon at Evensong generally began at about 7.50 p.m. and doubtless did so this time, and usually did not last more than twenty minutes, so that the service ended in good time for boys to get back to their houses and get their books etc. ready for Banco ('Prep') at 8.30 p.m. Mr. O. H. Latter, a junior master at the time, recalls that on this occasion 'Waggett, however, had become entirely oblivious of the passage of time—he had not written his sermon, but was preaching extempore . . . As the minutes went by boys began taking out their watches to see what record was being set up. At length, however, in the two houses nearest to the Chapel there rang out the 8.55 p.m. bells which were the signal for Banco to end and for the boys to put their books away and take their places for prayers . . . Waggett, being an old Carthusian, knew what the bells signified. He abruptly ejaculated, "Oh, I'm so sorry," and brought his sermon to a close, having preached for well over an hour. The boys were well pleased for, as there had been no Banco on Sunday evening, nothing could be demanded of them at first school on Monday morning.'

In the summer of 1891 he had a bad bout of neuralgic pain which made it necessary for him to give up work for a week or two; and again the same autumn he was obliged to take a short rest.

Another move—this time involving more than just the acceptance of a different sphere of work—was upon him at the end of 1892 and it meant the surrender of his responsibilities at Charterhouse in Southwark. The Revd. W. L. Vyvyan, afterwards Bishop of Zululand, who had been Waggett's assistant at the Mission and who became his successor there, said of Waggett's resignation: 'This last was a great loss to us . . . his influence will be felt as long as the Mission stands. The lessons that he taught us, his skill in understanding the ways and thoughts, his patience and large-heartedness in dealing with the troublesome things of the place, and his care for individual souls . . . the clearness and definiteness of his teaching are things that must last . . . he has left the work firmly established at a point where the opportunities of development are very great.'

On 14th November that year Waggett wrote in his last two-monthly letter to his people:

'You need not be assured that on my side there must be grief at parting. I am afraid you would scarcely believe how I have dreaded the time when I must lose the sight of your faces and the sound of your voices. Two things especially are good to have had, and hard to part with: but I do not think they will be altogether taken away from me. The first is our union together, as I said, in Church: and the second is that ministry at home, which especially in the winter times and in times of special trouble some of you have made it easy for me to give. There are some dear friends of mine who do not come to Church, or very seldom, and yet we can look back together upon some hours of very sincere feeling and earnest prayer spent together by the bedsides of the sick. I hope all will forgive me my many shortcomings, and will cheer and help me by their kindness: and by their steadfast continuance in holy life, and in faith gain for me the undeserved mercy of the Lord to whom I must give account.'

Then, referring very reticently to that which lay before him, he added:

'. . . I desire to offer myself to the work of Missions without any reserve and to go just where I am sent. But I shall, wherever I am, remember you with love: I shall visit you, God willing, before I leave the country, if God pleases to send me away: and in years to come it may be reserved for me to come back—to learn that some of those to whom I write now have closed a holy life in peace and joy, to see some who are wandering returned; some who are weak strengthened and built up and confirmed; to find all who are faithful rejoicing in God our Saviour.'

CHAPTER IV

Entry upon the Religious Life at Cowley 1892–6

IT came as a surprise to many who thought that they knew Philip Waggett well to hear that he was about to test his vocation at Cowley. The life of the 'religious' in all its strictness is not what they would have supposed to be the choice of one who so manifestly enjoyed, although in an almost entirely dedicated way, the exercise of the diverse and brilliant gifts with which God had endowed him. His own very brief words on the matter must be allowed to stand out in their deep significance. In a letter of 20th August 1894 to his sister, Philip wrote that he had 'No drawing to Cowley,' but that 'vocation is a very unaccountable thing,' and he continued, 'I do not think the bare reason can be given in any nearer words than just "I must." I do not know that I could get nearer in my own case.'

A large part of the remainder of this book is taken up with descriptions of Waggett's multitudinous activities away from the mother house of his order at Cowley and there is, naturally, a tendency to suppose that his Religious Vocation became obscured, in his own life, by the variety and number of the calls which reached him and by the demands on his gifts which came from many parts of the world. But two things must be remembered. First, the Cowley Fathers were not intended by their Founder to be 'monks' in the narrow sense of the word at all, still less an enclosed order : it is the 'mixed' life of prayer and pastoral activity which is the ideal of their rule—they are mission priests. Secondly, Father Waggett's affirmation 'I must' was a reality in his inner life which those who, within the Society, were close to him did not fail to perceive.[1] He came into the community by the deliberate choice of that which was against his natural desires

[1] I am greatly indebted to Father O'Brien (Superior-General S.S.J.E. 1931–49) for the substance of this account of Father Waggett's call and his relationship with the Society.

and attractions. He was conscious of a compulsion which he was indeed able to resist but which all that was best and deepest in him knew he must accept. He was especially rich in natural gifts and he was moved to a great and costly sacrifice. His relation to his community was certainly not a normal one but his love for the Society and his brethren was very real : he loved to be with them and always took a prominent part in all Chapter action. In the last sad days of helplessness when he was living under the care of his sisters it was significant that his longing was to return to Cowley. All this has to be borne in mind as we follow the story of his active life, the greater part of which still lies ahead.

We know from the part of Waggett's life which we have already traced that he had in himself something of the fashionable *bon viveur* and love of elegance which is to be seen in, for instance, the courtier priest of the Renaissance era. That was to appear again and again in his later history. To make a comparison with a different order, the genuine Franciscan ideal appears most frequently in those who have really luxurious tastes to restrain and who have had full experience of magnificence : this is how it was with the Poverello himself. It may be that Father Waggett saw in himself the need for some strong obedience to keep those cultured appetites for the good things of life well in check, and that we can see in his life under rule something made better through the existence of this taste for refinement, and in his new vocation something made nobler than it would otherwise have been through containing a will which was able to turn its back on worldly riches really enjoyed. No doubt also he felt a desire to identify himself voluntarily with the state of the poor and the oppressed amongst whom he had lived and worked in Southwark ; and, as we saw in his last letter to his people there, he certainly had aspirations towards missionary work abroad. However large a place a consciousness of the need for obedience had in his psychological make-up at this stage, it certainly was in the foreground of his mind in deciding to offer himself at Cowley. In a letter to Katharine dated 16th December 1892, only a month after he had entered Cowley as a postulant, he wrote :

'Obedience of course is the great thing; not because it relieves of responsibility but because it braces the will to seek strenuously the really important things. We have yet to see what London Mission work will be when it is done by men who are not spending 9/10ths of their force in unimportant excitement, but are content to do what they are bid, because they are bid, in those matters in which the conscience has no say except that it says we ought to do what is given us to do. Such a thing as subordination is next door to unknown out of doors in London: and yet there is no such exuberance of force in the various works. I do not say this critically but penitently.'

Much earlier in the year he had made a visit to Oxford with all this in his mind. He had spent the night with the Romanes family and 'I had a talk with Gore which much helped me.' Here was a very useful friend to consult on such matters because Gore, too, had made inquiries about the methods and ideals of Father Benson and his Society to see whether this would be a suitable rule for himself and some of his friends who felt a call to the religious life. Gore, however, had decided in 1889 that he and his companions must work on different lines [2] and their ideas finally took shape in the foundation of the Community of the Resurrection. (The discipline and ethos of the 'Cowley Fathers,' as the Society of St. John the Evangelist (S.S.J.E.) came to be known, are described in *Father Benson of Cowley* by M. V. Woodgate, pp. 64–5 and pp. 83ff.)

Waggett was clothed as a novice in this Society in 1892. Later, on 20th August 1894 he wrote that on entering upon the religious life he had

'. . . no longer the smallest wish to leave Tabard St. No dissatisfaction with common church life: a perfect horror of losing an inch of independence: and all the wise arrayed against me. But I knew that this was what God *asked*: that He left me free to stop away, but also free to come' (letter to K.B.W.).

He had put himself into the Bishop of Rochester's hands about the rightness or otherwise of his leaving Southwark at that time and he 'deliberately let me go.' His mind was torn—as any man's must be at such a time of decision and he feared that he might be deluding himself about the sacrifice he was making:

'Sometimes one's dread on the contrary is that it will prove easy, that one will get one's own way again by a new method, and recover all the things one meant to sacrifice, but God will take care of that' (same letter as above).

[2] See *The Life of Charles Gore* by G. L. Prestige, p. 110f.

49

For a time after his arrival at Cowley he was obliged, and was glad, to avoid his friends and his old connections, to bury himself in his new life and to take in the rhythm and the discipline of the community day, the inspiration and teaching of the Founder. He had his share of manual work, and he did not conceal how unaccustomed he was to it. When chopping wood he experienced buffetings of the body—'half a log came and hit me as hard as possible in the face,' and

'I have been digging, if you know what that means, a fearful grind I call it, but no doubt useful, and a change for the worms' (letter to K.B.W.).

Important intellectual work also came his way, not merely the course of reading which is part of the novice's routine. Within two months of the beginning of his postulancy he was picked out by his Novice Master, Father Puller, an eminent church historian, to give him help in the preparation of his book *The Primitive Saints and the See of Rome:*

'Father Puller is just about to bring out the lectures which he gave last Lent . . . about the Roman claims; and which were very useful. I went to the Bodleian to look out some things in a German book which he cannot read; and my own reading is pretty stiff by this time. When you are at Oxford you find out how fearfully unlearned you are. But I hope that here I shall fill up some of the worst gaps, and also restore my German: and get some rudiments of Hebrew which I only played with before . . . I read like winking—really getting something done after all these years. And Father Puller, the master of novices, is a *most* excellent Bible Scholar and historian and theologian and I have had some delightful conferences with him' (letters of December 1892 to K.B.W.).

Father Puller made a generous acknowledgment of Father Waggett's assistance in the preface to the first edition of his book which appeared in 1893. Waggett's learned work was encouraged even in his early days in the community and its importance was recognized. He recalls how by simple acts of kindness the Superior General, Father Page, indicated that scholarly work was to be one of the distinctive contributions which the new Father was to be accepted as making to the life of the Society : 'I shall never forget his (Father Page's) bringing from the town, during my novitiate, a case for papers which he thought would facilitate certain little researches.'

It is difficult enough to find information about the life of a man at the beginning of his response to the religious vocation, both because there is so little in the way of outward events to record and also because the developments in the hidden soul—the really significant happenings at such a period in a man's history—must be all but imperceptible even to his own secret consciousness. The poems which he wrote at this period reveal, perhaps better than anything else could, what was taking place within his soul—and he was able to exercise his mind during these years of preparation in this way. In 1893 Father Congreve succeeded Father Puller as Novice Master and began to give Waggett guidance in the development of this form of expression and he soon came to have a high regard for his aptitude for it. On 23rd January this year Waggett sent Congreve a sonnet with this short note enclosed :

'My dear Father,
 'In these lines there are three parts. In the first I address your paternity and one other of those "who have intelligence in love." In the second I address my soul, since I must not represent another as speaking in my halting words. In the third I implore that Eternal Beauty and Wisdom to save me from myself. The second part begins here "Oh my soul." The third where it is evident.

Yours obediently,
P. N. WAGGETT.'

Here are the lines referred to :

> Is it not strange and monstrous that a heart
> Which late the Uncreated Beauty touched,
> Should rise in petty strife, and cast abroad
> Rough inconsiderate words, or seek to win
> Some empty slothful pleasure? Oh my soul,
> 'Tis no new ugliness that startles thee,
> But old deformity at last laid bare
> Thou dost begin to see and tremble at.
> All through the years He has regarded it
> And with what patience, till but yesterday
> It irked thee to be so ungracious. Lord,
> Since Thy love has so long been streaming down
> Upon me, where I rolled in selfishness,
> Protect me now from that too fierce disgust
> Of my own self, not fit for holy work,
> And rather, while Thy Grace doth seal my lips
> And guard mine eyes and make me gently walk,
> Thyself unseen order my state within
> And fashion all anew in lowliness.

Another sonnet of Waggett's was preserved by Father Congreve, to whom it was sent during the writer's novitiate. In the manuscript copy the author described it as written during a moment of depression, 'in an uncomfortable mood to encourage one to go on to pray without waiting for the subsidence of silly thoughts, mixed motives, etc. . . . they are all Low Level Lines for a bad hour . . .' So he writes 'To one who was dissatisfied with his prayers' or 'An unimaginative man's encouragement of himself' :

> Strive not to catch the notes of that high song,
> Known to the Blessed only, nor thine eyes
> Strain after tranquil streams of light, that rise
> From out the Throne; nor seek to count the throng
> Of diverse Spirits,—angels, swift and strong,
> The ancients, and the martyrs, and the wise,
> Better than all the golden melodies
> Is simply unto JESUS to belong.
>
> The perfect numbers of that secret lay
> The central glories of those fountains clear,
> The source and substance of all joys above,—
> These are thine own, here in our common day,
> Since in thy dullest hour He still is near
> Whom now thou seest not, and yet dost love

There is an unsigned article on the word 'Moody' in the *Cowley Evangelist* 1893, p. 188, which contains without acknowledgment the verses 'When desire or memory' and 'While the vanities decay'—parts of a poem, 'Faith Overcoming Feeling,' published later. This article appeared eight years before the publication of the poem, but the inclusion of these lines makes a strong suggestion that it, too, was from Father Waggett's pen : and the style seems to corroborate this.

Father Waggett has left us one paragraph which speaks of other influences upon his life at this time—those of his Superior. In 1912 he wrote the following in the course of an appreciation of Father Page just after his death, which refers to his own early months at Cowley and to the atmosphere in which he then was :

'We who began our Community life under his rule, and those others, our elders, who saw him take up, in obedience, the burden of our affairs, learnt in him quite plainly the fact that rule is service. He was a messenger for us from God, always attending upon his task for us. In the house and Society which so profoundly respected him, he was still the lowliest in the House, the lowliest in the Society. Yet the humility and the subjection were *in* the office of government. They were not a light or a bloom upon a substance diverse from themselves. They were not a graceful counterweight to a *different* force, the force of his guidance, his insistence—a solace for his reproof. The humility was in the substance of government; and the government was real in our Father, because it came to him as part of his great subjection, his real share in the mind of Christ.'

Father Waggett was able to keep up his scientific interests, and we read in his letters to Katharine at this time—still as informative as any correspondence could be in a period of respite from external activities—that he was having discussions with Father Maturin on scientific matters. Father Maturin was to leave Cowley in 1897 to join the Church of Rome. The faithful Katharine was asked to send him the two series of Weismann's *Essays* which Philip had left at Bournemouth. One of his microscopes was also sent to him from amongst his former belongings.

About the middle of 1893 he had a period of anxious and nostalgic feelings about the Charterhouse Mission which, when he contemplated the understaffing of such parishes, very nearly made him give up the life at Cowley altogether. In November that year he wrote to Katharine that Poplar was still the home of his soul 'and I can't help it in spite of dear Tabard St,' but it was the latter which nearly drew him away from his course.

In 1890 George Romanes had left London and settled in Oxford at 94 St. Aldate's, being incorporated in the University and made a member of Christ Church. Here he was free from the distractions of London life, and able to take an active part in many academic debates on the relation between Science and Religion, to be in touch with many friends whose minds were congenial and, eventually to found the Romanes Lectureship, on the lines of the Rede Lectures at Cambridge. By the time Waggett arrived at Cowley in 1892 the first signs of Romanes's serious illness, from which he died, had appeared. Romanes was to find the presence of his friend in the neighbourhood an immense consolation and help in the remaining short time of his life; and his decline in health accompanied by his return to Christian faith must have occupied a large part of such spare time for thought as Waggett had during the first two and a half years of his novitiate at Cowley. When, not long before the end, Romanes was told that he must not see many people, he replied: 'I only want to see Paget and Dr. Sanderson and Gore and Philip . . .' (*Life,* p. 346).

In October 1893 Waggett was writing to his sister when he knew that his friend's condition was becoming serious :

'The Romanes go abroad on Monday. He is very ill. Can I hope to see him again? This some time past I have found out for sure that I really *care* more for him than any one outside my family. In so very *different* a way from Holland that I do not love H.S.H. more—but on a different line. I have seen him pretty constantly during his illness, and have been hoping always soon to help him—but he goes off.'

The following 29th January he wrote to K.B.W., referring to his friend's religious position, as he saw the end approaching :

'I am afraid there is not much hope for Romanes. Pray for him, dear, that he may have faith. Only don't tell that he has it not. Think how dreadful for him it is to be still without faith and so near the end as it seems.'

Evidently these prayers were quickly answered, for by Whitsuntide of the same year Romanes had completely regained his Christian beliefs. He himself wrote then : 'I have now come to see that faith is intellectually justifiable . . . It is Christianity or nothing' (*Life,* p. 349).

Romanes died on 23rd May 1894 and his wife spoke of the closeness between himself and Waggett at the end : '. . . . the two friends, united as they had been in earlier years by their common interest in science, and in those problems which all who think at all must sooner or later face, now found themselves in closer and fuller agreement than either could at one time have believed possible' (*Life,* p. 349).

The funeral service was conducted partly by Dean Paget (Francis) and partly by 'Mr. Philip Waggett, who had been to him (Romanes) as a young brother, more and more loved, during the seven years in which they had walked and talked as friends, the friend known as "Carissime" ' (*Life,* p. 351).

After it was all over Waggett wrote to his sister :

'It has been a good deal for us, this parting with G. R. . . . It wasn't his being gone which was hard to manage decently, but his being such a lover of God.'

Waggett wrote a tribute to George Romanes in the *Guardian* (6th June 1894) and he also set about a longer study of his life. There seem to have been difficulties in his mind about how to set about this task. In a letter of 6th February 1895 he says :

'Romanes' "Remains" will be out soon, edited by Gore; and I will review them. I have never seen them. Meanwhile I am just beginning to get really on with my own "study" of R.'s mental progress . . . after throwing out clouds of manuscript, much too general in aim. I have many difficulties. Want mainly to describe a bit of R. but it has to be very limited. I don't want to go far into the Religion—and yet silence may be misconstrued.'

On 7th September the same year he said that the 'essay' was finished some time ago but that the publication of it was not quite settled.[3] The preface to Romanes's *Life* by his wife makes it clear that Waggett gave her considerable help in the preparation of the book. The book itself sets some limit to the extent to which Romanes was influenced by Waggett, or indeed by any other personality, as regards the way he chose to come to his convictions :

'There will always be unconscious influence, and it probably was not altogether in vain that two or three of Mr. Romanes' greatest and most intimate friends were Christian as well as intellectual men. But of influence and argument and persuasion, as most people imagine them, there was nothing. Discussions many, during the past years, but to these he owed little. It is written that those who seek find, and to none do these words more fitly apply' (*Life*, p. 342).

Some years later Waggett wrote words about his friend in which we can read, perhaps, an expression of gratitude for what he learnt from the friendship himself :

'Those who would know them better should add to the calm records of Darwin and to the story of Huxley's impassioned championship, all that they can learn of George Romanes. For his life was absorbed in this very struggle and reproduced its stages. It began in a certain assured simplicity of biblical interpretation; it went on, through the glories and adventures of a paladin in Darwin's train, to the darkness and dismay of a man who saw all his most cherished beliefs rendered, as he thought, incredible. He lived to find the freer faith for which process and purpose are not irreconcilable, but necessary to each other. His development, scientific, intellectual and moral, was itself of high significance; and its record is of unique value to our own generation, so near the age of that doubt and yet so far from it . . .' (art. 'The Influence of Darwin upon Religious Thought' in *Darwin and Modern Science,* ed. A. C. Seward, Cambridge, 1909, p. 486).

. . .

In the latter part of 1894 and in the following year, though still a novice, Waggett was writing large numbers of reviews, papers, tracts and articles. An article in the *Guardian* on Don Bosco about this time was much and widely appreciated. Soon

[3] It has not been possible to discover that it was published.

after his profession he was at work on the revision of an office book in use at Cowley.

A retreat at Malvern, a sermon at Radley, the Three Hours' Service on Good Friday at the Society's Church; Lent addresses at West Bromwich and Birmingham all came his way during his novitiate.

Although his father and Katharine had both visited him at Cowley, his brother Ernest was the only member of his family present at his life profession in July 1895. He was soon much in demand as a missioner and preacher. He conducted a mission at Halifax that spring and preached at Leicester, Walsall and Newark.

He was not, however, allowed to dissipate his brilliant energies in merely parochial activities at home. It was indicated to him that he would be sent fairly soon to South Africa. Of the prospect of this he wrote so very wisely to his sister in July 1896:

'I have very little doubt that in a short time Africa will become the absorbing "thing" and then probably that also will have to be withdrawn from. We are here to follow after and possess God: working hard by the way if possible, but not finding satisfaction and a home or success lest we should grow happy with something short of God. The most terrible of all fates would be to get satisfied away from God.'

Africa—thither he sailed in September.[4]

[4] For the kind of impression which Waggett made on highly critical intellectuals about this time see George Santayana's *My Host the World* (1953), pp. 113–16. The meetings here described took place about 1895:

'As I found in a conversation we had afterwards in the garden about immortality, he was an *original*: I mean, that he drew his convictions from his own inspiration, even when they were, in words, perfectly conventional.'

Santayana's comments in these pages on the other members of the S.S.J.E. must be taken as evidence of his severe critical faculty which increases the significance of his appraisal of Waggett's mind.

CHAPTER V

Capetown 1896–9

WITHIN a year of his profession, at the age of 34, Father Waggett was appointed by his community Superior of the S.S.J.E. Cape Town House and Head (Father in Charge) of St. Philip's Mission. A brief history of the Society of St. John the Evangelist and of the expansion of its work overseas may serve to show the significance of this appointment.

Thirty years had passed since the foundation of the Cowley Fathers by R. M. Benson, and the Constitution and Rule, at first not clearly defined, had been established in 1884. Two years later the Fathers had been freed from the perpetual responsibility for fixed pastoral work by the handing over of charge of the parish of Cowley St. John to Vicars appointed by them, though not of their number, and the new church of St. Mary and St. John in the Cowley Road at Oxford had been built in 1883. The Father Founder had resigned the office of Superior-General in 1890 and Father Page had been elected in his place. The conventual church in the Iffley Road had been dedicated on 12th May 1896 but was still incomplete. There was no house belonging to the Society in London at this time; but work had begun in America in 1870 and in India in 1874.

Father Puller had begun the Society's work in South Africa in 1883 where, immediately after his profession early that year, he had become chaplain to the All Saints' Sisters in Cape Town. Three years later his influence and mission work had grown to the extent that a chapel was opened at St. Philip's School and St. Columba's Kafir Home had been established. When Father Puller returned to Oxford as Novice Master in 1891 his place in charge of the Society's work in Cape Town was taken by Father Osborne, who later became assistant Bishop of Springfield, U.S.A. It was under the latter's leadership that the plans for a permanent Mission House began to take shape. In 1894 a site in Chapel Street was acquired and the building of the house began. An adjoining plot of ground was reserved for St. Philip's Church and an appeal for funds to build it was launched.

This, then, was the history and situation of the Society's work in Cape Town when Father Waggett embarked on the *Lismore Castle* at Southampton on 12th September 1896 to assume the office of Superior there. With him was Father Page, the Superior-General who, after visiting Cape Town, intended to sail on to Bombay with Father Osborne. The Fathers enjoyed the voyage, and Father Waggett thus described the activity on board the ship at night, the bustle of crew and passengers moving about by the light of gas flares under the glowing circle of the sky :

'It was like a scene in a theatre said Father Superior, but he did not see the steerage; certainly it was just like some wonderful scene, only infinitely better and more artistically done than in any theatre. I do not always think real life beats Art in Art's own line; but the particular spectacle was artistic in the highest degree as well as full of the most intense human interest' (letter of 16th September).

On 5th October he wrote reporting his arrival : 'We entered the bay early on Sunday . . . when Father Osborne came on board and knelt for the Father Superior's blessing . . . and now how many years have I been here, and where else was I born? Everything is very unlike England, but so exactly what I expected that there has been no room for surprise . . . gentlemen who talk English in the night school but Dutch to one another; Kafirs, outwardly comic through excess of hat, with whom Father Conran can exchange some sibilant amenity; Government houses, museums, a Cathedral, the finest trams in the world . . . I shall write to you again when I have doubled my experience and added a week to my record of African life. At present courage and vigour must be husbanded for the visit to the Metropolitan which I hope to be allowed to make to-morrow . . .'

Father Waggett was soon at work, but his application to his new tasks did not prevent him from revelling in the natural beauties which were very close at hand. In a letter of 29th October to Katharine he describes some of the scenery :

'Sea point. You would love that. You get into a tram, and presently you are at a glorious tumbling bay of Atlantic water—the most magnificent surf—certain bays one mass of moving cream. Then you round a corner, and behold a mountain road, like the border road of Lucerne—

cut out of the high rocks, broad and stately, and walled at the seaward side, decorated with masses of wild geraniums, with *large* blossoms—and overlooking such a line of curving rocks as I have never seen, not having been to Cornwall—and over the fine sea line a range of real mountains. It is most magnificent and all within a short tram ride.'

He found the mission in a state of great poverty, but to this challenge he responded with his characteristic energy and confidence:

'Our little day's task is to believe a little more, or at least to believe as much again, as each day comes to a close. The covenant stands fast, we feel, though we can get nothing done—and we are implicated in the sure mercies of David. We are of those whom you at home are to look to with expectation that God will do great things by us—for we are really very poor in every way' (16th December 1896).

He was soon writing to his mother and sisters with an appeal to supply basic necessities of which the Mission was short. One of the first pieces of work upon which Waggett was to embark was the establishment of a dispensary. This was to be in the charge of a qualified doctor, Miss Pellatt, who had travelled out on the *Lismore Castle* to undertake this very job. It was intended that this should be a beginning of work among the Malay colony in the city —a responsibility which had been handed over by the Archbishops to the Society soon after its establishment in Cape Town. It had for a variety of reasons been possible to do very little for them up till this time. The resources at the disposal of St. Philip's Mission were very limited indeed, and it was necessary for the newly arrived doctor to establish herself in private practice in order to earn her living. No pay was available to work the mission dispensary; even the stock of drugs was almost completely inadequate. Early in 1897 Father Waggett was obliged to appeal in the *Cowley Evangelist* for £40 for absolutely necessary equipment for this new venture. His brother Ernest undertook to receive funds which were sent in response to this appeal, to buy the drugs required in London and to send them out. There is a letter showing that by the middle of August that year the dispensary was well under way and winning many friends among the Malay community. 'Mr. Russo, the chemist in Sir Lowry Road,' had made a series of generous gifts of medicine and had been kind and helpful in many ways. By 15th February 1898 Waggett was writing:

'The Dispensary continues to increase its work . . . Miss Pellatt is invaluable, both as Doctor and Missionary. I shall be greatly obliged if you put a note in the *Cowley Evangelist* and beg for prayers for the Malays.'

In the *Cowley Evangelist* 1899 Father Waggett gives the following account of the Malay people in Cape Town :

'By "Malay" in Capetown, we mean every kind of Mohammedan, whatever his race. We speak even of Indian Malays, and these in the last year or so have come to look more like the rest of the Malays by adopting the fez or Caffia, instead of the low embroidered cap formerly worn. The original nucleus of the Malay population came as slaves from the Malay archipelago, and there is much of the sturdy Malay character and blood still among them. A few of the common words of the Taal—the Dutch of Africa—are of Malay origin . . . But for the most part the influences of the old East, of Mecca and of the Turkish Empire have obliterated what belongs to the Asiatic archipelago. (It is interesting to note that the descendants of another set of slaves in the Cape Peninsula retain, after many generations in False Bay, the Catholic religion, and the obedience to Rome, which their forefathers received in Portuguese Asia.) Many Arabian faces are seen among our people; the women, without the veil, wear something of the headdress of Turkey, combined with the abundant skirts of the second Empire. (This absence of the veil is of vital importance, and carries with it the practical abolition of *half* the social system of Islam.)

'. . . The influence of the old East on the Malays is a growing one. People say that the influence of Christians is less and less. Formerly the Malays were the trusted servant class. There were bonds of affection and habit between them and their white employers. They were much humbler and more accessible than at present . . . The Malays are now rather exclusive and independent. They share in that growing separation from employers which marks working people all over the world; and at the same time improved means, and easier travelling, take larger and larger numbers of them to visit the central shrine of their religion. The Malay therefore is wonderfully uninfluenced by the people among whom he lives. On the contrary he exercises a powerful influence over them, and continually recruits his ranks from among them . . .

'. . . The Malays alone of any people in South Africa have learnt the art of keeping the number of their women in excess of that of their men. In every other section of South African population (in contrast to Europe) the men are in excess, and often a considerable excess. Altogether the Malays are apparently a solid, growing, and, in certain senses, formidable body of people.

'What is their religious state? It is safe to say that most of them know very little of the religion of Mohammed. But this does not prevent their clinging with extraordinary tenacity to their profession.

'. . . But for all his growing numbers, his industry of a sort, his dressiness, his horsiness, his fidelity to his creed and community, somehow you feel that the Malay is not a coming man. There is a resolute neglect of education among them . . .

'. . . It may be, in spite of their superficial and limited prosperity, that the time left for the Church to evangelize these people is *relatively* short.

But this is to look far beyond our own lives, those short lives which are all we have to give. For us the Malay population is a stubborn fact, an impenetrable obstacle, a dreadful outstanding defiance of our message. To think of it is a discouragement. We need all our hope in face of it . . .'

A little later he describes how the workers at the Mission were making progress in getting to know the Malays, but how this progress was revealing the immensity of their task and where they were also losing ground :

'Miss Pellatt is getting to know all about their life, and to help us to know as well. She knows the goodness of the people, and their weakness too. She knows, as few know, the seriousness of the situation, the danger to Christianity which arises from the Malays. She speaks of the "perfectly awful lapsing" of Christians. "For instance," she writes, "last month (February) I saw 89 *new* Malay patients. Of these 51 were either lapsed Christians themselves or had relations (generally father or mother) lapsed."

'. . . Let us try to maintain the quiet, loving, constant work which lies thick around the Dispensary—a Dispensary which amply justifies itself as a medical work alone, as a work of mercy and reform, and an exhibition in act of the Divine love. The Gospel work grows well about it . . .'

At the end of 1896 Father Waggett expressed his feelings about the progress of the work in general :

'There is much goodness, and sadness, and joy, and some badness, and altogether a moving moral scene all about us; and we hope to get a little altar spread in time for Christmas and a spark from heaven.'

About the same time came the cry, which is more frequently heard to-day than fifty years ago when Waggett made this appeal :

'I hope England, our carved-ivory England, in its green velvet bed, will not be deaf to our Bishops. Do you think that people at home will have any approach to a conception of the want of men here? If you will send us five new ones for one of our present ones we will try to spare one; and it will be a capital exchange for you, for every one of our vicars and curates is accustomed to doing the work of ten.'

Christmas 1896 brought much joy to the Superior, not only because of the devoutness of the services and the happiness of the social gatherings, especially the children's parties, but also because it was the occasion of the baptism of six Kafir men :

'The dark water like the grave—the devotion of the men, endowed naturally with so much earnestness, and led on by so patient a course of preparation. The figure so closely expressive of the great thing which it signifies and effects.'

In a letter of 17th February 1897 to Katharine, Waggett gives an impression on the spot of the stirring political events of the time in South Africa which were causing such a fever of excitement and anxiety at home :

'Oh! dear me no, you need not picture us in a fever about Rhodes and Transvaals and so on. Here it does not seem half so big as it does at home. It makes one stare to see the *Times* and the whole thing made so very important. The truth is, it is important to England with her great interest and her great earnestness. Here there is too little sense of all that—too much trifling and casualness, and playing with principles. I think it must be an education to S. Africans to meet the dead earnestness and real devotion to justice (not unctuous rectitude) of England. They know only the ring of African speculations, a vastly different thing from England—dear England.'

In May of that year he wrote to his sister describing a visit to Robben Island, eight miles off the coast near Cape Town, which was a leper settlement, lunatic asylum and prison all in one.[1] Without Waggett's description of the place and his feeling for the inmates one might have had a horror of visiting such a spot; but his letter makes it live as a home of beauty, sadness and sympathy :

'The place itself shows you much beauty, being itself but a little sandy island. But it lies now in a sea of the most wonderful pearliness—exquisite larks . . . and waders of different kinds flit about, and great gulls and cormorants let you get quite near to their flocks. The rocks are full of shells, anemones and other common objects of the strangest kind . . .

'. . . The poor dear Lepers are a sad sight I must confess—we find it hard even to *look* at them, and they have to bear the disfigurement in their own dear bodies—each in the only body he has got. Yet some are happy, and indeed I think they are happy, or pretty happy, or miserable, according to some difference within and not their poor health. It seems very hard to them that when God's Hand is heavy upon them, man should be hard on them next—taking them from their homes, and their wives, cooping them on part of an island, presiding over them with men in uniform, and making them sleep in wards. It is hard for them not to feel as if they were made felons; and it is all the harder because felons are trooping to and from their work on the same island, and the poor lunatics haunt it too. I hope it does not make you too sad to think of the poor little spot. A place to pray for—and for the good gentle patient Watkins, who was at Christ Church with me—unbeknown to each—and who is now their priest—visiting lepers especially day by day, utterly at home with them, treating them so fatherly.'

In the summer and autumn of 1897 Father Waggett was in-

---

[1] The island had been reorganized this year as an institution for 600 male and female lunatics, 1,000 male and female lepers and 100 long term prisoners. The 'village' contained the various civil servants and their families (about another 900).

vited to conduct several retreats and to preach sermons at some distance, and he welcomed the opportunity to get away from Cape Town for a time and to see some other aspects of African life. One of these was at Umtata in the diocese of St. John's, and other similar engagements took him to Kimberley, Johannesburg and King William's Town. From Johannesburg he wrote on 5th July :

'We had an hour or two of crowded life on the *Veldt* which did me more physical and mental good than all my journeys . . . You would have laughed to have seen us as we galloped hard over the undulating road, and took shoots, with a drop of three feet sheer (no exaggeration), almost without a pause. I never knew before what rugged places a cart could be taken over. This was a splendid clearer of the head after the retreat and made me ready for Sunday . . .'

Near King William's Town on 5th August he had an intimate glimpse of the living conditions of the Kafirs :

'On the way back, after visiting another station, where the culture of trout is being done by the Colonial Government, we went into a Kafir hut. I was not anxious to, but I was very glad afterwards. It was a large round hut, perfectly neat and clean. As there were no corners, it was easier to keep clean, and especially, of course, because the people were red Kafirs, without any European clothing, and therefore no rags and old boots to dispose of. The floor and walls were of mud, the roof of wattle thatched. Round the walls were a few bead ornaments, sticks and spoons, and a few ochre-coloured blankets. On one side a big tub for Kafir beer, and a few pots, but very few—no confusion of odds and ends. In the middle a raised circle for the fire, and round this five women, three of them with little children within their shawls,—not babies. There were two or three other children. The man was an oldish fat Kafir, and he and the women were all red, like the blankets, with ochre. Only one of the women was his wife, the rest were gathered for a kind of mothers' meeting. It was all very friendly and genial and polite. They gave us some sour milk, and my friends gave something to fill their pipes in return. The little visit dispelled my idea of a Kafir hut as a very dirty close place, and gave me a new ambition about St. Columba's. Something like this simplicity is what the men want for their sleeping places; and it is a great thing to do away with holes and corners.'

There is no surviving evidence of the subject matter of the retreats and addresses which Father Waggett gave on this tour; indeed the only reference available about all this is an almost casual remark about a retreat given about this time to the All Saints' Sisters at Cape Town :

'I have but one clear piece of advice for the sisters, "Love one another through thick and thin and God will guide you into all truth" ' (*C.E.* 1897, p. 189).

In the course of the summer of 1897 Dr. J. F. Bright, then a Fellow of Balliol, visited Cape Town and Waggett was, naturally, delighted to see his friend in this place so far from their previous haunts. He enjoyed Bright's presence and was also assisted by his advice at this time, for in the intervals between his travels Waggett was concerned with arranging a course of Church History lectures at Cape Town.

At the end of October Father Waggett went to Umtata to give the retreat he had promised there and the Bishop of St. John's prevailed upon him to stay for the Diocesan Synod. It was at this time that Waggett first met Father Callaway who was later to make an important contribution to the life of the S.S.J.E. Father Callaway was at this time an associate of the Society and had been in charge of the St. Cuthbert's Mission Station, Tsolo, in the diocese of St. John's since 1893. In 1900 he was to found the Society of St. Cuthbert centred in this mission which, in 1906, was incorporated into the S.S.J.E.[2] Waggett noted, almost prophetically, at this time that a mission station such as Callaway's 'would chime in well with the requirements of our Rule.'

It is delightful to hear these echoes of the first meetings between this great missionary and this famous Cowley Father in the sunlit and green and watered valleys of South Africa in those days when the task of the Church, though hard, was not hindered by the apparently immovable problems which beset evangelistic activity in so many parts of the 'mission field' to-day:

'I am now at Tsolo on my way to St. Cuthbert's, sitting in the cart while Callaway calls on the magistrate' (29th October 1897).

Father Callaway, writing at the time of Father Waggett's death in 1939, recalled an accident which occurred on one of the first journeys they made together:

'. . . he was thrown out of the postcart (a rough conveyance drawn by mules) near Idutywa and his leg was rather seriously damaged. He had to be carried for the addresses into the little Pro-Cathedral at Umtata by our St. Cuthbert's woodwork instructor, William Thwaites.

[2] Father Wallis, S.S.J.E., the last surviving member of the St. Cuthbert's Community, died in 1956. The author had the privilege of saying Mass for him in the Oratory at Cowley in October 1955 when he was almost completely blind. For details of the reception of members of the Society of St. Cuthbert into the S.S.J.E., see *Godfrey Callaway*, ed. E. D. Sedding, pp. 18, 23.

Then he came on to us, but was still limping with crutches (or sticks?). I learned then to see something of his beautiful mind.'

Waggett himself, writing on 2nd November 1897, describes graphically the contrasts of the place, its beauties, its richness and its tragedies :

'I wish I could convey some idea of this most beautiful place and mission . . .
'If Umtata is a revelation of beauty in nature and happiness in the Church after the slower scenes and more prosaic life of the Colony proper, St. Cuthbert's is an advance of the same kind on Umtata. Compared to this Umtata is a sophisticated metropolis. Here in St. Cuthbert's the swelling hills surround a really pastoral and patriarchal mission. Besides the priest's glebe, a big estate or small tract of country fifteen miles round has been ceded to the Mission by the Pondomise Chief. A great valley bounded by hills is all mission property. The missionary does not own the land nor draw rents from the tenants, but he governs them, appointing their pasturage and ploughing, and admitting, refusing, or expelling whom he will. The inhabitants of the Mission are Christians, but the country all about is almost entirely heathen. Directly one leaves the Mission, Red Kafirs' kraals are everywhere found. There is lovely grass, good ploughing land, and abundant water. The hills are bare of cattle now, here as throughout the land. One drives a hundred miles and sees not so many oxen. The green wooded undulating country misses them sadly, "the thousand hills" recall the cattle that lately fed on them. It is an almost awful desolation. The country is indeed plague swept. Every now and then the horns and skeleton of some forgotten beast, one left unburied out of a thousand, stare at you; here and there a newly dead animal which will presently be skinned and buried. Every waggon on the road is piled high with rinderpest skins, and about every kraal and isolated hut almost a score more skins are drying for the market. Sheep are few comparatively. The natives seem to be taking their losses very philosophically. The cattle are gone and there is an end of it . . .'

The extent and activities of the Missions are described in the same letter :

'. . . The centre consists of the Priest's house, a collection of huts for the boy boarders, a school, a church, which must be replaced by a larger and stronger one,—huts for girl boarders, catechists, lay helpers, carpenter's shop, and so on, with sheds, etc., for horses, forage and so on. A little way off is "The Cottage," where Miss Blythe lives, with one or two other ladies and some of the girls. The household here consists of Canon Callaway and Ley, and John Dobbs, a layman, all associates of ours . . .
'There are 127 children in the school, of these 50 or 60 are boarders, members of the Pondomisi tribe, whose chief gave the place to Bishop Key, who began the work here, built some of the rooms we now use, and was succeeded by Bishop Gibson. Besides the big Mission, with its many operations, Callaway and Ley manage nine other native stations besides three European places, one of which is the town of Tsolo, where

65

they are trying to build a church. The service on Sunday was most reverent—the singing quiet and gentle and careful . . .'

Father Waggett almost lapses into an idealistic fantasy as in the same letter he expresses his ideas of the possibilities of the place :

'One might very contentedly live and work very hard here for a term of years, and in due time, if younger men came on in sufficient regularity, one might very contentedly here sink down into a stationary life, which would have beauty and value in the centre of a growing work; and so in due time a man might die here, not without preparation and loving help, and fall into a fruitful soil. From time to time the younger men would go off a hundred miles or so to help a neighbour; one or two would repair to a synod; other priests would repair here for retreat; and the Bishop would bring his gifts of holy order and confirmation. New ways of agriculture would spread from the Christian centre—stouter horses, chosen oxen, fleecier sheep be given to the country-side, with music and letters and a growing free course of the Word . . .'

But he keeps such romancing well under control as he comes to earth at the end of the letter :

'. . . All this, thank God, and much besides, has its counterpart under different conditions in Cape Town, where I long to be again, in spite of the quiet here and the pure air . . .'

On 15th December 1897, after his return to Cape Town, Waggett wrote of Confirmations, inspections of the Mission's schools and of good attendances at the Advent services. There was much fruitful activity going on. Work among the Kafirs in Cape Town was progressing, too, and he refers to that in the same letter :

'The Kafirs are great men of business, you know : utterly different from our Cape folk, they would keep a lawyer employed. Logan, who came down with me from Kaffraria, is taking hold of them well, and all goes on I hope rightly. Six are to be baptized on Christmas Eve, I trust : I have a good mind to ask the Bishop to baptize them.'

The presence of a large and, apparently, increasing Kafir population in Cape Town at this time did, however, give rise to a number of difficult problems. Father Waggett refers to these problems in a letter of 10th August 1898 in which, however, he makes it clear how happy are the relations between the Mission and these people. It is sad to contrast the brutal attitude of the South African government towards the native peoples in recent years (1955–8) with the independence and security which they evidently enjoyed at the time when Father Waggett was writing :

'We have heard a good deal lately of the Municipalities' intention to form a Kafir location, or to do something else to bring into centres the large number of native men, now scattered about the Town. But there exists no power in the Municipality to remove the natives or any other clan from town, compulsorily—though if they provided a good location outside a number might take advantage of it.

'. . . Whatever happens, and I fancy nothing at all will happen for a long time, the interests of our Home are perfectly safe. For there never can be a *compulsory* moving of the natives, and while they are free to do so, there will always be a perfectly sufficient number of them wishing to enter the Home. We are full at present and shall very shortly have room for twenty more.

'There is no doubt a very large increase in the number of Kafirs in town since last year . . . It makes one at any rate very glad to have provided more and better room in our own little place, where the presence of the natives is a source of so much happiness to us, and I firmly believe to them also . . .'

In a letter of 9th September 1898, published in the *Cape Times*, Waggett strongly opposed the founding of a Kafir location near Cape Town :

'. . . Is it not far better for their race to continue to develop in beautiful countries where they have a good share of the land, where their native churches are organized, and their people protected by wise liquor laws, than for even a small section to make a permanent trek to a country where they cannot acquire land or follow their traditional mode of life, and where the future of their descendants is beset with dangers? . . . As for the cultivated and the exceptional natives, of course they will come here, and some will stay, and will be, as they are now, very welcome. But the location is not for them. It is to relieve the crowd in the street . . . Let the invasion be checked at the point of origin, by regulating the entraining natives in accordance with the strictly ascertained demand for labour . . . A governor on the supply tap is a better thing than a reservoir for overflows.'

Earlier in the year Waggett had accepted invitations from the diocese of Bloemfontein. He took a retreat for the clergy, attended a synod and addressed a conference on religion and science :

'On Sunday evening, after the services of the day, the Bishop arranged a meeting in the Town Hall. It was well attended and what I could say on the subject of the supposed conflict between Religion and Science, was kindly listened to.' (25th April 1898 in *C.E.*)

The following letters in the same volume of the *Cowley Evangelist* show how Father Waggett kept himself alive to the big questions of the day. On social questions he wrote :

'The Lambeth Committee's Report on Social Questions, of which an extract is given in Gore's "Ephesians," is a most encouraging and happy sign of the times, and a statement of the greatest ability. Let the Church get on to the highway of history where men toil and sweat, or freeze as by the Klondike; and where they think and doubt and grieve and resist temptation; let her help to teach them what to love and what to hate, and spend but little force and time on ritual controversies.'

In a letter of 30th April 1898, he expressed himself on the pastoral needs of Bechuanaland although it was far from his own immediate responsibilities and on 17th May he was writing home about the need for a training college for clergy, especially native clergy.

It seems amazing that on top of all these activities Waggett was able to undertake quite a considerable building programme during his relatively short time in South Africa. When he arrived in Cape Town in 1896 St. Columba's Home for Kafir Men, which had been opened ten years earlier, had become too small to accommodate the number who wished to stay there and it was plain to him that an entirely new building was necessary. By November 1897 he had arranged the sale of the old Home, the acquisition of a new site and the collecting of such funds as made the beginning of building possible. Early in 1898 the Archbishop of Cape Town (Dr. West Jones) laid the foundation stone of the new buildings, which were to include a chapel and accommodation for a hundred Kafir men. In October of the same year the new Home was completed and the Archbishop came to bless it.

Then there were the plans for St. Philip's Church which it fell to Waggett to carry to the very verge of fruition. As mentioned above, a site for this had been obtained in 1894, in Father Osborne's time. By the time Waggett turned his mind seriously to action £850 had been collected from offerings of people who came to worship in the school chapel; of this £200 had gone on the purchase of the site. In October 1897 Waggett found himself able to make a serious beginning with architects and planners, and the first step which he took was to change the original design in basilican style into an early Italian Gothic building which it would be much more convenient to build in stages. £500 was promised from the Marriott bequest on condition that the Church was completed by the end of 1900, and so operations had to go ahead with all speed. Father Waggett threw himself unsparingly into the task and, under God, it was his energy and enthusiasm as much as anything else which produced the result. The foundations were begun early in 1899, and the stone laid by the Archbishop on 4th February. The same month Waggett was writing enthusiastically about the response to his appeal for funds both in England and locally, and he added : 'I think there is no place in the world where the people deserve so much to be helped. They have collected such a large part of our present fund : and they have worked and worshipped so patiently all these years in the school-chapel.'

Father Waggett continued relentlessly with appeals both in England and South Africa and in the end the task was done; but as with the building schemes at the Charterhouse mission he had to be content with a Pisgah-view of the promised land. The new church of St. Philip was consecrated on 31st December 1899 after he had returned home. By this time Father Congreve had taken Waggett's place as head of the Fathers' house and priest-in-charge at St. Philip's. A full description of the building with plans and illustrations appeared in the *Cowley Evangelist* at about that time (1899, p. 249). As well as these large undertakings Father Waggett spent a certain amount of time on planning the building of a Home for Inebriates—again the idea had been first mooted by Father Osborne—on the Flats, an airy exposed place outside Cape Town.

These, with all his other multifarious activities, were great achievements and one is always tempted to ask why he could not have been allowed to stay on in South Africa to gain more and more for the Kingdom of God. It is not for us who are outside the Society to inquire the reason why his superiors in the community decided to recall him at this moment, or to question the wisdom of that decision. He had, for one thing, probably overstrained himself by making this tremendous output of energy, and on 21st August 1899—soon after his return—he wrote to Katharine :

'I fear, in looking back, that I was pretty near to being really ill. My stupid head will not leave off working : all night I dream about building funds.'

His sister had been out with him in Cape Town since the end of 1898 and he wrote in the *Cowley Evangelist* of the Christmas they had had together and of the contrast that made with a previous Christmas together in South London :

'We have had a happy Christmas. The people very good and quiet. How different from the anxieties and fearful scenes of a London Christmas. My sister's presence takes my mind back to our old quarters where the Light of Christmas happiness had to be maintained in the midst of a gross and noisy darkness of profanity and miserable excess. But there in South London was the beauty and the blessing of great and deep poverty. The cold and scarcity brought us near to Bethlehem. How wonderful that the Light first beamed in that narrow little darkness and closeness of the cave—dawned, not as the sun does daily on the expectant homage of the sea all shining, and the mountains on fire at his feet, but upon the ragged walls and the littered floor—like one's heart.'

Just before she came out he had given her, in a private letter, the following short impression of the general scene in the place of his recent labours :

'Our Blessed Lord save us . . . from sin and all other evils. He saves us from sentimental regrets, fond pictures of vanished beauties; morbid lovely colours of the past day. He gives us the future, we are attached *forward;* the new day is what we belong to—children of the morning: we are in Him who *cometh.*
'The spacious life seems to give character room to grow . . . The intense attraction which Africans have had for me in idea for so many years does not decrease but grows daily when I begin to know them as real characters.'

Soon after his return home Father Waggett contributed an article entitled 'Church Affairs in South Africa' to the *Journal of Theological Studies* (Vol. I, p. 212, January 1900). He begins this article with almost an apology for the appearance of an essay concerned with *Pastoralia* in a learned periodical, adding however : '. . . missions are a part of that great *Datum* from the contemplation of which alone sacred science reaches true and important conclusions. To refuse the gracious invitation of the Editor, might be to suggest that Theology can only regard records or that the Pastoral life of the Church can be independent of the best Christian thought.' He also apologized for putting his thoughts into print when he has spent such a relatively short time in South Africa.

Waggett explains that this account, which he is going to put on record, of Church affairs in South Africa is going to be almost entirely concerned with the doing of the English Church—'The Church of South Africa.' 'The Dutch Bodies . . . form a world by themselves of which we know too little.' But he does permit himself the remark—unconsciously, perhaps, foreshadowing the events of the 1950s : 'The Dutch have given us much that is worth keeping . . . If the English Church may claim a better name in respect of her dealings with natives, her record has been shorter, her difficulties less, though the temptations of her people have at times not been less tragic . . .' [3]

Father Waggett refers to the roughness of Capetown and to the relative primitiveness of the country. 'In organization the Church, as in more famous histories, is here also some stages ahead of the State . . . Some of the problems which will perhaps arrive at home have here been successfully solved . . . Here is a Church, then . . . which has successfully made the boldest experiment in lay government . . . where priesthood holds its rightful place in presence of the constitutional freedom of a genuine laity.'

'The parishes,' he says, 'do more on the average for themselves than English parishes do.' But he emphasizes the continually crippling effect all round of shortage of funds. 'The excellence of the clergy is no good reason for making each man do the work of three.' He regrets that the financial assistance coming from England is not larger but adds : 'A conscious dependence upon the home country is still of advantage to us in Church matters as well as in politics and trade.' It keeps the life of that Church 'open to the wide streams of English life, in guarding us against the rigidity which might otherwise attack a small and heavily burdened community.'

He goes on to say that it is in Rhodesia that the shortage of men is most keenly felt. It had been suggested that the shortage of men to work among the European community was such that all mission work among natives should be suspended. Waggett makes short work of that proposal, saying emphatically : 'The vigour of missions . . . is not the cause anywhere of weakness in the "white" churches, nor will the neglect of the natives provide better for the English.' For one thing, 'The men for the one work are not the men for the other' and he adds : 'The Church and

[3] The events at Sharpeville, Nyanga, etc., in March and April 1960 have made Waggett's words, and the comments on them here, seem a pale understatement.

Society of Rhodesia would be something other than Christian if it could patiently see missionary effort relaxed.'

He then proceeds to deal with the argument, not at all unfamiliar in English parishes to-day, that all missionary work is misguided, 'that liars are always more numerous than elsewhere in the neighbourhood of a missionary station . . . that missionaries have demoralized native society by upsetting the old native customs and thereby removing the only sanctions of morality which the native mind can apprehend.' He says :

'Grant the statement (liars around mission stations), which remains without proof. But the neighbourhood of a mission is the neighbourhood of a village, of a white centre, of a railway station, the neighbourhood of shops, of canteens, of idle questioners and idle answers. And all the natives one meets in such a district are not Christians . . . A Kafir in a coat, in the environs of a brandy-shop, does not fairly give the character to a mission which is trying to close the brandy-shop, and whose sons incur ecclesiastical censure by entering it. In the territories . . . where it is illegal and even uncommon to serve natives with drink, and where coats are not *de rigueur*, your tourist, surrounded perhaps by ardent Methodists in blanket robes, rejoices over the morality of an unspoiled heathen country!'

And he continues :

'Missions have destroyed the old sanctions of morality! What were those sanctions? . . . They were the practice or supposed practice of putting adulterous wives to death, and so forth . . . these savage punishments were very unevenly inflicted . . . a rich man could do what he chose . . . and at the best it was only the crime of being found out that was visited.'

The 'sanctions' of a primitive morality had to disappear on the advent of the civilized power. 'Missions could do nothing to preserve or to abolish them.'

He then proceeds to give examples, from his own experience, of the magnificent steadfastness of native Christians in the midst of the worst possible temptations, and of the real sacrifice which the native catechumen sees to be necessary before he is baptized, adding :

'There is in them an entire absence of that half-shame which tinges too often an Englishman's esteem of his religion. It is to them a matter inexpressibly solemn, real and precious; fenced by painful sacrifices, but every way honourable and great . . . It would seem as if these simple natures, with their direct and uncomplicated passions, their physical vigour and unshaken nerves, move towards Christ as towards a food which their whole being requires, and which they receive and hold fast with the force of a normal desire.'

And he says this last thing of the Presbyterian and other Free Church missions, and of Roman missions, as well as of the Anglican. But he adds : 'Many things indicate that the Catholic English Church may fit, better than any other, the needs, and weakness, and strength of native character.' And as one final shaft aimed at those who disparage missions he adds effectively :

'And as for seeking first the lost sheep of London, the plea for that course is shameful in the only mouths from which it issues, for one does not hear it from the laborious clergymen of our cities . . .'

Waggett then goes on to specify a number of districts, such as Capetown, Kimberley and Johannesburg where the Church is, to use a modern expression, 'understaffed,' adding :

'It is heartbreaking to state that for all this mass of natives no sufficient provision was made by the English Church—the Church which can better address them than any other, meeting them with the regulated discipline and the respect for individual liberty which they need.'

A brief reference then follows to the Kafir 'invasion' of Capetown on which Father Waggett has written elsewhere (see pp. 66–7 *supra*). Capetown, he says, is often found to be the resort 'of all the component elements of African life.' 'Here the Church might gather news of the faith in every tribe and place, and send forth reporters of the Truth into every quarter.'

CHAPTER VI

Interlude 1899–1901 and Westminster 1901–9

FATHER WAGGETT arrived in England in the early summer of
1899. A number of letters to Katharine at this time show his
relief at being at Cowley for a time of peace and refreshment
free from responsibilities, and also his need for such a break in
his labours. He was suffering from severe headaches which were
very likely caused by overstrain : the almost ceaseless activities of
recent years had taken a toll of his nervous energies. He wrote of
the advantages to one in such a condition which came from the
regular disciplined life in the community at Cowley :

'. . . Here is . . . the greatest possible regularity and such goodness . . .
this obedience is part of the whole from which such wonderful healing
comes out, from our Lord's Goodness . . . I cannot be grateful enough
for coming back to Cowley—and being among such good men' (letter
of 24th July to K.B.W.).

His superior, Father Page, did his utmost to prevent him, on
account of his health, from undertaking engagements away from
Cowley; but in July he went to London to attend a committee
meeting on behalf of the Archbishop of Cape Town. This, however had its compensation, for he was able to have lunch with
Scott Holland—a revival of his great friendship which gave him
immense pleasure.

It was chiefly because he was still suffering from headaches in
the middle of August that he was sent to take the summer duty
at the House of Retreat at Iona. This was a diocesan retreat
house which the Bishop of Argyll and the Isles (Chinnery-
Haldane) had built in 1897 and handed over to the Cowley
Fathers (*C.E.*, 1938, p. 199). A letter of 21st August 1899 to
Katharine seems to show that this was just the place he needed
at the moment and that it was doing him good :

'I wish I could at all suggest the beauty of this place—the narrow
sound which divides us from Mull—the soft air, the exquisite views from
every side of the island, and the lovely surface of the isle itself—rocks

and deep green grass, and purple and yellow flowers, and moss and heather: and yesterday the sun which was needed for colour came out, and drew the scent of honey from the rich deep cushions on which we sat . . .'

However, although he remained there until 25th September when the service of steamers to the island came to the end of its season and the house emptied, he was still not considered well enough to return to the south. He went first to the Romanes's house at Geanies—now, unhappily, for some years bereft of his friend. Thence he went for a spell to Mounteviot the home of Lord Lothian, with whom he had stayed for short holidays in the Tabard Street days in 1890 and 1892 and who was now very ill and only to live until the following January (1900). Then to Edinburgh where he spent only a few days with the dying Bishop of Bloemfontein (Dr. J. W. Hicks) whom little more than a year before he had seen, and assisted when he was in full strength in his diocese. About the middle of October Waggett moved to Onich where he was to be the guest for the next three months of Dr. Chinnery-Haldane, Bishop of Argyll and the Isles. Letters to Katharine at this time (November and December 1899) show that he was by no means recovered from the overstrain. They reveal the depression which came to him in this condition, but also the dedicated energy not 'far behind':

'. . . the distemper is fatigue, though it simulates other things. And I am not surprised at the fatigue. There have been so many questions to wrestle with, most of them momentous: and all of them greatly taken to heart. It is the fatigue of fifteen years at least of hard debate accompanied (as most debating lives are not) by a full supply of ordinary business and work. I am sometimes a bit depressed by the long pain: and rely on your love and sympathy and help . . . Just on the surface, you see, I am rather in a fix—all my life's preparation seems to have ended in a head-ache *et voilà tout*: no work, no future. But that is all nonsense. Nothing is wasted "in the great household where we serve" . . . and someone will yet make me good and purge the branch, and make me bear fruit . . . The most delightful news comes from St. Philip's. All are so good there: but it seems like a dream.'

Father Waggett dedicated his book *The Holy Eucharist*, which appeared in 1906, to Bishop Chinnery-Haldane, and there is a wonderful passage in the preface in which he expresses in glowing language from the heart his gratitude for this happy time of rest and real refreshment in the good bishop's house and company:

'When, after service in Africa, I had a period of severe pain which made me an exacting companion, he allowed me for months to be his. He brought me into all the warmth and happiness of his home and family. To have known him is one of the things which have made of life for me an experience much higher and more beautiful than the brightest dream in youth of what life might be. I did not know then that men could be so good as I have seen that he and others were. His tenderness, his entire humility, his reverence and profound faith, his patience and untiring charity make up a revelation for many of our time . . . To think of a kindness was, with him, to do it. If in his office as bishop or priest he heard of any good thing he *might* do . . . any one whose hope of Easter or Christmas Communion might be disappointed, he cast about *at once* for means to supply the need himself. He pushed the boat himself into the dark loch waters to be with an invalid priest on Christmas Day. He rode—and allowed me to ride with him—*impromptu* on a winter midnight to carry comforts to . . . the Presbyterian minister of a neighbouring parish who lay ill . . . An afternoon's round with him in Appin and Ardgour was a succession of missions or little spiritual retreats; pastoral visits which, though not rare, became in each house great or small, an event, a deliberate gathering and blessing of the family.'

This time of rest, however, was not a time of idleness for Father Waggett. Before Christmas 1899 he had produced the article on South Africa which appeared in the *Journal of Theological Studies* [1] the following year and another which was published in *The Commonwealth*.[2] He also wrote at this time an article on St. Denys the Carthusian which was later printed in the *Cowley Evangelist* (1899, p. 271). In the covering letter which he sent to Cowley suggesting the inclusion of this short article he says :

'Sailors before the mast delight, they say, in Lord Lytton's novels, and principally in those parts which least of all smack of the open air. In the same contrary spirit, one night in Capetown, after a day on the tramways, I sat down to write you a translation of a little treatise on St. Denys; and here, in Lochaber, I have found in my bag a few pages of introduction, written at Capetown, which you may think even now worth printing, though I have no St. Denys from which, at present, to supply the translation . . . A translation of some of the short works of St. Denys might almost become popular and useful. After all, how few short practical treatises are at all commonly used. In spite of an endless renewal of editions, how narrow is the circle of devotional writing known to many Churchmen. "The Imitation," "The Spiritual Combat," "The Confessions of St. Augustine," and one or two others, would complete the list for most of us.'

Waggett points out, in this article, the remarkable virtues of this saint and doctor who lived from 1402 to 1471, a period of some of the worst worldliness and disunity within the Church,

[1] See pp. 70ff. *supra.*
[2] A Christian Social Magazine edited by Scott Holland.

and which saw all the conflicts of the Conciliar controversies, militaristic popes and all that was worst in the medieval ecclesiastical system :

'Other points which will at once appear, even in a short extract, are the theological learning and the scriptural fullness of the Doctor, who, from his title of Ecstaticus, has perhaps appeared in our minds only as devout in a marvellous degree, and not also as one familiar with Holy Scripture and with the solid writers of Christian antiquity. A most interesting series of sentences from the Fathers is brought together in this small tract (*De Arcta Via Salutis*) and I dare say it would be difficult to find in the same compass . . . a more convincing exhortation to the plain reading of the Bible than we have here.

'It is good that we should see that, in what was perhaps the darkest age of the still unshaken though not unchallenged rule of Rome in the Western Church—a rule which is surely a *world*-phenomenon and a *world*-triumph rather than any part whatever of the Church's true strength—it is good that we should know of persons during that time as devout, as simple and as diligent in promoting plain Bible reading as any Protestant could be. It is good, also, to know that, in a time which was on the whole fierce and worldly, it was not only in Germany and Flanders, or upon the dim borderland of orthodoxy, that Evangelical religion bloomed in secret, but that a monk, a Carthusian, and a Doctor of the Schools, brought forth this and nothing different as the fruit of a life hidden with Christ . . .'

In a letter of 7th November 1899 to Katharine he asks her to cut out of the *Guardian* his contributions on science to that paper. He had evidently been asked by his friends to write a book on the subject, and in the letter he bemoans the fact that he did not have in his hands the earlier articles on the same subject which he had published in periodicals.

On Boxing Day 1899 he wrote to his sister a description of the wintry Scottish scene near the place where he was staying :

'. . . the poor Loch is a dull sheet of slate in the midst of a white world. It is wonderful how pure the white is of some birds. The oyster catchers' white is as brilliant against the snow as it is on ordinary days—while the "white" ducks are a rich ecru.'

By the end of January 1900 Waggett seemed to have recovered his strength and his diary reveals that he went to London, stayed with his brother Ernest and, to his great delight, made friends with his little niece Judith. He also saw his brother Francis, and 'kept in repair' his friendship with Scott Holland, the Romanes family and James Adderley. He revisited St. Pancras, had talks with Luke Paget and also with Lord Halifax who soon was to become an important personality in his life. By the middle of

February he was back at Cowley where he was immediately bombarded with requests for work of various kinds.

Letters written to Katharine week by week during the next few months give us some idea of the busy way in which he began to take up regular work again. There was an address to undergraduates at Keble College about Africa; many activities in preparation for the St. Philip's (Cape Town) meeting which was to be held at Grosvenor House on 25th June and which was to be addressed by Lord Halifax. In May he records 'altogether a terribly talking day' with a committee, a sermon, a discussion with Lord Halifax and 'immense talks with Father Page.' He comments that at the United Festival he 'saw crowds of Africans' but that he 'made a poor speech.' Early in June he paid a brief visit to his family in Bournemouth and the next month he preached both at Taunton and at a mission at Tunbridge Wells. At the end of this spell of journeying about he commented to K.B.W.: 'This life of perpetual snippets of work—or rather talking—is, I fear, of no value except to knock the self-contentment out of a person. I ought perhaps to make a great effort to get those two little books written—one on St. John and one on Heredity and all that—and then I shall be ready for a real job again.' At about the same time he paid a flying visit to Poplar and a comment afterwards shows once again, as we have observed before, that in spite of his having, since leaving there, worked in a number of places to which he had apparently lost his heart, his affection for Poplar remained quite unchanged: 'When I go to Poplar I always forget how many places I've been to in the interval and grumble because the slightest thing is altered' (letter to K.B.W.).

By the middle of August he was back in Iona, carrying out the same duties at the House of Retreat as he did at the same time the year before. It appears that he was now able, at last, to begin work on his first book. The following are extracts from a letter of 22nd August to Katharine and the book referred to is, presumably, *The Age of Decision,* a volume of sermons which was to be published the next year, 1901:

'. . . labouring with me [*sic*] pen till my hand is cramped—last night 11 p.m. to 2.30 p.m. [*sic*] and wrote 41 pages . . . It is an awful torment—the composition of anything one really cares about. And nothing at all would ever get done unless I sat up occasionally . . . However we managed here when there was anyone else but me, I cannot imagine . . . For here I have . . . the whole parlour to myself with three nice tables almost covered with my doings. You know how it is when one has tables. It always ends with writing on your knee or on a drawer pulled out. I have *really*—the unimaginable joy of it—got some of my dreadful book down on paper. Can you imagine the agony of woe of that Composition? If ever it gets written I am afraid the book will be too *intime* and I shall not like to publish it—only I suppose very few would read such a thing anyhow. You . . . have heard it all before at St. Philip's when the congregation was asleep.'

In September 1900 he preached at the patronal festival at St. Matthew's, Westminster, and in October he conducted a retreat for the ordinands at Cuddesdon College.

Almost immediately after this he conducted a week's retreat for the Sisters of the All Hallow's Community at Ditchingham in Norfolk. In November 1900 there happened the real beginning of his pastoral and personal connections with Cambridge which were to last, with interruptions, to the very end of his active life. He preached every week that month in St. Giles's church and stayed with Dr. Mason, the Lady Margaret Professor of Divinity.

On 27th November he went to Bournemouth to address two missionary meetings about Cape Town and Poona. A letter to Katharine dated the day before shows the kind of hectic life he was beginning to lead at this time and the spirit in which he approached these meetings, which might have caused another man apprehension or even nervousness :

'At present I do not know anything about Poona : and there does not seem much chance of learning before starting by the 9.6 to-morrow morning, as to-night there is an S.P.G. meeting at Oxford which begins the same moment as the train reaches Oxford (from Cambridge). Namport [*sic*]. Facts are a great trouble : and if I have no facts I can for once talk about missions in general.'

This last quotation from Waggett's correspondence suggests that this occasion may have been the one on which he uttered one of the aphorisms attributed to him—one of the many which collect round a personality like Waggett's and which may be apocryphal —'An ounce of theory is worth a ton of fact.' In the same letter he asked his sister to collect £5 with which he was going to obtain for a native teacher and his family in Kaffraria a supply of mealies which would last them six months ! During Advent

1900 Father Waggett preached at St. Mark's, Marylebone, where his old friend Adderley was now Vicar. He also preached the Founder's Day sermon at Charterhouse which was to be included in his collection *The Age of Decision* published the next year. Besides this he wrote articles for *The Pilot*—a periodical founded this year—and an introductory essay to *The House of Wisdom and Love* by M. E. Dowson which also appeared in 1901.

Early in the first year of the century Father Waggett was given charge of his Society's house in Westminster in succession to Father Hollings who had begun this branch of the Cowley Fathers' work four years earlier. Father Cary, S.S.J.E., writing in the *Cowley Evangelist* in August 1939 described Waggett's work in Westminster as : '. . . his most notable and permanent contribution to the work of the Society. His personality and far reaching spiritual influence, in conjunction with his intellectual and social brilliance, enabled him not only to undertake successfully the building of St. Edward's House, but also to establish the life and work of the Society there, as one of the vital spiritual centres in the vast diocese of London . . . While St. Edward's House remains a concrete reminder of his creative genius it may be said that the spiritual work which it carries on owes its momentum to his spiritual initiative.'

In 1897, while Waggett was still in Cape Town, some friends of the Society who hoped that 'the Fathers' might have a house in London drew up a circular on the matter which was sent out with the *Cowley Evangelist* (1897, p. 297). The founding of a house of retreat, easily accessible to people living in London, was the chief object of the scheme. The house itself was to accommodate clergymen and laymen who wished to stay there, and the chapel was to be open to both women and men. In the following year about seventy of the beneficed clergy of London took the trouble to express to the Society their opinion of the desirability of the plan, and the consent of the Bishop of London to the building of a branch house was obtained. Very soon a freehold site in Dartmouth Street, Westminster was secured and in July 1898 an appeal for £12,000 was issued. Almost at once nearly £2,000 was forthcoming in gifts and promises. It was not, however, until

1900 that a group of Fathers first took up residence in Westminster—in Charles Street, Berkeley Square. The house in Dartmouth Street, No. 13, was not ready until early in 1901 when it opened with Father Hollings in charge on 25th March.

It soon became apparent, however, that this Dartmouth Street House was in a position too much exposed to the noise of traffic to be suitable for its purpose. By the autumn of 1903 Father Waggett had found a new site at the corner of Great College Street and Tufton Street, near the Abbey, and he had plans well matured to move the establishment from Dartmouth Street to a new building here. He had had plenty of experience of raising funds for building projects both in South London and South Africa, and he was not dilatory in making appeals far and wide for this new venture. But more than that he had a vision of the importance of the contribution which the new house might make to the whole life of the Church of England. He wrote in a letter of 23rd September 1903 which appeared in the *Cowley Evangelist:*

'I cannot be silent on a point which lies near my own heart. Nothing has been so welcome as the gathering of a small band of the younger clergy to our present house for prayer and consultation. This work will find a better home in the new house. And what I specially desire and pray for is that we shall encourage one another to cherish and to obey those great *principles* of Divine truth which the English Church has been called to witness to; principles the possession of which makes the English Church so much more than—as is sometimes said—two isolated provinces of a western Patriarchate. We shall do no good while any considerable number of our clergy imagine the position of an English Churchman to be a kind of makeshift or inferior substitute for that of a person in the Roman Communion. I hope that our House when it comes may have a small place among those influences which inspire men with a sense that the English Church is, in our age of the world, entrusted by God not only with clear historical claims, but also with principles which are worth dying for; that the responsibilities of an English Catholic priest are those of a most solemn and a most arduous charge on behalf of the whole Christian people.'

In the same letter he gives a glimpse of his own spiritual approach to the material work :

'We need—if I may speak especially for this London effort—the interest and prayers of all who love the Society, and we need them especially at the present time. If the prayers and the thought are given to us, I have no fear at all upon the subject of means. But if we work in isolation and without the full sympathy of those who desire the Glory of God in our whole Society, the work we have taken in hand will be

F

set back, or, if it seems to be accomplished, it will be done at a dangerous expense of that inward force which ought to be growing in reserve for the tasks which God may yet show us after the House is securely established. We need most urgently the assistance of many prayers, and I beg for these prayers in full confidence that if they are given thanksgivings will later be given by many on our behalf . . .'

As once before in Waggett's building programmes, the site had been acquired on terms which made it necessary to begin building immediately and from February 1904 the work proceeded apace. It is clear from the accounts of the progress of the work in the *Cowley Evangelist* and elsewhere that Father Waggett himself was the centre of inspiration the whole time, and he kept himself in the closest touch with every stage of the building operations in spite of the ceaseless pressure of other business which necessitated frequent absences from Westminster. All the competence in dealing with plans and complicated accounts which he had gained in Tabard Street and in Cape Town came fully into play. The building committee and the special appeal committee under the chairmanship of the Duchess of Bedford worked untiringly, and their appeals with those from Waggett's own pen met with an astonishing response which made it possible for the contractors' bills to be paid, in almost every instance, up to time. In spite of this tremendous success, Waggett did not make the mistake of allowing himself to be obsessed with the immediate task in hand. He reminded the people that the other demands on their energies must not be overshadowed :

'There are other causes—the cause of the Poor in England, and of Foreign Missions—which must on no account give way to this effort for the Westminster House. We can, if necessary, wait; and our present object is only to let our friends *know* how the matter stands, and the conditions of entering the House.'

The foundation stone was laid on 17th June 1904 by the Bishop of Stepney (Dr. C. G. Lang). Once again Father Waggett was denied the happiness of seeing an important stage in his labours completed : he had suffered another period of exhaustion (no wonder!) and was away, in Florence, having a very necessary rest and change of scene. But his brother Ernest was able to be present at the stone laying and the members of the committees, friends and subscribers must have felt Philip's personality all around them at that moment. At High Mass, celebrated at St. Matthew's, Westminster, to mark the occasion, Father Benson preached and at a gathering afterwards Lord Halifax spoke of : '. . . the first, I may say, conventual house for men which will have been built for many a long year in connection with the London diocese . . . Such a house is a centre of spiritual life and force for the clergy and the laity . . . May Father Benson see a still greater increase in the number of his spiritual children; but among those children there will be none for whom he will more thank God than for Father Waggett—Father Philip as I prefer to call him—to whom this particular work, we may say, owes its existence, and to whom we should be ungrateful indeed if we did not say on this occasion how great is the debt which is owing to him.'

In May 1905 the whole cost of the chapel (£3,500) suddenly arrived from an anonymous donor, and the foundation stone of that was laid by the Bishop of London (Ingram) on 20th July. The house first began to be inhabited in December of that year and it very soon became much used and appreciated. The chapel was consecrated by the Bishop of London in July 1906—Father Waggett, for once on such an occasion, being able to be present. A year later, as a result of a final meeting to collect funds held by the Countess Grosvenor in her house with the Bishop of Stepney presiding, Waggett was able to announce the closing of the building fund with a surplus of £62. It was a notable achievement to have raised a house and a chapel, such as St. Edward's House is, in just over four years : but it was a characteristic feat of Father Waggett's energy, vision and thoroughness of plan and execution.

In some paragraphs in the *Cowley Evangelist* Waggett sums up the feelings of all who had worked for the house now that the task was complete, or rather now that the work was really beginning :

'We have been allowed to see the end of a great piece of work. The House is built and paid for. The Chapel, which we expected to wait, has been offered as one great gift to the service of God, and was duly dedicated last summer by the Bishop of London. How wonderful that all this provision for a life of devotion for many men and for many years is placed in our keeping, and that what was at one time so far beyond hope has become actual—a gift from God through the unflinching generosity and devoted work of many. The minds of those who know the history of this work must be full of the memory of the patient labour of the Committee which has guided us at every step, and of the great association of ladies in the work of collection which has done so very much to carry the work through. I have been specially desired by those who have taken the largest share not to write their names here. They will be remembered. The work with all these has been one of *constant* sacrifice, involving no merely general support, but real daily industry and the most careful attention such as is given to great enterprises of profit.

'In the great relief of a work so far finished we ask all to help us to give thanks. Many prayers have gone up for many days for guidance and for the power to finish it, and the wide area of the intercession will now be a foundation for thanksgiving by those who have "helped together by prayer for us; that for the gift bestowed upon us by the means of many persons thanks may be given by many on our behalf."

'May the same prayers and many others help those who are responsible to use rightly the opportunity which the Divine mercy has thus put before us.'

The rest of this chapter must be taken up with some account of Father Waggett's other many and varied activities which were going on at the same time as St. Edward's House was being built and for the remainder of the time he was Superior there until his removal to Cambridge in 1909.

From the time he went to Westminster Waggett held the position of Chaplain General to the All Saints' Sisters,[3] which involved frequent visits to hear confessions, his presence at meetings and much correspondence. Apart from this he was continually in demand as preacher, missioner and conductor of retreats. It was in this period also, as will be seen from the list of his published works, that he was making his most notable contributions to the study of the connection between science and religion. Lectures— *Is there a Religion of Nature? Science and Faith, Science and Conduct*—were all delivered and published in 1901 and 1902. In 1901 Waggett gave the Holy Week addresses in St. Paul's Cathedral, which were published the next year as *The Heart of Jesus. The Scientific Temper in Religion,* which has often been adjudged his best book, appeared in 1905; *Religion and Science* in 1904; *The Holy Eucharist* in 1906; *Hope and Strength* in 1907—to mention but a few.[4] The production of these books meant that it was necessary for him to keep abreast in his reading

[3] The community founded by Harriett Brownlow Byron in 1851 in connection with the Church of All Saints', Margaret Street.

[4] He also wrote an essay on 'The Church as Seen from Outside' in *Ideals of Science and Faith,* ed. J. E. Hand (1904), and contributed three sermons to *Churchmanship and Labour,* ed. W. H. Hunt (1906).

84

with the latest developments in science, philosophy and psychology. At the same time as all this written work he was constantly interested in experiments in social services, and many individuals had the privilege of his friendship and his help. The author has heard of a number of doctors, especially amongst those connected with the Westminster Hospital, who confided in him some of their difficulties with their patients and received immense encouragement and spiritual strength through his counsel. Father Waggett was appointed Select Preacher at Oxford in 1902 and at Cambridge in 1903 and again in 1913. Impressions of his activities in these years frequently come from his letters to his sister.

During this period he was in touch with Gore, who remained a Canon of Westminster until his appointment as Bishop of Worcester in 1902. In his correspondence with Katharine he reveals that he hopes the vacant bishopric of Oxford will be filled by Francis Paget, if not by Gore. Paget was in fact appointed, and in one letter to K.B.W. (24th April 1901) he makes short work of a suggestion—not very probable—that the appointment might fall to himself:

'I love promotions and things for other people. Ecclesiastical choices etc. really interest me immensely. But that's because I've got nothing whatever to do with them. Do I pretend to be unambitious? Not a bit. I love doing things and getting things done: and I should love to write a good book. But great places have nothing to do with me; and no one would ever think of me in connection with the smallest of them.'

In the summer of 1901 he was seeing the Archbishop of Cape Town in London; in July he made a brief visit to Iona during which his time was filled with writing and talking to the guests which included one of his nephews. Then came a warm invitation from Bishop Welldon of Calcutta, Metropolitan of India:

'My dear Father Waggett,
'I will not be importunate—for you know best—but come if you can and when you can and help the people who govern India to govern it in the faith of Jesus Christ. Whenever you come, my house will be yours.
                    Ever most sincerely yours,
                         J. E. C. CALCUTTA.'

But this he was obliged to decline, especially as he had promised to take part in the General Mission to South Africa in three years' time. On 10th August 1901 he is complaining to K.B.W. of the heat and sultriness of Oxford:

'It is so perfectly exhausting here, one is perpetually famished and yet heavy—a most weary air . . . I am always dead beat here all day long.'

No doubt he had every reason to complain of the Oxford air in a hot August, but one wonders whether his languid feelings were really entirely caused by conditions of the weather. His exhaustion was very likely brought about by his too generous out-pouring of his energies wherever he went and worked. However, he is reporting on 13th August to the same correspondent a talk with Dr. Strong the new Dean of Christ Church :

'. . . who is quite himself, not disintegrated by his new dignity—to me the greatest dignity nearly in the world . . . He is a very able man and understands the College work as well as being a theologian. I think he may do good work against the extreme critics, and altogether will be a good influence.'

And 26th August produced this comment on Dr. Sanday whom he had recently met :

'. . . now our most distinguished Biblical Scholar—one of the two or three men in England whose opinion is waited for in Germany.'

Towards the end of the month he gave a retreat to '59 sisters' at the Convent of the Holy Name at Malvern ; filling in the spare time between the retreat addresses by writing book reviews. At the same time he was reading *Pride and Prejudice* and a comment on that to K.B.W. ought not, perhaps, to be thrown away :

'How delicious Mr. Bennett is. Poor Collins. What had the clergy done to Miss Austen?'

In the winter of 1901–2 there was a heavy programme of preaching, with an especially busy time in February 1902. One Sunday he preached in Westminster Abbey in the morning and at Balliol College in the evening, while the following week there were sermons every day. From all this pressure of work he slipped away quietly to Bournemouth several times, for his mother was dying. She was buried on his fortieth birthday (27th February 1902). The letter which Father Benson wrote to Waggett on this occasion should be read in full, both as part of the experience of Waggett's own life and also as an addition to the published correspondence of the Father Founder of Cowley :

'My dear Fr. Waggett,   *26th February 1902*

'May God grant you and yours much consolation in your present time of sorrow. He watches over us amidst all the changes of life. If He calls away from us those who have been with us here below filling earth with the brightness which came to us from Him through them, it is His Will to make them still the channels of His bright love towards us, calling us while we contemplate them in the anticipation of His glory to learn increasingly the brightness of that Love in which we are to live with them eternally.

'He would make Himself known to us more and more, both by what He gives for a season, and by that which for a season He removes. It is only for a time. He shall come quickly and bring the Saints with Him. The Heavenly Jerusalem is growing to its completeness quicker than we can imagine. We may not grudge the stones which are one by one put in their place, ready to shine out as the jewels of the Great King in the coming day of revelation. They speak to us not merely as Old Testament memories did, from the darkness of death, but with the voice of the Incarnate Word speaking through them from the glory of the heavenly height where they are waiting to cheer us onward that we may follow.

God bless you,

Yrs affect. in Christ,

R. M. BENSON.'

For the rest of the spring of 1902 he was driven with work, often sitting up far into the night and for ever on the move. His diary reveals the following as a characteristic week: Monday in Oxford, Tuesday in London, Wednesday in Cambridge, Thursday in Oxford, Friday in London; a meeting about China in London on Saturday morning, to Oxford for the night to preach the Sunday morning sermon, then back to London to preach again the same evening.

No doubt much of the industry in the night hours referred to above was expended on an article in the *Journal of Theological Studies* which appeared in April 1902 on 'The Manifold Unity of Christian Life.' This article may be said to be, unconsciously perhaps, Waggett's *Apologia* or *Confessio Fidei* concerning his work on the relationship between Theology and Science. The beliefs and hopes which he expresses here about the attitude of mind which exists or which, in his conviction, should exist between men of religion and men of science is expounded more than once in his longer writings on the subject; but this article is the most concise, as well as the most clear, expression of his ideas on a theme which—although he was not able after his ordination from sheer pressure of practical duties to give it the attention he knew it demanded, and which he *could* profitably have given it—was never far from the surface of his mind as one of the most important, perhaps *the* most important, of the issues in debate in the period in which he lived.

There are two parts to the article. First an expression of a movement which he believes that he sees in the general thought of the time—a philosophical tendency. Secondly a statement of a theological position definitely held by himself. Waggett begins as follows, and it is interesting to make a comparison between the style and manner with which he launches out upon some deep philosophical waters here and those which he adopted in a 'maiden' utterance to the Aristotelian Society twelve years earlier [5]:

'In what follows immediately I express—as preface to a definitely held opinion about *religion*—only the conjectures and impressions of a listener with regard to existing tendencies in the *general* movement of thought; impressions which are perhaps little better than sanguine hopes, such as the real student, punctual in the observation of contemporary learning, will reject as baseless or recognize as more fitly expressed elsewhere. Such impressions are only confessed in order to give shape to my own thoughts in the latter part of this article.'

He goes on to say that he thinks the most important, if not the most evident, movement of modern thought is one which at least aims at some reconciliation of idealism and realism and continues:

'We need a tolerant idealism; and within idealism a tolerant monism . . . a monism which shall find large room for the practical dualities of goodness and happiness, of sin and misery . . .'

And here, immediately, he adds in a footnote:

'. . . the unity which resolves this discord is one which overcomes evil by a substantial victory, and not one which makes evil irrelevant by passing beyond the distinction of morals. The moral sense is precisely that element of consciousness which survives within our discord as witness to the final harmony.'

Waggett then proceeds to enunciate, in the clearest and most enlightening way, a point very important indeed for the support of his main thesis:

'The monism which is thus tolerant is not a "moderate" monism; it is rather one which takes care to make evident the high level at which it is pitched. Such special care is needed to allow for the interpretation

[5] See pp. 42ff. *supra*.

88

made by minds to which the Eternal is not sensibly near. It is perhaps a natural tendency of clear-eyed spirituality to announce what sounds like too near-hand a unity. The clearness which in the seer is due to long sight makes to the short-sighted a suggestion of proximity. And thus the confidence of the teacher becomes a source either of deception or of "offence" to minds of another temperament or of a lower accomplishment. Monism apparently secured at too low a level either discourages or discredits the cause it has at heart. The practical man knows that his progress depends upon gripping certain distinctions which are proximately of an invaluable truth; the distinction between justice and mercy, between sin and spiritual want . . . The work of our best teachers is to find the unity in which these contrasts are resolved, but to find it far enough aloft; so as to raise us to the high plane of completeness and not to challenge our sense of limitations in a region which we seem to know . . .'

And then he comes to the hope which he has from what he believes he sees as a changing tendency in the thought behind some of the writings of the time [6]:

'A liberal idealism, a liberal monism—it is by these alone that sure progress, not by any means of spirituality only but of science also, can be secured. I am on less safe ground when I say that some real progress has been made towards these good things. It may be impossible to point to great works which are an advance in this respect upon old books which still have influence among us. It may be that among the thoughts of others we catch only those which are most sympathetic with our own, and overlook more powerful movements which make for estrangement and conflict. But I am under the impression that this is not the case; that while there is indeed a lamentable facility of personal segregation, and to dissociate himself from someone else is the frequently accepted duty of every eminent man, yet there is under the surface a real drawing together of supposed opposites, a real effort of inclusion—perhaps very gradual—of some antithetical terms into that light in which they are seen to be complementary. I believe for example that the peace which has fallen upon the debate between naturalists and theologians is due not solely to a fatigued indifference which has its share in the effect, but partly also, and in its more valuable part, to a real recognition by science of its own departmental character, to a real respect yielded by spirituality to those limitations which constitute the very charter and strength of science. In the deep places there is a change which makes for conciliation, which ought to be prelude to a new period of activity.'

His own views of the value of scientific inquiry and of the need for a rational interpretation of the world—in a word his own

[6] It is a pity that Waggett does not specify, in this article, the books in which he sees this tendency. He mentions some in his own larger works and certainly he would have found plenty to confirm what he sensed thirty-five years later, and even more in the present day, e.g. Prof. Lovell's Reith Lectures for 1958. The reader wishing to see Waggett's article in better perspective of its own time might be referred to another article in the *J.T.S.* (April 1900) by F. R. Tennant entitled 'The Theological Significance of Tendencies in Natural Philosophy.'

part in the 'real respect yielded by spirituality' of which he speaks above, comes quite soon :

'To shut up as far as possible the senses as inevitable deceivers, to turn away from the scene of daily experience as unable to contribute to the knowledge of solid truth—this, after three centuries of successful science, is no longer anyone's desire. Instead, the idealist accepts Green's account of philosophy as "a progressive effort towards a fully articulated conception of the world as rational." It is a *rational* conception we require, a description in terms of mind; but it is a *fully articulated,* therefore proximately and practically pluralist, conception that we seek; and it is *the world* we are to account for.

'Modern scientific thought is on the whole favourable to such an independence as we covet of "outward" and "inward" knowledge. For ideas of Evolution have increased the impression both of the actuality and of the rational character of the world . . . It is the notion of ordered change, of history in the universe, which seem to me most markedly to increase the impression of external reality . . . The old equivocation on the word "cause" is justified by the disclosure that purpose penetrates all the details of process with which it was formerly contrasted. We get the result, therefore, that modern knowledge of natural sequences renders nature more stubbornly resistant to an intolerant or independent spiritualism; but at the same time more inviting to a spiritualism which is content to live on terms with "fact." The very process which makes general scepticism *less* possible makes rationalism (the search for an intelligible meaning of the world) *more* possible : the world being seen as at once more actual and more ideal. In this way it may be that science promotes the conciliatory attitude we desire . . .'

Waggett then passes on to the second part of his article which is his expression of an idea he has of an analogous process going on within theological thought parallel to that which he has traced above as having occurred, in his belief, in scientific thought. First the analysing and investigating of the 'inward' phenomena with the mental presupposition that the whole of truth is to be discovered by the observation of individual particles to the exclusion of the possibility of there being any significance in the juxtaposition of large conglomerations of particles or in any 'outward' view of the whole within which the observation is taking place. *Then* the discovery that the analytical investigation has revealed the existence of a process which is much larger than anything which is to be observed within the particles themselves and which demands an explanation of the whole—the outward 'world' within which the particles have their existence. 'Can we not recognize,' he asks, 'a parallel necessity in theology to that which I have conjectured in philosophy; a parallel necessity, and something of a similar effort?'

This is how he puts 'stage one' of the analogy when it is applied to religion:

'There has been a revival of attention to the inward substance, as distinguished from what were known as the "evidences" of religion, a revival also of what some would call subjective pietism in exclusive distinction (a distinction, as I wish to submit, falsely exclusive) from "Institutional Christianity." The necessity for greater "inwardness" has been felt, even apart from the needs of devotion, both by orthodox and revolutionary believers in face of modern difficulties. The latter have proposed to save faith by withdrawing it from the domain of history and criticism; and the former, in revolt against the crude criticism offered by science, have asserted, or ought to assert, that in matters of the spirit the "inward" must rule our debate; that an unbelieving theology is no theology at all, but an attempt to bar the very beginnings of a science which can be nothing unless it is, to start with, the description of what is contained in Christian consciousness and experience. There is a revival of mysticism.'

This almost excessive concentration on the 'inward' has led to curious effects in relation to criticism of the scriptures. Some scholars have been led to view the evidence of the scriptures in a special way because of the prepossessions with which they are unconsciously furnished. 'And among such prepossessions,' he asks, 'has there never been a quasi-mystical objection to facts as such; a maidenly distaste for that heavy food; a dim feeling that actuality and significance were mutually exclusive alternatives?' He says that all this has a most queer effect upon some critics' approach to the evidence and produces strange inversions, such as the idea 'that it is so plainly good that men should think Christ rose from the dead, that we have no need to suppose that He really did. The principle of economy forbids one to admit a foundation in external events for a belief which is sufficiently justified by its moral value.' Indeed the whole of Waggett's treatment of this question is so intellectually amusing and so brilliantly expressed that every modern student of these matters ought to be compelled to read this essay—to preserve his sense of humour if for no other reason.

But Waggett goes on to see the 'beginning of all good' in this revived attention to the inward foundations of religion. The hope of progress which he here sees is based upon his observation that parallel movements in the past have very often gone through three successive stages of development. First there has arisen a mutual distrust between the 'outward' and 'inward' schools of believing thought. The ecclesiastical mind has been jealous of the independence which it perceived in the 'mystical or Quietist or Evangelical position.' He sees here some good, because in this distrust there is not merely jealousy but a suspicion—in which Catholic believers and scientific observers are drawn to join hands—of claims of which the offence really lies in some pretension to exclusiveness or singularity, and not in the stress laid upon an inward foundation.

The second stage Waggett declares to be a clear advance upon this. It is a stage of conciliation, and he remarks :

'The writers who seek to do the work of conciliation are not properly called mediatizing writers, nor are they found conspicuously in a middle school of Church action. They seek to allow for both sides of the contrast rather than to find a middle line which shall avoid extremes. It is Augustine, if any ecclesiastic, who is at home among mystics. It is Teresa and John of the Cross, if any mystics, who are cordially Catholics. Nevertheless . . . the conciliatory and comprehensive school . . . pleads for the lawful right of two modes of Christian life to exist side by side in different individuals within the Church.'

However he points out that this mode of comprehension, because it seems to require the existence of two sorts of Christians charged with expressing two sorts of Christianity cannot be regarded as a final or satisfactory solution. 'To the present writer,' he says, 'it seems that what might be called the co-inherence of thought among the sacred writers grows clearer with every year's study.' And he continues by saying that the most profound study of unity in diversity which 'the best teachers of our time are giving to us' is that which 'will introduce the third stage of our progress.'

This third stage, Waggett says, is one 'towards which . . . it is the Christian's duty to press on, is one in which men see that diversity is not a relaxation allowed for safety's sake within unity —a concession to passing needs, but is the necessary foundation for all vital oneness.' And he adds in a footnote an anatomical analogy of a kind which nobody of his generation was better qualified to frame and employ for the purpose :

'The idea of unity by diversity of members in a body is not what I have supposed it necessary to mention. What is not quite so familiar (nor indeed *practically* so true and plain) is that each member contains *in posse* the characteristics of all. If the part selected is really natural (e.g. a polype or a cell, and not some large conventional division, such as the head or the foot), then it may (very roughly) be said to represent the whole potentially. Specialization of form and function depends not only (as every one knows) upon co-operation in a body, but also (when the body is a whole and not an aggregate) upon identity of type. The digestive cell has something of the contractility of the muscle and something (often a good deal) of the irritability of the nerve. It is only, so to speak, *per accidens,* only really through special nutrition, that the cells of certain tissues are more effectively and obviously representative of the whole. In a body of which the life is *intelligent,* though the analogy of organisms, as observed, will not carry us far, and in any case will not carry us all the way, it appears that every member must, in proportion as the intelligence is developed *at all,* have also an *intelligence* of what belongs to the whole. The difference between one kind of Christian and another is really a difference (so far as essentials go) of less and more.'

He concludes this section of his thesis thus :

'There must be during this life different degrees in conscious knowledge of the twofold unity for different believers, but the most "inward" will more and more plainly recognize that he owes the continued exercise, as well as the origin, of his faith to facts beyond himself, and holds it only in communion with the rest of believers . . . That life is "inward" or spiritual which is ruled from within; not necessarily that which is even relatively inactive in the sphere of sense; and accordingly we find even in practice that it is Mary nowadays who accomplishes the Martha tasks—Gordon who rides to Khartoum, and Westcott who mediates in industrial war.'

Waggett then moves on to a discussion of the doctrine of the Trinity to which these considerations lead :

'The intimate and inextricable coexistence of the inward and the outward in the economy of grace in seen in its fullness in the New Testament . . . the correlation between the Christian spiritual condition and the "external" revelation of the Trinity becomes increasingly clear. This means not that the conception of God existing as Three in One is a mental externalization of a fact of consciousness, but that the fact of consciousness, namely faith, is nothing else than the existence of God in Trinity subjectively considered . . .'

Here he seems to be saying much the same thing as was, for instance, expressed by Evelyn Underhill in a book on mysticism which was published a few years later :

'. . . we have in the Christian doctrine of the Trinity . . . the crystallization and mind's interpretation of these three ways in which our simple contact with God is actualized by us. It is, like so many dogmas when we get to the bottom of them, an attempt to describe experience.' [7]

[7] *The Life of the Spirit and the Life of To-day,* E. Underhill, 1922, p. 11.

Then, to move on to the main conclusion of Waggett's thought, he says '. . . in order to manage any reconciliation upon any special point of misunderstanding, it is necessary to have made a large and habitual and varied preparation of the ground . . . It is only by large and slow movements that we can reach the point where men of both tempers will wait for God's loving-kindness in the midst of His Temple.' And a comment worth noting in passing is :

'There seems indeed to be no well defined variety of Christian thought outside Scripture which is not to be found also within it; and this is not due to a deliberate adherence in all ages and quarters to the words and reasoning forms of the sacred writers, but seems to spring from the nature of the case and to constitute something like a minor support for the unique authority of the Canon.'

Waggett then proceeds to a lengthy treatment of the ideas connected with Baptism in the New Testament and in the manner of the 'large and habitual and varied preparation of the ground . . . by large and slow movements' counselled above brings the argument round to a careful consideration of the 'earthly things' and the 'heavenly things' spoken of by our Lord in his discourse to Nicodemus on regeneration in John 3. After a detailed analysis of the discourse, for which the reader must be referred to the original text of Father Waggett's article, he comes to this conclusion :

'The divisions, then, into which men's thoughts naturally fall are all represented in the Divine teaching. They are represented in the order of discovery, a discovery which starting at the making of a Christian proceeds upwards and downwards in time . . .
  1. The mysterious origin of the heavenly things . . .
  2. There is an event in the life of the Word, in His mission; involving, including His Incarnation . . .
  3. There is a sacramental bestowal of this life . . .
  4. There is an inward spiritual experience . . .
  5. But further there is to be a conformity of will and temper and character . . .
  6. . . . The new-born must serve one another . . .

Here, in one short conversation, every word and phrase of which expresses a reality which is essential to the experience of the full Christian life, is included in one manifold whole St. John of the Cross in the Dark Night, the 'Jesus of History,' 'High Churchmanship,' the positive side of Christian mysticism at its best, the ethics of the moralist and good works done for the right reason and with the right energy. They are all there, and none of them are in isolation or set against any of the others.

In this article, the only one of its kind which he ever contributed to the *Journal of Theological Studies,* we see Waggett in full flight as scientist, philosopher and theologian : all these at once and not one of them at any point in conflict with either of the others.

On 31st May 1902 he was writing to Katharine : 'I hope sermons may count for some kind of work, for they certainly gradually pull one down.' Later in the year he addressed the opening meeting of the Theological Society of Trinity College, Dublin—a meeting which 'by the help of Lord Hugh Cecil was made the most important of the year.'

All this at the time when he was supposed to be based at Westminster and was in fact building St. Edward's House ! However after Christmas 1902 he managed to spend some time abroad with Bishop Gore. He wrote enthusiastically to his sister from Rome on 8th January and the jaunt evidently did him a great deal of good and refreshed him. He must have given vent to a certain amount of boyish spirits on this expedition, for Gore reported of him on a postcard : 'He behaves well at times.'

Back in London in February 1903 the rush seems to have been the same as before. On 4th February he reveals in a letter to Katharine :

'I had a day yesterday. Up betimes I celebrated at St. George's Home, Bourdon Street, and Ernest and Constance came, which made me very happy . . . Then in a hurry to St. Pancras for St. Albans (the town) whence by cab to Colney Chapel—the All Saints' Sisters: saw 28 sisters and then walked to Radlett and took train to St. Pancras, and *just* caught the 4.45 for Oxford; stepping in as it moved. Then after tea, a lecture at Wadham College on Heredity, etc. Very well attended, with one good Biologist, Dr. Diney, with whom it is very interesting to get a talk. I hardly ever look at a book on these subjects, and if any work is done it's by unconscious cerebration . . . I read Beauchamp's *Career* in the train . . .'

After conducting a retreat at Chester later in February he spent the night with Gore at Worcester on the way back to London. Many questions were pressing on his mind for attention :

'I am fearfully exercised by my various sermons—making a great effort. Now I must go to a South Africa Mission Committee. They want me to go on the General Mission of 1904—and I shall be there about six months if the way remains open for me to go . . . It will upset very much my London work: but it is a duty, and it rests with my superiors ecclesiastical and in the Society. So many things to think of, sermons all the time . . . Schools question. Clergy Discipline Bill question. Our committee for building this house comes to-day' (letter to K.B.W.).

It is good to see that he pays this deference to his superiors in the Society, for it was an open secret years later that they found it difficult to restrain his immense energies and curtail his activities. Certainly, one is tempted to think, a member of a religious community should have been prevented from undertaking such a vast amount of work outside the community. But Father Waggett was *sui generis* as a Cowley Father and probably the Society did best by regarding him in this way, and probably he served them and God best by being allowed a very free outlet for his varied abilities. Instead of regarding all this as an aberration, then, we can admire a strict society which was liberal enough to contain such a man and superiors who were humble enough to permit his gifts to be given so generously to the world. Here, in a letter to Katharine of 3rd March 1903 is a burst of the irrepressible schoolboy in his nature:

'Many thanks for the pins—I will take one to Committee to wake up the Chairman with.'

Then:

'. . . the preaching is a work which never stops—one is always preparing for the next sermon. After Friday I turn my attention to Edinburgh—and think of two sermons daily till after Easter and the Three Hours and then they'll say "That boy's tired." '

In June 1903 he went to Eton to address the communicant members of the school. The letter to Katharine which this experience produced (27th June) is characteristic through and through:

'Addressed the communicants among the boys. Very good. Also in the Museum they have a section of a hive, between two panes of glass—with a passage to the air: and all the bees in it working away like mad. It looks an aimless hustle, but they get the comb built—and you see the honey growing in each little cell. Tremendous struggles to get the wax off the waxy ones: like boys pulling off each other's jerseys.'

In a letter of 13th July to his sister he gives an idea of how life proceeded for him during that month. He was referring to an offer which Mr. Gerald Ponsonby had made to help him with his correspondence. The 'Mission' to which he refers is pre-

sumably the Charterhouse Mission, because in his letters he hardly
ever speaks of Poplar in any other way than by its name :

'*All* the Ponsonbys of that generation have the same beautiful humble
spirit and a sort of absolute straightforwardness, so also indeed all the
younger ones I know . . . Gore of Worcester who is more Ponsonby
than anything else . . . I have had a tremendous week . . . Yesterday I
preached twice at Woolwich Garrison Church—once to the Garrison
of Gunners, and once to the cadets and Fusileers—and in the evening
I went to the Mission which was *swarming* with old friends and children.
I *never* was so popular or so nearly so and came home sticky all over
and all through . . . I took down (1) . . . a Professor of International
Law . . . (2) . . . an American lady who has spent long years in what
she calls the Orient, meaning Japan, and (3) . . . a French lady of
Russian birth. All three Pagans I gathered—the Russian avowedly so.
They were immensely impressed and gave us a great deal of good advice.'

The autumn and winter, according to occasional references in
his diary and letters, continued in much the same crowded way,
and so it is hardly surprising to discover that in the spring of
1904 he once again nearly collapsed with exhaustion and overstrain. He was obliged to spend some weeks abroad resting and
the greater part of the time he was in Florence once again. There
he had to remain until the latter part of June, missing the laying
of the foundation stone of St. Edward's House on the 17th of that
month. There is a letter to K.B.W. from Florence dated the
second Sunday after Easter 1904 in which he describes a visit
to a small convent of Carmelite Fathers in the village of Arcetri
near Florence and the clothing of a novice there which he wit-
nessed and which very much impressed him :

'. . . The Prior spoke throughout solemnly, but most naturally, introducing the postulant's name in the midst of the sentences like a man
who was quite sure of it . . . He spoke of the dangers of the world, its
enmity to Christ, the pure air of the Cloister, the call to follow Christ
in humility and mortification. The figure of the Prior, very slight and pale,
was full of the impressiveness of a really humble man who feels the
reality of his office. He was most entirely in earnest . . .

'Then the Prior addressed the new novice again, giving him his new
name, and ended by embracing him. Then he went to each of the Fathers
and Brothers for the kiss of welcome. The first Father gave it to him
more or less ceremoniously. The next, who was our friend, added a smile
of personal joy, and from that moment each welcome was given with more
and more beaming smiles, and the most brotherly little hugs and whispers.
The novice smiled more and more broadly and brilliantly, and ended up
with a triumphant happy nod to his weeping mother. It was the prettiest,
most natural, spontaneous thing in the world.'

Father Waggett was back again in England in full strength by the end of June, in time to embark for South Africa with the missioners of the General Mission arranged some years before. There is a letter of 19th July to Katharine from Cape Town in which he records some impressions of his return to the scene of his earlier labours. He saw the Archbishop and many old friends —'the people very affectionate, the little boys grown up to big fellows.' He said it was a great joy 'to see so many still faithful who have grown up from childhood since I was there five years ago' (letter of 29th July in *C.E.* 1904, p. 213). That comment on how he found things in Cape Town is at the end of a letter from Bulawayo in which he had described the work of the mission in that part of the country and his own share in it :

'. . . Now I have two addresses to give, and then if possible to bed early; because to-morrow we start at 7 to see the world's view, in the Matopos, and Rhodes' grave. Simpson has been hard at work with the children, the railway camp and the drawing-room services in the distant suburbs. I have had the daily mission service (with two addresses) in the church, and an address at midday for men in the stock exchange. This has been very well attended, and last night we had the mission service there also because of the small-pox, which necessitates the closing and fumigation of the church.'

The midday addresses for men in the Stock Exchange at Bulawayo to which Father Waggett refers above received the following comment in *The Church Chronicle* for the Province of South Africa. This report was contributed by a layman and it gives such a clear impression of the content of the addresses that it merits an extensive transcription :

'. . . Father Waggett took for his subject "Progress." The speaker first showed that although material prosperity, the increase of the means of communication, the accumulation of wealth and the growth of the Empire did not in themselves constitute true progress, still they were all parts and very important parts of progress. True progress he said was the growth of moral character. This was a definition which would stand all tests, and in proportion as material progress assisted in the development of the moral character of man it could be described as a part of true progress. The zero in the scale of progress was the slave, the man who had no rights; and the first step necessary was the obtaining of his rights. Until he had obtained such rights it was useless to expect him to think of anything else. The next upward step came when the man, having obtained his own rights, then had time to begin to think of the rights of others, or in other words of his duties : the exchange of his own rights for his duties to the Club, Society or Trade to which he belonged. The next stage was the exchange of the rights of the Trade Society, and so on in ever widening circles to exchanging the rights of the Empire for the duties of the Empire to mankind in general. This being so, men's duties being shown to lie in ever-widening circles from that of the individual to that of mankind in general, was it unreasonable to suppose that mankind as a whole had a duty to something outside itself and greater than itself, which was God : so that the true progress of mankind resolved itself into its realization of its duties to God?

'The next point the Speaker made was that although true progress meant a movement in ever-widening circles it was equally true that there was also a movement inwards. Just as we had alternations of movement in nature, expansion and contraction, light and darkness, heat and cold, so it was necessary sometimes to have concentration on drawing together in order that we might afterwards advance better. The preacher also showed by illustrations from the natural world that true progress did not mean the loss of individuality, but that each of us could best contribute to the general good by cultivating our own individuality to its fullest extent. Everything in nature was made up of minute particles each separate and distinct; from the lowest organisms consisting of a single cell, to those composed of an infinite number and vast variety of cells. What was required was the co-operation of the various component parts, each separate and distinct in itself, making a harmonious whole, and not a mass of jelly or conglomerate.'

Writing from Gwelo, Rhodesia, on 12th August, Waggett makes another reference to the Stock Exchange meetings which shows that he was very much gratified with the reception he had there :

'. . . These after the first day—and we had them throughout the week— were well attended, all the seats in the Hall being filled by men, and they are the most interesting men in the world. The free and open life here develops character, so that each person is himself and memorable. We had hearers of every kind. Government officials, merchants and working miners. The existence of smallpox in the town, and of a case in the school, made it necessary to close the Church for two nights, and on these the ordinary mission service was also in the Stock Exchange. On the first of these there was no electric light, and the glimmer of a few candles (afterwards supplemented by oil lamps) was very favourable for a shy preacher . . .'

Waggett enjoyed immensely intervals in the mission work during which there were trips to the Victoria Falls and excursions on the river above in a canoe with big native paddlers. The wild life, the vegetation and the scenery all received vivid description in his letters. The mission activities in Gwelo seem to have been very gratifying, too :

'It is a very small place—only about 300 whites—but on Sunday evening we had in the Masonic Temple, where the service was, 135; that is pretty nearly all the adult Europeans. In the morning the police and volunteers came in uniform, the Congregational minister shut up his chapel, and he, with his brother from Selukwe (like his brother at

Bulawayo) has encouraged us by his presence at the daily service . . . I have a service for women in a minute or two, and must now leave off. On Monday, if possible, I shall go to Selukwe, and on Wednesday to Sebakwe, where we stay for two nights; and thence to Salisbury, the seat of government, where there will be again a regular mission. The missions have been well prepared for . . .' (letter of 12th August).

In other letters he gives accounts of services at which he preached and gave mission addresses at Salisbury, Kimberley, Johannesburg and Pretoria. Before leaving for home Father Waggett paid another visit to Robben Island. Mr. H. F. Webb of Claremont, C.P., has sent the author reminiscences of this and his previous visit. Waggett was not himself one of those who conducted mission services for the inhabitants of that sad but redemptive island, but he was well remembered there as late as 1958. Canon R. P. Smart [8] of Capetown, who died in 1958 aged 87 sent two photographs of Father Waggett on Robben Island to the author through Mr. Webb. The first shows him standing outside the parish church in the centre of the island, frequently referred to as the 'Garrison Church'; in the second he is seen with the Revd. W. U. Watkins [9] and the Revd. Mr. Simpson.[10] Mr. Webb comments : 'Father Waggett's then boyish appearance (despite his deep learning and spirituality) is very pronounced.'

Waggett returned to England at the end of October 1904, and no sooner was he back—no doubt refreshed by the voyage—than the usual busy round of engagements was resumed. On 7th December he told Katharine that he met :

'a doctor and an engineer and another or so and Mr. Turner of the National Gallery . . . To-morrow I am hoping for an instructive hour with him and have engaged to take with me that dear eager fellow my Lord Shaftesbury.'

One Sunday in January 1905 :

[8] Canon Smart lived and worked for some years with the S.S.J.E. at St. Philip's Mission, was assistant chaplain on Robben Island from 1901–6 and later Rector of St. Philip's, Cape Town after it had become an independent parish. He has supplied me with much information about Fr. Waggett's work in South Africa.

[9] The Revd. W. U. Watkins is mentioned by Waggett in the letter quoted on p. 62. Mr. H. F. Webb has written an account of his ministry, and says, 'What Father Damien was to Molokai, so Father Watkins was to Robben Island.'

[10] Who had come out from England as one of the missioners' assistants.

'I worked hard . . . a dry sermon in the Abbey—*not a wet eye* in the sacred edifice and a visit more exacting to Edward Clifford of the Church Army, in which for once in my life I expressed differences of theological opinions, and stood up for my own. It must have been a horrid jar for Clifford, like seeing a lamb show its teeth.'

Evidently about this time Scott Holland had been writing some articles about developments in Russia which worried Waggett. On 1st February he wrote to his sister :

'I am very sorry, very deeply concerned about Holland's writing for the Russians. But I cannot say anything unless he asks me. I think that the Press as a whole has been mischievous about the Russian crisis. That does not mean that one defends the Russian government.'

At the end of May 1905 he went for a short holiday to Paraggi in Italy as the guest of Lord Halifax, a fellow-guest being Dr. Lang, Bishop of Stepney.

In Lockhart's *Life of Lord Halifax* (part II, p. 166) there is the following reference to attempts made by Waggett's host to teach him to dive into the sea :

'In 1905 he (Lord Halifax) recorded that his last bathes were "chiefly employed in trying to teach Fr. Waggett headers." As a pupil, Father Waggett, like James (his valet), does not appear to have done him much credit.'

After returning from Italy early in June Waggett was busy for the next few weeks with preparations for the opening of St. Edward's House which was to take place on 20th July. Perhaps it was during the Society's retreat that year that he put these ideas into a letter to Father Congreve dated 31st July 1905 :

'There is a thrush in the garden which hops about like a sparrow. It cannot run. It has one broken leg hanging by its side, the right leg, to which it pays the no-regard which the very active boy on crutches, who is found in every school, pays to his infirmity.
'This brave bird cannot get about quite quick enough on the ground to catch all the worms it needs. But it *fetches* a snail from the Irises to make up, and cracks it on a stone. Sometimes the want of a leg over-balances it: but it *uses a wing* to put that right—a wing on the ground where the legs usually serve.
'When it comes to going away, the one-legged thrush can fly with the best. In the air it knows nothing of any infirmities at all.
'The organ of faith is brought into use by some to make up for feeble-ness, which others don't feel, in what are called "ordinary affairs."
'When it comes to the flight of prayer, there is no inferiority in the soul which was crippled for some lower uses.' [11]

[11] *Christian Progress* by George Congreve, 1910, p. 324. In the intro-duction Father Congreve remarked that the inclusion of this paper brought him 'one touch of unmixed pleasure . . . into the collection.'

This month his diary records a meeting with Sir Francis Younghusband at the Duchess of Bedford's house. Then his voice began to cause him some trouble and it is a change to come upon a letter *from* Katharine giving her brother some advice:

'I am grateful to hear your voice is all right. *Do* be careful with it and don't begin preaching again yet or if you do preach in quite an undertone. It's such a good plan and makes them listen. With a bellow if they look stupid and then very small and quiet again' (13th August 1905).

That September he conducted the ordination retreat at Fulham Palace; and in October he performed the same office once again at Cuddesdon:

'The Bishop of Southwark was there and his two suffragans elect. The Dean of Christ Church, Warden of Keble, Dr. Rashdall the Great Heretic (such a dear) and other great persons, all content with the simplest form of addresses' (letter of 11th October to K.B.W.).

The list of sermons, addresses and talks which Waggett delivered in November and December 1905 it would be tedious to record. At the end of January 1906 he went to Edinburgh to

'preach at the Cathedral and another Church, and have two missionary meetings, one for the clergy, and one for the public. And also to visitate [*sic*] the All Saints' Sisters who are in Edinburgh' (letter of 13th January to K.B.W.).

In February he met Lord Hugh Cecil in Westminster and this *rencontre* gave rise to a flippant remark to his sister:

'He is a *dear* person. He looked quite a wreck, after the Party Meeting and all the anxieties of the last weeks. Perhaps it will end in our getting him for Archbishop of Canterbury after all' (letter of 15th February to K.B.W.).

He was delighted at this time to hear of the appointment of his great friend Luke Paget as Bishop suffragan of Ipswich. On 16th March he was writing to his sister in reply to her request for advice on what she should do in relation to the problems of religious education which were exercising many people's minds at that time:

'It does not matter which of the memorials the parents sign: either *National Society's* or Lord Halifax's. (Lord Halifax's is not E.C.U.'s, not to be called that). If the vicars don't provide one or the other, it is bad: and I think your best way of asking would be to write to National Society. It ought to be done. We know for certain (though it's one of those things that can't be said) that Birrell *wants* to be memorialized by the parents.'

He was preaching very hard all through that Lent—more than once a day on average—frequently at Manchester. On Easter Monday he went for ten days' holiday to Florence with his friend Edmund Brocklebank. After Easter 1906 Father Waggett went to Cambridge to stay again with the Masons, and on Sunday 29th April he delivered the University Sermon in Great St. Mary's (*The Cambridge Review*, 3rd May 1906, p. 368). On this occasion he preached without notes—unnecessarily apparently—for when he got into the pulpit at the University Church 'something fell over which I supposed to be my MS. (but was really my cap)' (letter to K.B.W.). At dinner on this visit he met Professor J. J. Thomson, the famous physicist and pioneer of atomic science, whom he described as 'the foremost scientific man of the world at present—a most simple . . . jolly, natural, kind man.' The University sermon, though it would probably be an exaggeration to say that it shows the work of a moralist 'at its best' yet certainly shows how a moralist can say things of very great value indeed. This sermon also shows one of the lines along which Waggett at this time conducted the debate of religion against scientific agnosticism or amoralism, particularly in the field of theories of heredity. The end of the sermon appears to be rather disappointing and tells us that Waggett has not yet reached the height of his powers as a preacher. His text is 'If ye then be risen with Christ, seek those things which are above . . .' (Col. iii, 1). He begins :

'The supernatural condition and the high destiny which is no less than to be with Christ in glory, require in the Christian a daily rejection of evil; they lay claim upon the body, upon the hours. Our persevering practice of good is more than the condition of our acceptance with God; it is the very process of Christ's redemption in us. His saving grace, first protecting, afterwards enlightens us; it is developed in growing recognition of His purpose, in a constantly more deliberate obedience to His law.

'These are the thoughts which I would follow a little further; but it is not fitting for me—being what I am—to offer opinions or persuasions to many of those in whose presence I speak to-day. I wish rather to repeat to the younger members of the University some of the old lessons of faith, old to them as to me, but to them not so old that they cannot verify them by an early obedience.

'They are among our first recollections—the call to faith, the promise of grace, the assurance of the power of prayer, the lessons of the happiness of the humble and the pure in heart, of the power of love, the sovereignty of goodness in a world where for young eyes goodness is obscured by many splendid competitors—wit, bravery, strength and address, the prestige of birth and station, the imperious charm of beauty. These were among the first lessons offered us; and how late we accept them seriously; how late we grant to them the test of our obedience.

'. . . It seems to me that most of our plans are of the wisdom of the world; most of our strife is against flesh and blood and for our own honour; and it is only when all is tried which fancy can suggest that we turn at last to the commandments which long ago were given to be a light to our feet.

'Late we learn, and slowly when late we begin; and because late, therefore when already our lives are encumbered, and steps have been far astray, and strength is ebbing and the eyes no longer clear . . .

'How great a consolation for those who late obey if their past sorrows could issue in this fruit—if the unspeakable regrets might urge us to speak words which now could rouse one man to prove betimes the great directions of eternal life.

'. . . Christ Himself, who saves our nature by making it His own, yet saves it, even in His own person, in the reality of action. He redeemed it not by the momentary exhibition of a divine prerogative but by the enduring heroism of a lifelong sacrifice in obedience to the will of the Father . . . The conflict was not less actual in Him because it was triumphant; the choice of good and rejection of evil was not less persevering, less personal, because it never wavered; the fidelity to God not less costly in devotion because of its unfaltering sacrifice.

'. . . So far probably we are all agreed, and it is an old story. It is true that lately great attention has been given to the natural forces of human life which influence it from within. There has been an advance in the natural history of man, for those who are specially devoted to natural history. And among thinking men and others who welcome the news which comes from science, there has been a considerable impression that men's lives are entirely directed by hereditary disposition in combination with circumstances; that conduct is a result only, and in no sense a cause; and that the hope which inspires moral effort is a delusive hope.

'. . . It is enough for our present purpose to say that the new knowledge we have received is not of that kind which practically liberates new forces. Sometimes a force newly recognized is equivalent for some purposes to a force newly created. For example, the isolation of vibratory or explosive energy which has always been present in combination with other forms of motion may affect commerce and social intercourse.

'But the increased knowledge of the facts of inheritance is not, at least at present, of that kind.

'. . . If moral effort is useless now it was useless always. If we have not entirely mismade history in the past moral effort has directed in some measure the course of human development, it directs it still and will direct it in the future.

'A practical effect can only follow the new conceptions by way of an alteration or abandonment of the moral effort itself . . .

'There is no reason for any surrender of the kind. Moral choice is not abolished by the limitation and the relative stability of the moral material.

'Character is not temperament. Character is both indicated and actually determined by the way in which a man—granted that the spring by which he works is unknown or unknowable, granted that it may be beyond the limits of his own being in time—yet in fact manages a given temperament in a given world, in a set of circumstances relatively to him fixed but affording—as does the fixed structure of his mental and bodily constitution—alternatives for choice.

'. . . The question we ask ourselves is this. Which of the powers within me do I wish to find eternally strong? Which, then, shall I give scope to? . . .

On Whit Monday 1906 Father Waggett visited King's College, London, and addressed a gathering of old students. After this he had another onset of headaches and general tiredness which hampered him throughout that summer. At the end of August this led him to accept an open invitation to visit the Duchess of St. Albans at Clonmel. In November he lectured to the medical students at St. Bartholomew's Hospital. Then may we be forgiven for detecting a wistful note of vanity creeping into his chronicle to his sister? : 'I look in on Lady Wantage . . . I dine with her about once a year and she gets savants to meet me.'

Waggett had a short time before this been elected a member of the Synthetic Society, a group founded in 1896 by Talbot with Gore and Wilfrid Ward with the object of co-ordinating different points of view of eminent men on the issues of the times and making a positive contribution to the thought and discussions of the day. In its time the society included A. J. Balfour, Lord Haldane, Sir Oliver Lodge, George Wyndham, William Temple, Alfred Lyttleton, Baron von Hügel, Hastings Rashdall, Scott Holland and G. K. Chesterton. In November 1906 Waggett was corresponding with Balfour and Ward about proposals which were to come up at the next committee meeting of the Synthetic Society. In a letter of 8th December to Katharine he gives a good indication of the width, and depth of his varied contacts in these years :

'I have had beautiful days at Oxford. There is a wonderful set of young creatures now at Balliol—mostly from Eton—all as clever as can be and Socialist and also Christian. Laffan, Knox, Lister, Browne—these strike my mind most: but last night I saw 20 of them—all most delightful—with the extraordinary *sudden* simultaneous bursts of deep laughter that only boys from 18 to 22 have. All so good to each other.

'Then I have been to Eton and seen the young ones coming on: and I gave a sermon . . . in Lower Chapel there . . . to all the Communicants and the boys who were to be confirmed next day—including William Congreve, Father Congreve's great nephew. It was jolly beyond words.

On the 28th we had a meeting of the committee of the Synthetic Society—Balfour, Wilfrid Ward, Wyndham, Sir K. Lyall, Dean of Westminster—that is to say the original members and one or two added. I hurried away to see . . . Lord Roberts.

'Then on 2nd December last Sunday I went to Cambridge to preach to undergraduates in the University Church and enjoyed that very much: and saw other delightful men—Selwyn, Leslie, Spens—especially Spens: a wonderful Christian set of extremely clever men. There is a real *spring* time both at Oxford and Cambridge, such as there has not been for years . . .

'I am very well on the whole. Very sorry about some things: and feeling that some sort of change is dreadfully needed in society and in the country. We have got into precious tangles both of thought and practice. I don't mean a change in religious thought—though there also it would seem that there are men taking much more superficial views than we thought they did.

'Here in London I have been lecturing almost daily. What I have been most thankful for is three lectures to the Medical Students at St. Bartholomew's Hospital. I am going to give in January similar 3 at University College. There also, in the Medical Schools, is a strong and hopeful Christian movement . . . I expect I shall have to give up my visit to Rhodesia in 1907 which is not a bad thing.'

On 14th January 1907 he wrote to his sister an interesting note about a meeting with an old friend :

'I have been to Cambridge . . . Last night after work I had a long talk with Harry Head the doctor at his mother's. You remember Head was the other science boy at Charterhouse. He is now a very leading, perhaps the first, brain specialist. He has vivisected his own nerves to find out things. A most cheerful robust eager person.'

Holy Week 1907 saw him conducting a retreat at Chester. He was tired again, but had something penetrating to say about the keeping of days and seasons :

'. . . it is unfortunate for these dear Chester people that I am so much at an end . . . I am not helping them. But they *look* for help in the kindest way. I know so well what you mean about special seasons. The *reality* is the reality of prayer in common: and a new gift of the Holy Spirit must be hoped for—only the gift won't be like others before. There is a time of life when the season is a great deal and then later life and prayer must both of them become more level. Part of the difficulty of preaching is that the young people are still *there*—longing for the Holy Week of youth. I wish we could call up one of the very young men from Oxford to preach.'

In the months that followed he was as much pressed as ever with retreats, sermons, lectures, journeys, writing,[12] his chaplaincy to the All Saints' Sisters and the supervision of St. Edward's House. In July 1908 he permitted himself to write :

[12] In 1908 he contributed two sermons to *Mission Preaching for a Year*, Part II, ed. W. H. Hunt.

'I don't think people know how really hard we work in an ordinary way quite apart from all the things they hear about—how hard we grind for £30 a year here and £28 there—all necessary to make two ends meet at Westminster. But it would be very silly to appeal *ad misericordiam*. I heartily enjoy work. The thing I have to write is the contribution to the Darwin memorial volume published by Cambridge University—next year is the 50th anniversary of the great book. If I do it well, it may be of real use to the Church.'

St. Edward's House was full, really carrying out its purpose. Father Waggett had become known throughout England—and in many other parts of the world as well—as a great religious teacher; but he was on the eve of another change in his life. A period lay before him in which, for a time, he was not to shine quite so brightly.

CHAPTER VII

Cambridge 1909–14

FATHER WAGGETT had for some years been connected with University life at Cambridge. He had been chosen as preacher before the University a number of times and he had also preached to undergraduates and addressed meetings from time to time on missionary and scientific subjects. He had friends among the senior members of the University, notably Dr. Mason with whom he had stayed on occasions when he had visited Cambridge to preach. He had easy contacts with public school boys, among them those of Eton and Charterhouse, and with students of various kinds; and it was quite natural that he should be thought eminently suitable to undertake some kind of chaplaincy work within a university or on its borders. Bishop Hensley Henson, though having a great respect for Waggett, used to describe him scoffingly as the "decoy duck of young intellectuals" ' (*Retrospect of an Unimportant Life,* Vol. III, p. 366); and this, although it is a slightly barbed Hensonian witticism, is also a tribute to his influence over young men.

In the early part of 1909 there was a project afoot for the establishment of a house at Cambridge which should be something of a counterpart to Pusey House at Oxford : a house of Christian conversation and study distinctly in the Anglo-catholic tradition, with a chapel and library, where those who were considering ordination could stay from time to time, and where there would be a small staff competent to lead discussions and give counsel to young men both in connection with their vocations and with regard to the place of the Christian faith in a university and in the professions and jobs to which graduates, on leaving the university, would be going. The project was being discussed by the committee of the English Church Union which then had Lord Halifax as its chairman and H. W. Hill as secretary. Funds for the purpose had been put by the Rowe Bequest into the hands of the committee, who were to act as trustees.

The house acquired for this enterprise was one which had belonged to R. D. Archer-Hind, the well-known Cambridge classicist and Fellow of Trinity, and before that to Harry Goodhart, in Malting Lane and the trustees obtained it upon a lease. The establishment began its existence with the title of St. Anselm's House and it opened its doors to six quasi-permanent residents in October 1909 at the beginning of the Michaelmas University term. These comprised four young men who had recently graduated and who were either thinking of offering themselves for ordination or desiring to take part in study of the kind outlined above; Father Waggett who was appointed Warden of the House, and Leonard Pass whom he had as sub-Warden or second in command. Pass was then a layman, but subsequently (in 1916) he was ordained and eventually held the offices of Principal of Chichester Theological College and residentiary canon of Chichester Cathedral.

Here follow some reminiscences from the pen of the Right Revd. J. C. H. How, D.D., formerly Primus of the Episcopal Church of Scotland, which are included with the object both of filling in the background of the religious situation in Cambridge at this time and also of recovering a small part of the memory of H. L. Pass which might otherwise fail to find permanent record :

'It would be true to say, I think, that for the first few years of the century the only really active missionary forces in the life of the University were the Cambridge Pastorate (centred on the evangelical church of Holy Trinity) and the C.I.C.C.U. . . . an undenominational society . . .

'On the Catholic side in the Anglican Church the three churches (St. Giles, St. Clement and St. Mary the less) . . . each attracted a certain number of undergraduates who sought ways of worship on richer and fuller lines than they found in their College chapels.

'In the colleges the dons, even the clerical dons, seemed to be rather aloof from the undergraduates, and (as it seemed to most of us) did little to make intimate contacts with the younger men or to give them pastoral attention. No doubt there were exceptions . . .

'Not that there were not catholic-minded priests, and some laity, amongst the senior members of the University . . . These all (and others with them) had their quiet influence in their colleges and beyond, and undoubtedly helped to prepare the way for the very definite 'Catholic Movement' that was to begin and spread . . .

'If, as has been said, those college dons already mentioned contributed to this movement, its real forward march was due to the untiring and devoted work of a *lay* senior member of the University, who never received any official appointment to any college office, whether of his own college, St. John's, or elsewhere. He was a Jew by birth, and, one may suppose, in his early days, by religion; but those who knew him before and during the very first years of the 1900s, will remember that he was then rather of an agnostic turn of mind, and was an amusing and convivial member of a little group of like-minded "philosophers." But all that was to go. He was converted (largely, we understood, through the influence of Canon E. G. Wood). He was baptized by him, and forthwith began his most remarkable work for the Catholic cause in the University. His name was Herman Leonard Pass. Many years later he was ordained and became Principal of Chichester Theological College; but we are now concerned only with the earlier period.

'Externally and physically he had everything against him! He was a tiny creature (only about 5 ft. high) with a heavy black moustache, a very definitely Jewish face, very weak eyesight which demanded very large and highly magnifying spectacles, and a frail body with an inside which was constantly giving him trouble. I have often felt that he had all the physical disadvantages of St. Paul and I think we may reverently say that he had a very full share of that apostolic fire and zeal which characterized the great converted Jew of those first days.

'He lived in lodgings at 31 Thompson's Lane . . . and an amazing amount of converting and deepening influence flowed out from that unpretentious abode.'

Bishop How recalls that a group of college chaplains and scholars gathered round H. L. Pass and met from time to time at his lodgings. This group came gradually and informally to call themselves 'The Brethren' and they formed something comparable with the 'Holy Party' which met at Illingworth's Rectory at Longworth in preparation for the publication of *Lux Mundi*. 'The Brethren' would have acknowledged the description of 'Liberal Catholic' as indicating their theological position and it was they who in November 1907 had sent a letter of sympathy to Father George Tyrrell in his struggles for liberalism within the Roman Communion and who received a gracious reply from him.[1]

This, then, is an indication of the 'Liberal Catholicism' of 'The Brethren' who wished to form a centre and a house of study in Cambridge, and such was the Herman Leonard Pass whom they would probably, but for the fact of his still being a layman at the time, have placed at the head of St. Anselm's House. Father Waggett, whom they did eventually choose for the position, was, as a scientist and a Cowley Father, in full sympathy with the 'Liberal Catholicism' of the group which was sponsoring the

[1] See Maude Petre's *George Tyrrell,* Vol. II, pp. 371–2, for the text of both.

foundation of the house, which was to be a precursor in some sense of the Oratory House (Oratory of the Good Shepherd) in Lady Margaret Road in later days. The tenuous connection, such as it is, between St. Anselm's House and the Oratory House is referred to briefly in the recently published *History of the Oratory of the Good Shepherd* (1958) by H. R. T. Brandreth (pp. 7, 8). W. L. Knox and A. R. Vidler, both members of the O.G.S. (the former was Superior for some years) who both lived for a period at the Oratory House, were of the second generation of Cambridge Liberal Catholics and they show their debt to Waggett's thought in their book *The Development of Modern Catholicism* (p. 116f.) published in 1933 :

'The breach between science and religion was too deep to be healed by a single book; but *Lux Mundi* marked a great step forward in so far as it delivered Christians from the desperate duty of ignoring the scientific teaching of the modern world . . . Even when it appeared the controversy was dying down, the situation at the end of the Victorian era is described thus a few years later: ". . . the tragic breach between those strong souls (the scientists) and the men who try to pray becomes deeper just because it is forgotten . . ." (*Religion and Science* by the Revd. P. N. Waggett, S.S.J.E.).' [2]

The Revd. Michael Champneys,[3] who was one of the four younger members of the household at St. Anselm's and who lived there during these first twelve months of its existence, has supplied most of the information about this period of Father Waggett's life. There is remarkably little evidence in the sources used hitherto [4] probably because the First World War brought this period to an end. Letters and papers were lost in the sudden upheaval and people's memories became confused at the beginning of this war even more than at the outbreak of the second, because the earlier one came as a more sudden surprise.

But even this is not quite enough to explain the hiatus. There is no doubt that in some strange way, and for a variety of causes, Waggett suffered a measure of eclipse at this period. The tremendous pressure of the preceding years must have left him to

[2] Reference to *The Development of Modern Catholicism* would help any one wishing to plot Waggett's place in the evolution of Anglican theology. See chapters XIII and XIV *infra*.

[3] Died in 1958.

[4] I am indebted to the Right Revd. John How, D.D., not only for the notes above but also for details of the whole of this period.

a certain extent nervously exhausted. We have seen before that he was subject to spells of what can only be described as nervous prostration—verging on breakdown—and this time it seems to have been a longer spell of less intense fatigue. Those who remember him during these first years at Cambridge recall that he was often easily irritated and Mr. Champneys, who had opportunity to observe him at close quarters, remarks that it was difficult to imagine him as being really relaxed. He seemed to feel loneliness and more than once was heard to say that what he wanted was affection, not respect. He even seems to have been ill at ease with his religious vocation at this time and friends questioned whether he had rightly decided to commit himself to life vows in a religious order. There is enough evidence to suggest that he was passing through a mental and emotional crisis such as comes to many men slightly earlier in their lives and which was never completely revealed or which, at any rate, is not described in his surviving letters and diaries.

Waggett went to Cambridge early in the summer of 1909 to make arrangements in connection with the beginning of the St. Anselm's House venture. He was looking forward to a spell of life which should be less rushed and in which his energies might be more concentrated and his work more stationary. On 16th June 1909 he wrote a letter to his father in which he makes remarks which perhaps half unveil the distracted and strained state of his being:

'It irks me very much (as the English of the Latin grammar used to say) that I cannot come at once to you. I have to see after things in Cambridge to-day—to-morrow I shall be in London—but at Colney all Friday and then on Saturday to Leeds. While all next week will be occupied with the "Darwin" commemoration at Cambridge. London to-day is full of fine people going off to Ascot, where I am told there are horse-races . . .
'I think Cambridge may be a great blessing for me—at present a blessing in disguise. It will stop this moving about and the endeavour to meet the multiplied demands of many different kinds of people : and—well there will be many advantages consequent upon that.'

Dr. Waggett died on 2nd November 1909, only a month after his son had taken up residence at Cambridge.

If Father Waggett was to be able to play any official part within the life of the University he must needs be made a member of it. Early in 1910 he was admitted to the degree of M.A. and became a member of Trinity College. One who knew him well at the time wrote this recollection of the degree ceremony :

'. . . one of my most vivid recollections is of his matriculation in the University as a preliminary to receiving the degree of Master of Arts *ad eundem*. The spectacle of Waggett in an undergraduate gown would have been unforgettable, but it was not vouchsafed. His dignity called for a better way. Accordingly he walked up the steps of the Senate House preceded by his servant, who bore in his arms the gown of an undergraduate of Trinity. Within, as Waggett took pen to sign his name in the book, the gown was momentarily laid on his shoulders' (*Church Times*, 14th July 1939).

It was also necessary for him to have some regular status in the diocese of Ely, however nominal. Accordingly he was licensed to a curacy at St. Peter's, a little ancient church which was the parent church of St. Giles' and is now little more than a chapel of ease within that parish. Waggett used to celebrate the Communion at the altar of that church and assist in other ways also in St. Giles's parish.

But the St. Anselm's House part of his work—and that was the chief reason for his being in Cambridge—was not what the world, or even the Church, would call a 'success.' To begin with there was personal incompatibility between himself and his colleague Leonard Pass. Exactly where the cause of this lay it is difficult to determine : there is no reason to think that Waggett had any particular lack of sympathy with baroque art, the Romance languages or the Mediterranean peoples, all of which were so close to the heart of Pass.[5] There is the suggestion, though, which seems to emerge from Dr. E. G. Selwyn's recollections in Mr. Gillett's memoir of Pass that Father Waggett was only appointed as Warden of St. Anselm's House because Pass was still a layman and therefore unable to perform the functions which were required : that in fact the drive and inspiration for the whole undertaking came from Pass and not from Waggett. If this interpretation is correct, and if Waggett was aware of this fact, here are the makings of a situation in which Waggett would have been ill at ease from the start. Here are Dr. Selwyn's recollections (*op. cit.*, p. 20):

[5] See *Herman Leonard Pass*: a Memoir by C. S. Gillett (Mowbrays 1939).

H

'As Pass's work developed, the time seemed ripe for setting it upon a more recognized footing. One difficulty about this was that Pass was still a layman . . . and seemed likely to remain so; so that if a chapel were to be provided it was necessary to find a priest. Father Waggett, s.s.j.e., was at this time disengaged, and it seemed that he might bring to such a house just the gifts that we needed . . . Two men more different in temperament than Leonard Pass and Father Waggett it would be difficult to conceive; you might as well try to mix water with quicksilver; and the arrangement did not last very long . . .'

Waggett is described by those who knew him at that time as being frequently uneasy with the undergraduates who came into the house for meals—as well he might if he felt that his position in the place was in some way a false one—and he is remembered as making frequent references in conversation to his prowess as a biologist, as though to compensate himself for some inadequacy which he supposed he had. Little stories about his idiosyncrasies at this time have survived.[6] When the conversation of the young men at table—and perhaps of the older ones, too—was beginning to get on his nerves he would scratch his head in an agitated manner and say: 'A spider in my hair: I think that means I must join some other Church.' Or there was the young man who would repeatedly ask questions about Church ceremonial and try to lead the conversation along the lines of what might be called 'sacristy gossip' who received the reply: 'I'm afraid I don't know, I'm *not* high church myself.'

Somehow, in spite of his immense abilities and his personal attractiveness, Waggett did not either in this period or when he returned in 1927, make the impact in Cambridge that would have been expected. His headship of St. Anselm's House lasted for little more than a year. After that he moved to a house, No. 55 Chesterton Road (close to St. Giles's church) in which he lived with Father Longridge, s.s.j.e., for a time. Here things were happier: he did more effective work among the junior members of the University and established better relationships with the colleges.[7]

[6] There are also the stories of his tame birds. At this time he had a blue Mediterranean thrush which had the habit of lying on its back for him to stroke it and which followed him about from room to room like a dog. During his second Cambridge period he had a parrot, acquired in Alexandria, which was similarly attached to him.

[7] I am indebted to Sir Will Spens for the recollection of his Lent lectures in 1910 described on p. 165 n. *infra,* which gives a picture of Waggett's work at this period.

In spite of the apparent failure—though this is probably too strong a word—of this period, perhaps the quieter rhythm of it prepared his nervous energies and husbanded his resources for the great work which was to be done in the following years. But during these five years in Cambridge he did not wholly escape from outside demands.[8] On 6th August 1911 he was at Oxford preaching in the Society's Church a single sermon on the Transfiguration and on the death of the Bishop of Oxford, his friend Francis Paget, which had occurred a day or two before. His sermons had lost none of their accustomed force:

'. . . It was on a mountain of earth, lifted towards heaven, but rooted in the plain, where pain and disfigurement, sorrow and madness share what seems their home and kingdom with sin and unbelief, that the glory shone—a glory hidden by the veil not of His body, for the flesh is the way through the veil—but of that body's then mortal condition.

'The vision and the voice that certified its meaning were given that we might have hope of life beyond the grave . . . Our Feast, then, of the Transfiguration may take for us this year a colour of consolation and teaching about the mystery of death; because the Feast this year finds us in mourning for our Bishop, the Father in God of this diocese, and the visitor and protector of our Society . . .

'In the light of this life so closed; so vigorous, so disciplined, so complete; so filled from end to end with duty and faith, let us seek a lesson about death and the life that interprets death . . .

'This life is at best so short, and it is haunted with uncertainty . . . That is certainly the *first* thought . . . Human life is perhaps least lamentable when it is most pathetic; when the buds that never bloom are cut off unopened, the dew of the morning still undisturbed . . .

'The second Christian thought about the dead is a thought of the blessedness of the life they are removed to in contrast to the sadness of the life they leave behind: its solidity, its golden solidity, in contrast with the vanity of this . . .

'Is that the last word? He has left what was vanity and found what is real? Nay, for here, on this side of the grave, his conversation, his commerce and citizenship, was in heaven; and we have passed already from death into life . . . when Christ admits us to His kingdom of love . . .

'. . . And we need not be ashamed to bring to the grave side, the sword, the garland of a leader, the mitre and staff of a prelate. They are not the toys of a pageant that is gone, a disguise, fanciful or pompous to be abandoned before the great reality of death; they are, or they may be when rightly used, the tools or ensigns of a service which already here, in this perishing world, belonged to a kingdom that shall not be shaken.'

[8] Miss Gertrude Arkle (aged 91 in 1958), an aunt of Alan Leslie (see p. 197 n.) recalls that in 1911 Waggett went to Russia for Holy Week and Easter. 'I think there was some sort of secret mission involved, for Waggett travelled as a King's Messenger with every kind of comfort . . .' Leslie had been living with Waggett at Cambridge for some months and he took him with him on this journey to Russia.

In 1912 he preached a Lent course of sermons at All Saints', Margaret Street, afterwards published as *Our Profession: a penitent's desire of Christian loyalty*. In the same year he preached on the death of Father Page, the Superior-General S.S.J.E. (a quotation from this has already been made on p. 52 *supra*. Father Page had resigned the office of Superior-General in August 1907):

'. . . He was a true and energetic leader and ruler. He could most wonderfully "get work" out of people. He could lend the impulses of his eagerness in order to bring to a conclusion, or at least to bring to the point of effort and production, the preparations, aspirations, collections, in which writing men too often wander interminably. The infirm of purpose know an intense gratitude towards the man who thus "lifts" them into self-committal, expression, movement . . . perhaps to strangers who saw him from only across a space, he had something of the air of an ecclesiastic inured to office and smoothed to the grooves of influence. What they saw in fact was the uncomplaining, self-pitiless submission of a tender and most affectionate spirit to a yoke which fitted close and well because it was ever gallantly leaned upon. The man was one whose joy it would have been to live with a few people in a country place or to renew the hard-working simplicities of Coatham and Leeds and India. Once, at the end of a Conference of the Diocese, in which the Father had declared that the priests of very poor country parishes were to be envied rather than pitied—it's a subject on which a great variety of views is possible—our splendid Bishop Stubbs tossed across the Oxford station platform (that last relic of the middle age) a jesting-severe challenge to the Father Superior: "When will you take some of those poor villages and try to live in them?" The Father bowed with submission to his superior, but said aside to a companion, "And the real joke is that I would ask no better than to live and die in one. I would share the life of the people. If they were very poor I would go short. If I had nothing left to eat, I would say from the altar, take your choice, feed me or bury me." And then, from his short dream of a country shepherd's lot, he passed on to that work in London and St. Albans for the All Saints' Sisters, which seemed to have no end.

'. . . The Father was a man of wide sympathies. Not himself a reading man, he was intensely interested in the studies of others, intensely concerned for their success . . . His heart, you would say, was at Cowley, and yet who had a keener joy and greater fullness of hope about the great London world, with all its glooms and lights, its pitiful luxury, its splendid self-sacrifice?

'Of what Father Page was in the far more sacred sympathies of prayer, I cannot speak even to the intimate and devoted circle for whom these pages appear . . . It is best to say little. He was no friend of many words. Once, when a friend of his was trying with some eloquence to express his own shortcomings, idleness, futility, the Father interrupted him with, "Yes, all that is no doubt very true, but you should leave other people to say it."

'It was an elder brother, quite brave, brisk, and charmingly intolerant.

I wish I could have seen him in his boyhood. He must have been a brother to get one out early in the morning, one who knew the way to the streams, who flew a gate in front of slow runners, knew no shirking, praised no shirkers . . .' (*C.E.*, 1912, pp. 248ff.).

In the *Cambridge Review* of 22nd February 1912 (p. 289) there appears an article by Waggett on Cardinal Newman evoked by Wilfrid Ward's *Life* of Newman which had recently been published. The article is much more Father Waggett's assessment, very penetrating and sympathetic, of Newman's personality than a critique of the book. It merits being read, indeed ought to be read, by any one who wishes to approach discerningly the various studies of Newman—and there have been a large number of them—which have appeared since the centenary of his submission to Rome in 1845 :

'. . . Mr. Ward has given a sufficient representation of all that is sad and disquieting in Newman's Roman Catholic life, and in his own view of it. We need not fear more grief from a fuller disclosure of the man; and anything we learn here makes him, after reflection, more lovable than before.

'. . . By joining a world-wide communion Newman did not come into a more extended mental sphere, and when he acknowledged a very ancient claim, he found less use than before for history. We have all heard of the years of gloom and sadness when Newman was convinced that he lived in vain, when Church authority seemed to make his efforts fruitless, a gloom and disappointment about his own practical efforts which never altered his attachment to the Roman Church. Nothing can exceed, and nothing but quotation can represent, the pathos of these journals of exhaustion and distress. At last, after the years of trouble comes the Cardinalate and a happy evening, and the peaceful end.

'. . . The pathos does not lie in the neglects of authority or the disappointments of effort. The pathos is in this, that a rare spirit should have wasted strength in such attempts. Success in them would not have been pathetic, but tragic. If recognition had come earlier, this spirit, finely touched and surely to fine issues, would have been incurably entangled in affairs for which he was wholly unsuited. What had he to do with the burly intrigues of a religious organization? He had no business in a turmoil of hierarchies; defeating Kingsley; resisting Manning, cajoling Irish Bishops, Irish squires. If it is true that his authorities ruthlessly caused his failure, then surely we and he owe them a great debt . . . But it was too bad that in the course of teaching an invaluable lesson they should have allowed him to touch the Achilli business . . . After this unseemly business, following so many finer and sharper trials, what wonder if there are here and there signs of petulance. Our wonder is at the elevation of character, the strength of fibre which made collapse so slight and rare. No, the pilgrim of eternity had nothing to do with the management of a Church, the conduct of an agitation; and the robust prelates did well to head him back to his own home of light.

'And besides, to do them justice, it was no wonder if misunderstandings arose. Newman on his side had seen a new movement come to great proportions in five years, had found himself a king in Oxford; and he supposed that, in his new position of what he thought greater strength, something of the same sort would happen. On the one hand, the old Catholics supposed that the transition of the Oxford Fellows was to be the beginning of a great march across the line. *They* hoped to convert England, and Newman proposed to educate Catholics; and neither of the subjects of these benevolent designs had the smallest wish to accept the benefit proposed.

'. . . His was a character singularly transparent, sincere, and unconventional . . . He has no *phlegm.* Possessed of every refinement and delicacy, he lacks entirely the inhuman *morgue,* the solidity, the *vis inertiae* of the aristocrat. He could never be a man of the world. The unique subtilty and versatility of his intellect and the victorious flexibility of his written style hid from those who saw him this simplicity of his character; he is a child with an amazingly powerful mind. It is because he is unsophisticated that he bewilders the admirable children of this world who expect the stolid repetition of some formula which cannot two days running express a living mind . . . Had he possessed the smallest sense of pose, he would have refused the cardinal's hat; or, if, indeed, he saw that refusal was the most becoming attitude, then it was his conscience, his relentless sincerity, that forbade his adopting it. A little pomposity would have saved him much anguish, but it would have entirely destroyed his excellence.

'. . . Here is material for tragedy enough; and if we add to this the strange conviction which so often haunts the minds of men framed for the hidden life, that they must needs take up some cause best left in hands of another sort of strength, then there must follow life-long anguish, and an almost intolerable strain, of which the least painful element is the failure of external enterprise. In men, thus complex, thus transparent, thus driven or drawn to action, the upper surface of the mind is ruffled by what seems desire of fame, but the deep heart cries, "Should I forsake my sweetness and my good fruit, and go to be promoted over the trees?" Such men are unconscious of their own true value, and see nothing of the success that properly belongs to them. Newman did not make the fortune of the Roman Church in England, and there was no heralded defeat of religious Liberalism when he ceased his life-long fight. But he remains a witness of the Unseen to multitudes, a succourer of distressed faith . . . He is one of the men who hold an elevated way, their eyes against the sun; whose faces show to us who walk in shadow the light we see not yet, and whose voice assures men of the lower path that their dark pilgrimage also has a certain goal.'

Also in 1912 he wrote a paper entitled 'The Issues of the Day.' This was not published until November 1945 when it appeared in *The Symbol* [9] (Vol. 32, No. 11). Perhaps it was originally written for an undergraduate audience at Cambridge, but there is no evidence that it was ever delivered there. The paper, though

[9] Inset for parish magazines published by The Faith Press.

quite inspiring, seems to lack the profundity and quickness of perception usually found in Waggett's writings. There is little doubt that Cambridge did not bring out the best in his work.

On 13th February 1913 Waggett took part in the discussions of the 'Theological Dinner' at Oxford at which Sanday, Strong, Lock, Holland and others were considering the miracles of the New Testament. 'Waggett made a long speech . . . repeated what they had said before about the special character of our Lord's life requiring the Virgin Birth, and . . . added a little about the physical sides of propagation not supporting the idea that a Virgin Birth would involve incompleteness of humanity' (Stone writing to Gore: *Darwell Stone* by F. L. Cross, p. 106).[10]

There survives also a sermon which Waggett preached in St. Alban's, Holborn, on Whitsunday (11th May) 1913. (*Church Times*, 16th May 1913) on 'Three Whitsun Prefaces.' He speaks about the proper preface at Mass for Whitsunday which is sung in Rome 'and was sung in England formerly, being in the Sarum books as well as the Continental books,' about that which is in the Book of Common Prayer, and about that in the Ambrosian Liturgy which is sung at Milan. The first, he tells his hearers, ran as follows: 'Through Christ our Lord who ascending above all the heavens and sitting at Thy right hand, O Father, poured forth the promised Holy Spirit to-day upon the children of adoption. Wherefore with floods of joy the whole round world to-day rejoices . . . and the angelic powers sing all in chorus to Thee the hymn of Thy glory, saying without ceasing: Holy, Holy, Holy.' And he comments:

'See the splendid theology of that Preface. Our own present Preface is a fine one, but it remains one of the mysteries of liturgical history that a learned person like Cranmer should ever have dreamed of leaving out so magnificent a statement of the connection between the mystery of the Ascension and the mystery of Penitence (a misprint for "Pentecost").

'Here in this preface we are reminded that it is because our Lord hath ascended up into Heaven above all heavens and is seated at the right hand of God the Father that He sent down, as on this day, the Holy Spirit He had promised. The exaltation of Christ is the cause of the inspiration of man, not a cause as some men conceive cause, as something that went before and is afterwards followed by a result, as you may speak of a seed as being the cause of the harvest . . . To speak in terms of time

10 There is also a letter from Stone to Waggett, on the Assumption of the Blessed Virgin Mary, dated 23rd October 1915 (ibid., p. 257).

and space, no sooner is Christ, God and Man, in His adopted nature, the nature of man, seated upon the throne which was His according to His divine nature from all eternity, no sooner is Christ's manhood lifted up to the right hand of God, than the manhood which is the same in His members is immediately filled with the glory of the Holy Ghost . . .

'Dare I use a figure to make it plain? A man down below in a great body of water is without breath. His limbs are without life. He struggles, and is dying. Not so was it with our Saviour, though He rested in human death within the grave. But conceive such a man under the water and then conceive him rising to the surface. As his head, his lips, his eyes emerge into the sunlight and air, instantly, not as a consequence, but as a part of the same fact, his limbs, his fingers, every part of him is full of the vigour of the air. All his blood now again courses free, being refreshed by the healing air which is his because his head has emerged from the medium which it cannot breathe, into the freedom, the clearness and thinness of the sun-bathed atmosphere. You remember as boys how your eyes came up above the dark green clouded water and saw the delicious sparkle of the surface of the sea stretching miles away, looking so lovely when you saw it from an inch or two above the surface. You remember the delight of the warmth and the sunlight and the deep breaths as your head came up into the upper air. Were not your limbs full at once of the vigour which the air alone sustains?

'Perhaps you have not had the dismal experience of being nearly drowned; even so, take the homely image for what it is worth. When our Saviour having in our flesh slept the sleep of death, when He broke the bonds of the tomb and walked for a time by the lake side, and on the road with His disciples, He still breathed, as it were, our lower mortal air . . . as soon as our Head, Jesus the Divine Saviour made Man, was in the sunlight and glory of Heaven, so soon did the golden glory of the Throne pour down upon the earth, shining forth in those who are His . . . They joined actually, substantially, really, in the heavenly worship.'

Then there is the Prayer Book version. It speaks of the wondrous manifestation here in men's sight—'giving them both the gift of divers languages and also boldness with fervent zeal constantly to preach the Gospel unto all nations,' and Waggett continues :

'. . . There ought to be, there is, where men faithfully look up to Christ, the manifestation of the Holy Ghost; that wondrous, unimaginable glory of God—Three in One—becomes known, in the pouring forth of the Word of the Gospel with a heavenly courage, and in all the works of mercy, and in all the glory of worship . . .

'I see in my mind the ministering angels who usher in before the Divine Presence congregation after congregation, headed by their priests, into the Presence of the Heavenly throne. They come up there, some of them poor and despised; little bands of dark-coloured people from the Philippines in St. James's Bay by Capetown, who all among the Mohammedan millions have been keeping up the Catholic worship since the days of Francis Xavier, poor little fishermen, despised by their neighbours, making their living out of the bay, dragged from their Eastern home long ago, as slaves by the Dutch, and still there, in their little white-washed chapel, lifting up the Everlasting Sacrifice, still in their humble lives coming up as their fathers did into the heavenly place, although in earthly life, because their worship is full of the Holy Ghost and contains not only the merit, but the energy of the priesthood, the king-ship, the sovereign Presence of Christ our Lord Himself. So much, then, for the earthly Churchly pilgrimage, counterpart of the heavenly act of Christ.'

Then he goes on to speak of the Ambrosian Pentecost preface : 'We come to Thee, O Father . . . and by the illuminating descent of the Holy Spirit, as heavenly eternal security has been restored to us by the Passion of Christ, by the gift of His Spirit, so Thou wilt of Thy mercy grant us tranquillity in this present life, tran-quillity through which we who have been made partakers of so great a gift may by a quiet devotion be made perfect . . .'—con-tinuing :

'Now, this quietness, this meekness, this gentleness, this keeping still, this silent devotion, have we sought after that? Have we meditated God's holy word? Have we in stillness thanked Him that we have a Saviour in Heaven? Have we avoided that showy and loud self-assertive kind of life which is inconsistent with the blessing that is poured down upon us? Heaven is near to us when we are quiet and meek. Heaven is far from us when we are loud and hasty. We have got two great reasons for being quiet. We ought to be quiet because so many sins have been forgiven to us. Do you remember the worthy in the Old Testament who said : I shall go softly after this all the days of my life. I shall go softly now that the Lord hath had mercy upon me?

'When a man has been near to death and has been brought back from the brink of it he feels this—I must go softly; I am not my own man; I will not go lazily; I will not be less busy for shouting less, not less useful for reporting less frequently what I have done; I shall go softly because God has brought me back from the grave . . .

'Let us as the inheritors of the heavenly gift go softly, speak gently, and above all things avoid all judgment of others. When we seem to see a fault let us hide our eyes, for our eyes are seeing amiss. They ought to be fixed upon the Saviour. There was one who said, Your brother must die, your brother is a forfeit to the law. And the answer is, Why! all the souls that ever were were forfeit once . . .

'O think of that, and mercy will breathe within your lips like men new made. I have been inconsistent; I have been unmortified; I have not kept the rule of the Church; I have forgotten my prayers; I have hurried over my thanksgiving; I have come perilously near to more dreadful things. I do not know that my lips have not been stained with lies. How shall I stand up and once more ask for the Holy Ghost? And the answer is : Thy lips shall once again be crossed with the crimson cross of the Precious Blood to make them fit once more to speak to God. And remember, thou forgiven sinner, to go quietly in the time that comes, refraining even from good words in judgment against thy brother and seeking that quiet devotion by which the heavenly gift will be perfected in you unto ever-lasting life.'

In October 1913 Waggett read a paper on 'The Christ of Experience' to the Church Congress of that year. In that disquisition he set himself not to explain and defend the Christian case against unbelief, but to speak of the place experience takes in the life of believers.

'The kingdom, now founded but not yet completed, has a forward aspect; an anchor fixed in ground not yet reached . . .

'In certain respects Christ is absent and to come. But He is still in the world He saves; already present in power to the Church, working in the work of His members . . .

'It is this presence and the knowledge of it, partial as it is, which in fact must have sustained the Christian Life from age to age. It is not possible that the impulse of acts, however great, done in this earth long ago should, without a continuous influence "from above," have kept moving till now a march which when it is true to its purpose—that is when it is real at all—goes counter to the natural desires and even the naturally discerned interests of man.

'It is unreasonable to believe that men can long be kept from sin by the record, however well authenticated, of things done long ago, or animated to virtue by the hope of an unseen heaven and the fear of an unproved hell.

'The real existence of grace, the influence of Christ, is required to account for the survival of His following . . .

'. . . moral results do not arise except by the working of a Power which is far beyond that of Precept or of Example.

'And those who exhibit the moral results are the men who recognize the Otherness of the Goodness they reach. This is the evidence which the believer has within himself: this is the evidence, the witness, the testimony that God gives of His Son in the experience of believers; namely, the fact that God hath given us eternal life, and that this Life is in His Son . . .

'The evidences of this power have in reality all the continuous variation of life . . . some are visible to all men, though not seen by all . . . And so it comes to pass that the Lord manifests Himself in some ways to His own and not to the world . . . In both these classes of evidential fact—the facts that are visible to all, and those that are known to believers—there is a kind that is wonderful, and a kind that seems ordinary . . . It was after the publication of his book on the *Varieties of Religious Experience* that I spent some hours with Mr. William James . . . I ventured to say that his great study would gain force for many readers if it included some things which are thought common; fewer strange doings that are not religious, and more religious doings that are not strange.

'He told me, with the gentleness and candour which belonged to his character, that he meant to bring together into evidence some of those common things, which surely are the matrix in which the wonders are nourished, and which disclose in their extent and mass and consistency an unmistakable signal of the Divine Presence . . .

'The facts are susceptible of an interpretation different from ours; and it has always been so of things common and things strange . . . If we were more willing to meet the moral test we should handle a weightier mass of proof . . .

'We turn to evidences which appeal to the Church alone. Here also some may be called ordinary and some extraordinary, or wonderful.

'The ordinary (save the word) may be grouped under the head of Prayer in the sense of supplication; with the recognition of Providence; the conversion of sinners; the comfort and strength that come of the Sacraments and the blessings of the Church.

'To some men these are matters not only of obedient faith but of knowledge too. To others they belong to a faith kept up by authority.

'But in both the experience of the mercy of God through Christ works conviction; produces for the mind a condition of stable equilibrium which, as it were, recovers, after disturbance, its own poise . . .

'The extraordinary part of this evidence within the family is the experience of supernatural prayer, by which Christ, working in the whole company of the faithful seen and unseen, shines in the minds of those who walk according to the Spirit . . . sometimes they are raised to great privileges of perception . . . What they know is not available in an immediate way for evidence, for they hear unspeakable things. But still they help us . . . And their faith supports our own, making us both discontented with our ignorance and resolute to persevere in trust. They help us through troubled times: they are watchmen in the night and cry "The Day cometh." '

Waggett then refers to the great difficulty of speaking of the 'central experience' :

'Let me speak very simply of the importance to us all, whatever our special vocation, of this light which is the life of Christ in the greatly prayerful. They are our eyes.

'This knowledge of Christ, of which St. Paul was eager to speak among the perfect, is the λόγος ἐνδιάθετος of the Church risen to a certain degree of consciousness. Upon it depends, as St. John of the Cross declares in another way, for from it must proceed, all the force, because all the reality of the λόγος προφορικός; all power in preaching, persuasion, doctrine, rebuke, proposals of reform. The *ratio,* the inward ruling idea, governs the *oratio*; it is joined in one reality with all true utterance and all righteous action.

'St. Paul writes as if this knowledge, so rare for us, and reckoned so hard of attainment, must be normal for the Christian.

'When it is absent, or not growing, then the *moral* life is in danger. If the privilege of the elect, who in Christ are blessed with all spiritual blessings in the heavenly places, is not followed by a holy life, it is because the gift of Christ has not become the *knowledge* of Christ; and there must be instant prayer for the spirit of wisdom and revelation to be poured on those who, being rooted and grounded in God's love to them, have not advanced to apprehend the form of the divine purpose or to know the love of Christ that passeth knowledge (Eph. 3 : 14ff.) . . .

'The experience and the science are so sure that when the Christian is perplexed and in danger of being daunted by the suffering of the world, he is offered the answer to that perplexity, and the key to that suffering is the suffering of the Christian known to co-exist with the unchallengeable warrant of future happiness which is the gift of the Spirit (Rom. 8: 23).

'. . . We must not rest except we are returning towards the normal life . . . except those who dwell in the house of the Lord begin to behold the fair beauty of the Lord, and thus to approach the sanctuary of conformity and sacrifice . . .'

Also in this year (1913) Waggett wrote an article on 'Heredity' in Hastings' *Encyclopædia of Religion and Ethics*. In addition to these larger literary works he produced during these Cambridge years introductions to a number of devotional and mystical books by other authors. In 1910 there appeared from his pen a preface to *Meditations on the life and teaching of Jesus Christ* by G. B. Budibent; in 1912 a preface to *Pilgrim Songs,* a volume of thoughts on the Psalms of Degrees collected chiefly from addresses given by H. Montague Villiers edited by Evelyn Villiers. In 1912 a translation of *Ascensiones in corde* by Cardinal Bona, with a preface by Waggett, was published. In the same year there came *Guide to True Holiness* by a Marist Father, Paul Huguet, translated by Agnes C. Fisher, which also carried a preface by Father Waggett; and *The Mystical Personality of the Church* by R. de Bary also had an introduction by him.

In 1914 Waggett was appointed Hulsean Lecturer at Cambridge. The outbreak of war made it necessary for the delivery of these lectures to be postponed, and they were eventually given in the academic year of 1920–1 and published in 1924 under the title of *Knowledge and Virtue.* So although this first Cambridge period of Waggett's was not a time when his lights shone at their brightest, he was not either idle or unproductive. He no doubt thoroughly needed the holiday he took in June 1914 when he went with a friend to Munich and the Tyrol, as unsuspecting as most of his contemporaries of what was soon to emerge from Germany.

And so came the eve of the first great cataclysm of this century which was to upheave the lives of the young men amongst whom Waggett was working at Cambridge. There was also to come a great change in his own fortunes and way of life. It would be most interesting to know what Waggett himself thought of these last five years, and from this point of view alone it is unfortunate that letters of this period must have perished among his papers which were destroyed in 1940.[11] This phase of his life leaves behind something of an enigma; but one or two references by Cambridge contemporaries lend a few details to an otherwise rather blurred picture.

Percy Lubbock, the editor of some portions of *The Diary of Arthur C. Benson* which were published soon after Benson's death in 1924, has given us this little *vignette* noted by the diarist under 24th January 1910:

'. . . Then went off with S.A.D. to dine with Waggett. He has taken the pretty old house at Newnham, once Harry Goodhart's, and has an assemblage of young High Church men there. It is a quaint house; he has a chapel, with a fine Sassoferrato, and an oratory with nice Sienese pictures. His own room full of books, deal tables, crucifixes. I am told he is rather inclined to break down in nerves. There was a big gathering, rather obscure young clerics, and laymen, with that odd, bright ecclesiastical smile which means so little. A huge party at dinner . . . I liked the old ecclesiastical feeling—it reminded me of Truro—the mild and godly mirth, the general submissiveness of tone. I know exactly what to do and say . . .

'Then we adjourned to a little bare room, and pious undergraduates came in. Father —— made a long rambling speech about a mission somewhere. The two things he said were important were: (1) to conciliate the natives; (2) to hold one's own against other denominations. That was a Christian programme. Waggett spoke very well, dwelling on the almost Greek beauty of the Kaffirs, and their primitive joy in Church things. A long story, called a "very sad" one, was told of a young chief excommunicated for polygamy. I felt a mixture of admiration, bewilderment and hopeless disgust at the frame of mind of these missionaries. But it was an interesting evening. I should not like much of it, but a little gives me back the old days, and the air of religion.'

Very good for the clergy, no doubt, to be told sometimes how many ecclesiastical assumptions appear to a thoughtful layman!

On 21st October 1911 Benson noted: 'At dinner I sate [*sic*] next Waggett—rather fractious but appealing . . .' And on 1st February 1914 there is this entry in Benson's diary:

'A most brilliant, provocative and amusing sermon from Waggett, about reality in life, and the coming democracy; it was *full* of good points and all so easily and finely done—highly artistic. He said in the course of it that he didn't suppose there would be a revolution—only some unbending Tory Head of a House might be hung from a lamp-post. (The Master objected to this afterwards, and Waggett said that he was thinking of Shipley!) I'm not sure if such sermons do good; Salter objected to it. It was over the heads of all but the cleverest, and was felt perhaps to be simply fantastic. But it was full of good stuff . . .'

[11] In response to the Civil Defence directions on the removal of inflammable material from attics, at his sisters' home in Parkstone.

A picture of Waggett's place in G. K. Chesterton's circle of friends at this period is given by Maisie Ward in her *Gilbert Keith Chesterton* (1944), p. 235. She describes the two men at a hilarious dinner party in London, each illustrating the other's triolets on the backs of menus. 'They were both as clever with the pencil as with the pen.'

Stephen Gaselee, contributing one of the essays in *Arthur Christopher Benson as seen by some friends* (1925) gives this handsome tribute to Waggett's social gifts at this time (p. 96):

'Although he (Benson) shone in all company, there were certain diners who perhaps brought him out more than others. If I had to give a name, I should say that Father Waggett, whom we had made a member of our High Table during his residence in Cambridge, himself a talker of a very high order, made Benson appear at his very best.' [12]

[12] I am indebted to Mr. T. Daish, M.A., of Magdalene College, for this reference.

CHAPTER VIII

The War 1914–18

IN the late summer months of 1914, which were to be the last of Waggett's first spell of work in Cambridge, there was an ominous feeling of uneasiness throughout Europe; but few guessed the magnitude of the storm which was so soon to break. In June Waggett had been on holiday in Germany itself; at the beginning of August he was back in Cambridge. War was declared in the night of 4th August 1914.

Waggett's earliest reaction to the new situation is remembered by the Revd. F. A. Simpson [1] who recalls an impassioned sermon in the little St. Peter's Church at Cambridge calling upon all his hearers to 'carry on as usual.' This was a mysterious eruption, Waggett continued in his sermon, the extent of which nobody on earth could at present judge, from the ordered life of mankind, and the duty of every loyal citizen and faithful Christian was to allow the upheaval to affect and upset *him* as little as possible. To maintain 'business as usual,' to carry on in the normal way for as long as possible, were the first duties of all, at any rate until the situation became much clearer.

But there was a sanctified restlessness about Waggett which would not long allow him to remain outside the fray: he was now 52 but full of vitality and all eagerness to serve abroad. Canon Hulbert Powell of Cambridge, who was Vicar of Great St. Mary's at the time, recalls that General Congreve, the brother of Father Congreve of Cowley, was in command of the Guards Division which was encamped on Midsomer Common, almost opposite Waggett's house in Chesterton Lane, in those very early days of the war and that Father Waggett mentioned having had talks with General Congreve with a view to finding some useful work in connection with the armed forces. Like almost all his contemporaries he felt confused and while saying 'carry on,' he was

[1] Fellow of Trinity College, Cambridge.

feeling that he ought to be preparing for something entirely different, not knowing in which direction that was to be found.

A letter of 10th August 1914 to his sister shows his state of mind at this moment :

'I feel sure it is neither right nor any good to bombard the great Head Quarters at this time. I am *hoping* still the Bishops will put themselves in regular communication with the Army authorities so that those authorities may know where to turn when they want more people like me—clergymen: and not have to advertise or meet a rush of separate volunteers . . . last night after the excellent service . . . attended by the Vice-chancellor and Mayor and Corporation I spoke to our own bishop . . . Let us hope and meanwhile . . . we must root out the wish to be in the front or at the front: and see that things go on as usual in the background—doing whatever pastoral job we have and so on. Very dull and very hard to concentrate on. A large part of my pastoral job may simply disappear and *if* things develop I trust we shall be able to shut this place up or rather hand over the house. If that happens then one may hope for some job—perhaps a hospital on this side.'

To the September 1914 issue of the *Cowley Evangelist* Waggett contributed a really notable paper on the significance of the catastrophe which would have been equally valuable twenty-five years later and could hardly fail to exalt and guide any man or woman at *any* time of great crisis in his or her life. The strength of the message and its revelation of Waggett's mind at this time merit its being quoted at length :

'THE LORD AND LAW OF REAL ADVANCE

'Since we last read the *Evangelist* a great change has come over all our lives.

'In the interval we were forced to face the dread of war, and a little later we faced the dread of peace, a peace which would have been purchased by the desertion of duty, and the fatal acknowledgement that might is right.

'Now those initial fears are past, and all the natural and right shrinking from suffering—a suffering borne in our case by others—is swallowed up or overshadowed by the awe too great for fear, with which we recognize a great day of God, a time of reckoning with the Eternal Justice, a time of testing and of inevitable transition. For the Day of God, when it comes and passes, leaves nothing as it was before. There are *natures* which may be unchanged, but their *position* will be different. The frame of things which seemed to us practically stable, will, when the Day passes, have been shaken down and reset. Heaven and earth must pass away, only the Word will abide. There will be beneath men's feet a new earth for pilgrimage, a new heaven for light, a new earth for foundation of service, a new heaven of the vision of destiny. And in the shaking and resetting, what is the fate of mankind, and of a nation, and of man? Who shall be saved? What national life will live on in the new tasks and partake of the new burdens and the new blessings; find membership in the new kingdom, the kingdom wherein—it is our only hope—righteousness will more evidently live and reign?

'Our Lord tells us He is the Guide and Ruler of men through the changes. When he first proclaimed the Divine Kingdom and offered His Sovereignty, His leadership, it was at a time of impending catastrophe, in the initial stages of a violent world-change.

'He taught that those who would trust Him, abide in Him, follow Him, should be saved through the change: that they should have a part in the new kingdom; and that they should have such part through death. Of Himself He said, "I am the beginning and the ending: the first and the last; I am he that liveth, and I was dead, and behold I am alive for evermore (for *all* the ages, though age succeed to age); and I have the keys that unlock death and Hell."

'He presents Himself as the living one, ὁ ζῶν, and He, as Man, is the *living because* He died. He is the new man of the new age, the new humanity, the first begotten of the dead, the Father and origin of life for the world to come.'

'Old things have passed away. Behold all things have become new.

'There is new earth, new heaven and new man. And as this is the law of life disclosed in Christ, the fount and sum of life, so it is the law of life for every one who would be saved. For the salvation is not the rescue of a man's own bones or of a man's own soul. It is the entry into the new service, obedience to the new law, sharing the new burden, fighting the new battle, going on in God for God to the new sacrifices of love. Only the new man can share all this, only the man who has died and been born again.

'Alas! for the one thing that may haunt the new world. The old unchanged, undead, unrisen heart, the old, old selfishness and littleness cumbering the new earth; the old, old hopelessness and lovelessness breathing unjustly the new air; the old unfaith staining the light of the new heaven.

. . .   .

'The great change comes and the great testing. Already in our mood and hope and feeling we have died the saving death. In mood and hope and feeling all littleness has passed away. It is burned in the furnace of affliction. It is evaporated in the *greatness* of the event. Where now are selfishness, and pretence and animosity, and luxury, and sloth? Surely they are gone for ever. Where are they? They are hiding still at the bottom of the heart. It is not enough to pass through the change in hope and mood and feeling. What is abandoned there must be abandoned in reality, in living habit, in steady perseverance. Otherwise when the trial is past, the old miseries will revive, and in the New Day will be the old heart; in the new kingdom the old man. We are to pray and strive that what we turn from in disgust of thought we may *die* to in reality of discipline that by the grace and power of the divinely assumed manhood of Christ, bestowed on us in Holy Sacraments, we may indeed pass from the old things through death unto life—a life which shall not be a resumption of the old joys and fears, but the revelation of a new and unhoped-for gravity of service, the blessedness and the glory of obedience. If each prays for this death and resurrection, if the Church with one heart thus prays, then the nation, now softened and ennobled by affliction, will not, when the great floods pass, climb back again to the old shores of worldly care and pleasure, of worldly pride and sorrow, but will pass *on* to the further shore, and plant the footsteps of a new march upon the soil of the promised land of truth and justice and mercy—the land wherein we shall know God as our Father, and man as our brother, and press on towards the mark of our heavenward calling in Christ Jesus' (*C.E.,* September 1914, p. 193).

Within a few days of writing the above he found himself, to his own great surprise, plunged very much *in medias res.* Without any warning, on 6th September, having 'no reason for thinking I should be wanted, only the old conviction that I must go,' he heard that he would be leaving for France two days later with General Congreve as a chaplain attached to the Brigade of Guards which was part of the Sixth Division of the Expeditionary Force. After this hurried departure he spent about a fortnight at the Divisional Headquarters in France, where he had work entailing much movement from place to place and where his sufficient skill as a horseman acquired in younger days was of great service to him. This is his impression of his work in those first few days, in a letter to his sister dated 24th September :

'Really it is like Cambridge or a parish: not doing the very work but making many friends high and low—so as to be serviceable to them later. But all sorts of chances will develop . . . Found yesterday most surprisingly a shop with some paper in. I told Madame it was like the Magazin du Louvre—a remarkable joke which has been repeated round the little town.'

Such was the unpreparedness of the military organization in those early days—vividly described in many chronicles of the war —that Waggett and others seemed to be able to choose their work wherever they felt inclined to go or wherever they saw a need which really called them. This system had advantages, perhaps, but there were other aspects of such an unready and disordered campaign. On 25th September, riding out with 'big guns all round and sometimes shell overhead' he found a big hospital with no chaplain and asked leave to stay there. Accordingly he went the next day to the 4th Brigade of Guards, his address being now the 4th Field Ambulance. He soon found himself 'quite at the front and the wounded and sick come in constantly—and then soon pass on.' On Michaelmas Day 1914 he wrote :

'It is most lamentable to see the suffering, but the courage is too wonderful and not least—perhaps *most*—the courage of doctors and stretcher-bearers. To-day we went to see the curé—a most delightful man—and he gave us leave to celebrate in the parish church to-morrow. I went about with him among the troops well and ill and introduced the Irishmen to him and he gave them absolution and those that will can go to his mass for communion to-morrow' (letter to K.B.W.).

In the same letter he asked his sister for some prayer books and hymn books, and also for some light novels and similar literature to lend to the ward orderlies who were not allowed to smoke during the long nights. He also gave Katharine the addresses of relatives of several of the wounded men in order that she might send news to them as he lacked time to write himself. A glimpse of his pastoral work among the wounded soldiers is given by his reference in letters to one badly wounded man for whom the doctors held out no hope of recovery. Waggett sat up most of the night with him and 'it was like Tabard Street and he got round a corner I thought.' 'There are many cases here not to bear describing,' he went on, 'but they are living still. The doctors are capital. There is little time for the niceties of hospital nursing.'

He was constantly under fire now, both in the daytime and during the night. On Sunday 4th October the bursting of a shell nearby made it necessary for a service he was conducting to be abandoned in the middle. An account of this episode was sent home by a former Cambridge undergraduate who saw in Waggett the army chaplain something which, evidently, had not always been revealed in his approach to the young men at the University.

'Funnily enough last Sunday, as I was running through a little village, quite close to the firing line, and there were a good many shells bursting over it, I passed a padre, of course in uniform. I only saw a flash of him, but I could have sworn it was Father Waggett, but could not possibly wait then to make sure. Since then I have heard that he was there that morning and held a service till he got shelled out of it . . . He was always a good sort, and I have got a lot more respect for him after that, than I ever had in Cambridge.' [2]

On the following Sunday, 11th October 1914, he was able to hold four services without interruption; that night, after the burial of two men in the trenches:

'the colonel took me round all his advanced trenches: very misty

[2] Published in a Cambridge newspaper. It has not been possible to find the reference.

and moonlight and oh! how cold. And it was *very* jolly to see the beloved men in their place of work. I wish I could have been up every night. But mostly I am busy in hospital' (letter to K.B.W.).

Next day he wrote to his sister asking her to make excuses for his absence from various engagements entered into before the war began. It was, apparently, a great relief to him that he would not now have to read a paper at the Church Congress—which was later to be postponed—since such an occasion was evidently a more 'frightful trial' than the kind of life he was now leading in which a night's unbroken rest was the rarest of privileges.

Not a word of complaint about his own discomforts finds its way into his letters at this time: instead of this a deepening perception of the supernatural mysteries betokened by the grim realities which surrounded him. A letter of 24th October to Katharine shows how this perception is developing:

'The days of riding about and making cheery friends seem long ago and strange: so *much* suffering: such *processions* and masses of hurt men: so many dear dear friends who *can't* stay with us. I am convinced all the lives are laid down for a mysterious purpose of regeneration, and I *understand* sometimes, without ever being (able) to explain, why the Death of the Lord was necessary for our salvation. I understand sometimes quite well. But it is surprisingly little I can say to the poor wounded: and—I spent a good part of last night by the railway train which took away a good many officers and a whole body of men.'

And on 29th October he adds:

'Each death is to me *more* grievous than the last, not less: and people keep writing to me from home of the fun I must be having and the interesting life. I cannot tell *how* these poor widows are to bear their grief hearing of death as the first definite news of their husband.'

He was in the Battle of Ypres in November 1914 and from there sent appeals home for things to ease the pains of the wounded.[3] On an undated post card which seems to belong to this period he wrote these words:

'I drowsed off yesterday and had these words in my head when I woke: "Faith to see God under the material pressure and great fatigue of war. Hope to hold the vision of Peace in the dread extremity of war. Love to conceive and serve the divine purpose in the bitter conflict and costly sacrifice of war." '

[3] After this battle he was mentioned in despatches for his share, it is believed, in evacuating the wounded under fire. He was also responsible for saving the lives of nuns in a convent at Ypres.

By 19th November he was allowed to snatch a little rest and he wrote from the Sixth Division Headquarters. On 7th December he returned to the Ambulance—'I cannot face the idea of leaving my poor struggling grubby 4th ambulance with all its horrible discomforts . . . I have made my work there now at great cost and must stick to it.' About the middle of December 1914 he had a brief period of leave in England during which his chaplaincy was put on a regular footing. He was back in France by Christmas and, the Ambulance being settled in a fairly large town, he held services in the *Temple Protestant* of the place.

Waggett had nothing more than many others to record of the early weeks of 1915. In his letters home he commented frequently on the waterlogged state of the ground everywhere he went on his horse. On 13th January he wrote to Katharine about a thing which was worrying him, the fear of wasting time :

'which is always ready to stare all of us in the face—as with me at this moment—and the danger is only met by prayer and by doing instantly every tiny thing that offers. Often I have had nothing to do but write a few letters for soldiers and it seems as if one were shut in a magic glass box. Then one gets busy and looks back with pity on those vacant days. But they come again. Soldiers do not a bit mind doing nothing. They simply wait for their turn.'

In the same letter he described how saddened he had been by the sight of 'the endless pitiful processions of homeless villagers in Belgium and northern France' :

'Well dressed people suffered too . . . You saw three daughters with their best hats and papa with his cylinder hat all *dragging* along with (them) bundles of things they *couldn't* leave behind and such heavy bundles : I tried one or two—walked a mile with one of these respectable parties.'

In February 1915 Waggett was ill for some weeks and he was sent to Nice to recuperate. Katharine joined him there for a short time and then travelled with him to Boulogne. By the middle of March he described himself as once more on duty at

'a fine hospital utterly different from Ypres experiences—can hardly believe in them now—we talk about that time to our newly joined officers as the *first* people talked to us about Mons, poor dears, and the retreat' (letter of 13th March to K.B.W.).

About this time, having met the Prince of Wales somewhere behind the lines, he describes the Prince's incipient enthusiasm for motor cycling. Any book including reminiscences of trench warfare, or of combatant life generally, must rigidly ration its space given to horror stories; but one cannot omit the account of

'the cheery fellow who was hit in the knee among the wire entanglements and lay there helpless through five nights and into the sixth day, with nothing to eat but grass. The Germans thought he was dead and took off his boots and carried off his iron rations. He went down to the base yesterday doing fine' (letter of 22nd March to K.B.W.).

Arthur Benson, whose frank expressions in his diary about Waggett are recorded above (p. 126) wrote at this time (30th March 1915) from Magdalene College, Cambridge, to Katharine about what he had heard of Waggett's ministry in France. Benson stayed behind in Cambridge during the war, carrying on such work as was left to him there, and he seems almost to envy the courage which took Father Waggett right out into the midst of the conflict of his own free will :

'Dear Miss Waggett,
'Thank you very much for your kind letter. I have, since I made inquiries, heard both *about* your brother and *from* him, from Boulogne, where he fell in with my friend Percy Lubbock, who wrote most gratefully and delightedly about him—his talk, his energy, his charm.
'I knew that at one time it was a great strain on him; but I hear from different quarters about all the work he is doing, and how much he is valued and loved so I hope he is well again. I do immensely admire his choice and the way he has carried it all out.
Believe me with kind regards,
Sincerely yours,
A. C. BENSON.'

During Lent 1915 Waggett was preparing seven men for Confirmation. The Bishop of London went out for Good Friday and after a very busy Easter Waggett was moved to the 4th Casualty Clearing Station. On 15th April he wrote to his sister his expectations of the new task compared with the old :

'I shall be sorry to be further from the troops in trenches, but it is no terrible distance. I expect it was time I had a bit of quieter time—tho' every one here says I have shown no signs of wear and tear. Still there are not many people who have had the good fortune to go on so long in these parts. In a way the very front is very *simple*: this and that cottage chimney stack broken, bridge, factory, trench, communication trench and so on. All gets very familiar. Directly you go a little way back you see how *big* and wonderful and complicated is the Army . . . great *lines* of machinery, etc. I shall be glad to be in that sort of thing and there is a big hospital and much to do in my line and I have a course of lectures to give to the chaplains of this region and so forth. All very good and restful and I shall get clean and mended up.'

On 1st June 1915 he writes to his sister some thoughts on what the discipline of the war crisis has done for individuals :

'We have now the opportunity of doing and not for the war only what we poor little people have preached and prayed for all our lives, that is of giving every man an opportunity of work suited to his capacity and to apply that discipline to the feckless or the proud which *cannot* justly be applied while the proud can say he's not wanted or the feckless that he can't get work. Of course discipline and organization is only *one* side and can be overdone but within it has been cruelly underdone—so that the joint must be sent to the kitchen again . . .'

By 27th June he felt able to make this observation, which is of interest as it is in such contrast with what was being said so widely only a few months before :

'the newly arrived men look well and strong and splendid : they arrive absolutely broken-in, brown, strong, tough : having had magnificent preparation at home.'

On 13th July he was writing again to his sister about a brief spell of leave he was having in England. Although intended to be a rest it involved him in a tremendous rush, reports to the Chaplain-General, the Adjutant-General and Lord Kitchener's private secretary, answers to difficult questions put to him by the Bishops, and hasty visits to his sisters and to Cambridge. By 22nd July he was back in France and writing with tantalizing secrecy about the part of France in which the hospitals under his care were now situated :

'We are setting up our new hospitals in a beautiful little clean country village on the chalk and limestone—a country some distance from our last and very different—true French France . . . I am now in a new and uninhabited and almost empty house and shall be very comfortable . . . I made the journey by road by myself with the servants and horses' (letter to K.B.W.).

He mentions having a church parade one Sunday during that summer at a Flying Camp 'in such a very beautiful great lofty barn with lovely upright beams in the roof made in the natural shape.' Afterwards there was lunch at the village inn with two agreeable French officers of Gendarmerie, a visit to G.H.Q. to see the Bishop of Khartoum who was then presiding over the chaplains, also to see the Quarter Master General and to transact other business.

In a letter dated 6th September 1915 to K.B.W. he looked back over his experiences during his first year as an army chaplain :

'The first year has been all experiment and learning with many mistakes. Now I ought to be able to put my hand more firmly to the one work, all the sort of excitement of being with the Army having gone. Most of those I knew at all well in the former Brigade are gone to a better world . . .

'Among the many mourners' letters I had one while I was at 4th Field Ambulance from a Dissenting Minister saying "May the Crucified be with you in your work." I was very much struck. It woke me up to how very little of the Cross there was in those days so interesting and sometimes so amusing. And I took to praying it very much myself. You can't have the Crucified *with* you if you're not in the smallest degree being crucified yourself—if it is only like a thief at the side. "Alas, how very hard a thing it is to be a Christian." But it's the only thing worth while.'

21st November brought forth this vivid appreciation of a great soup kitchen which had been established at the bottom of the communication trenches :

'. . . worked by whatever regiment is on the spot. Each regiment in the Brigade sends all its bones, 5 lbs. meat, and some quantity veg. And day and night the devoted cooks boil and skim and every one can just come and have oceans of excellent soup. They served nearly 1,500 the day I looked in . . . When I see the bones with meat on, I always think of that old woman in Thackeray who said, "A leg of beef is not a company dish" ' (letter to K.B.W.).

On 10th December he was writing to Katharine on the recently received news of the death of Father Maxwell, the Superior General of the Cowley Fathers :

'It is a great *blow.* I use at last with reality the expression "I cannot at all realize it." . . . Fr. Maxwell was a rock man, absolutely straight, full of goodness. I shall miss him terribly . . .'

On 15th December 1915 Waggett shows in a casual paragraph to his sister that he is still keeping alive the interests of his own mind :

'I am just finishing *Guy Mannering.* It is certainly a most splendid book. In spite of knowing what's going to happen I am still thrilled by it and Brown is by far the best of Scott's characters—manly, strong, not pulling and half lying like Waverley or the fellow in Montrose : but very brave and straight and a handsome fellow too.'

In January 1916 he had some leave in England, most of which was spent visiting a married sister and her family at Eastbourne. The difficulty he had, during this visit, in obtaining a pair of boots which would fit him gave rise to a characteristic disquisition on Christian footwear:

'There is no doubt that *sandals* are indispensable to the ideal Christian life. Introduce boots and you say good-bye to Gospel simplicity. Francis was a wise man when he made his friars barefoot and in a later generation there was more in the terrific controversy between the shoed and unshoed Franciscans than meets the eye' (letter to K.B.W. 20th January 1916).

On his return once more to the front we have another reflection on the 'waste of time' feeling which beset him at this time in the previous year:

'In a place like this "in and out of trenches" there is not much encouragement to write and the things I could write would not be interesting far off: just mud, shells, long walks, ditches to walk about in— mostly not much damage done: and mostly every one quite cheerful. Only every now and then in a bitter shower on a hill-side near the trenches one catches a glimpse of the awful waste of precious time it is for every one. Somehow, in God's mercy, this waste of time which would be criminal if it was our fault is redeemed by some outpouring and uplifting of the human spirit which goes on all the time, some inpouring of Divine Spirit for which we ought to pray much more constantly. I should like people at home to make *their Communion* every morning, not only go to Mass, and to do that "for" a soldier' (letter to K.B.W. 18th February 1916).

In the same letter he reflected on the Lord's Prayer and all Christian prayer in the circumstances of the war:

'The point about the Lord's Prayer is that you must pray, first for the Coming of the Kingdom: and details—even like Pardon and Peace—only *inside* of that.

'Seek ye first the Kingdom: that means first the establishment of the kingdom and the manifestation of God's righteousness. Then other things like Peace and dry feet will be added to you. But we are here in this world to pray for the kingdom to come, and so to bring it down to earth. He showed me the heavenly city the New Jerusalem *descending* from God out of Heaven.'

In March 1916 he was allowed to pay a flying visit to Oxford to exercise his vote in the election of the new Superior General S.S.J.E. to succeed Father Maxwell. The lot fell upon Father Bull. On 20th March, back on the Somme, he reported to Katharine that he had had a kindly and encouraging letter from the new Regius Professor of Divinity at Cambridge (V. H. Stanton) 'greatly hoping that I shall return to help reconstitute the place.' During April he became a senior chaplain; but towards the end of the month he was put out of action by contracting trench fever and he was sent to hospital at Havre and afterwards to the Canadian convalescent home at Dieppe. At Dieppe he met his old friend James Adderley 'looking dreadfully old and broken up rather.' When he was recovering he was able to enjoy half a day's motor trip with Adderley and another old friend, Alfred Acland, visiting some of the historic places in the lower Seine valley.

Early in June 1916 Waggett was back on duty and on the 21st he was speaking to Katharine, in a letter, of the training of younger chaplains which fell to his lot :

'Oh! if we had had the smallest guidance when we came out instead of finding our feet as best we could on a slippery slope. The new chaplains will do much better. I had a quiet day for a neighbouring division on Monday.'

Although he does not mention it in his next letter, he was at this time having some trouble with his right arm—first thought to be neuritis, but eventually discovered to be the slight splintering of a bone. On 27th June he sent a brief chronicle of his recent experiences to the *Cowley Evangelist* :

'We are extraordinarily busy here; and there are many things to manage and arrange from hour to hour. I am in a place where the chaplains can all easily reach me—and do. Things being more crowded, we have Holy Mass every morning in my bedroom, and my little servant is getting expert in hiding my impedimenta, and spreading my red blanket on the floor, "To make it church," the while I wrestle with a censer for the primitive use of incense . . .

'Nor, I am thankful to say, have I anything wrong with my feet. Trench fever is a very exhausting thing, with some serious symptoms, but it does not touch the feet. All these symptoms disappeared long ago, and I am getting steadily better, while getting through my work all right. All my brethren "play up" well: and being an old boy now in the school, I find things pretty easily arranged with military and medical authorities, which two years ago were subjects of much perplexity and talk. Everything from saddlery, up to what I named as our daily morning Blessing, has its channel just now in this office and bedroom.

'Last Monday week, wonderful to relate—you will know later how wonderful—I was able to conduct a day of retreat for the Chaplains of two neighbouring Divisions. We had one for ourselves just before my illness in the beautiful underground Church, I perhaps told you of. But that Church, gracious as it was, probably polished me off in that cold weather by its continual dampness . . .

'I am always spending money on things for Church and troops; so I should be quite glad of a small donation for such expenses; only I should not have any time to render any accounts. I suppose the daily tale of my official letters and wires here in the course of an "out of door" life is thirty. And this is quite a lot for a Boffice (bedroom cum office), without a clerk, and with a horse waiting outside to take me to the Wood of this or that, or the Greyhound or the Dead Cow (all these are altered and inapplicable names, and are thrown in to give colour to an otherwise bald and unconvincing narrative).

'We daily have very good talks about the Great Good Things, and I am sure we are beginning to make progress by means of difficulties. A young chaplain, who is very full of difficulties, told me yesterday to my great joy that he now understood that the difficulties had not to be got out of the way, as a preliminary of the work, and that a work without difficulties would be really like a coffee mill with no friction and no coffee.'

Another similar letter, dated 8th July, appeared in the *Cowley Evangelist* soon afterwards. A comment on the system of dealing with German prisoners of war is worth preserving :

'Before the Push I used to wonder what would be done about Prisoners. But it all works smoothly enough. Little processions. Enclosures for collecting and sorting as you read in the papers. Camps and trains : and so for home. The German prisoner is first of all a soldier and does exactly what he's told to at once—and the organization of this part of the business is *nothing* to the problems of a Sunday School treat' (letter to K.B.W. 18th July 1916).

On 22nd September he is referring, in a letter to Katharine, to the preparing of the future clergy who were now laymen in the forces :

'A few days ago we had a conference with the Bishop about the national mission. You see the best part of young male England is *here* and in your camps . . . We have also got here (or in those camps) the *whole* of the future clergy. There is no other field from which to get candidates for Holy Orders but the Army *alone*. I count the Navy in the Army, the Navy is the Army afloat. Perhaps Bertie would say the Army is the Navy on shore.

'So if there ever *does* come a possibility of quiet speaking here, it must be taken. And it is fine for the chaplains to have something more positive to do than the consolation of suffering, and fine for them to have something more definite to do than the encouragement of the troops.'

During the years of his service in France Father Waggett kept in touch to a remarkable degree not only with his community at Oxford but also with the work he had begun at Cambridge and also with the All Saints' Sisters to whom he remained chaplain. On 23rd May 1916 he was writing to his sister on the success of his efforts to avoid being 'invalided' home on account of the trench fever he had earlier :

'It would never have done for me to come to England sick. They are quick enough to put older men like me at the Base or to a Camp in

England: and I am perfectly happy in the Front line and as active as any one there—fighter or non-fighter. So I stick to that. I will ask for ordinary leave in a reasonable time.'

In January 1915 and again in November 1916 Waggett was mentioned in despatches 'for gallant and distinguished services in the field'; though writing to Katharine in response to her questions about this he said, 'Asked what he was mentioned in despatches for, the clergyman replied that he had not the faintest idea.'

Early in 1917, however, he became unable any longer to resist the official pressure on him to take work at home, and he was appointed Senior Chaplain in the Tidworth Area. The documentary references to this new period of work are extremely scanty because, being within easy reach of Bournemouth, where his sisters were still living, he visited them frequently and there was no need for the lengthy correspondence which has supplied so much information up to this point.

Waggett enjoyed this period at Tidworth and seems to have been as active as ever in his new surroundings. It was from here that he wrote enthusiastically to K.B.W. about private soldiers in his confirmation class : 'that God should have given me such sons in my old age!' Writing to a nephew at this time and suggesting that he came to visit him at Tidworth he mentioned one of the army doctors there whom he much liked—Brett Young —an admirer of Robert Bridges (as he was himself) and a writer of poetry. This was the Francis Brett Young, afterwards author of *My Brother Jonathan* and other novels. As he was now in England Waggett was able, being such an old friend of Scott Holland's, to cheer him during the last months of his life. He died in March 1918. (See *Henry Scott Holland* by Stephen Paget, 1921, p. 323.)

May 1918 brings to an end what might be called Waggett's ordinary war service and makes way for the beginning of another phase of his life. In that month, to add to the already remarkable variety of his career, he was sent to Palestine as a political officer with a special mission and attached to the General Staff.

CHAPTER IX

Palestine 1918–20

IN May 1918 Father Waggett was sent to Palestine as a Political Officer with a special mission to improve relationships between the various sects, factions, racial minorities and other conflicting groups which were continually at strife with each other at the time owing to long standing rivalries which the war had done much to inflame. How he came to be chosen for this delicate task of pacification was, no doubt, one of the many well guarded secrets of the war years; it remains a mystery to the present day. That it was a good choice, though, the following section of his remarkable life story leaves in no doubt. Waggett was appointed to the General Staff of the E.E.F. (Egyptian Expeditionary Force) as an A.P.O. (Assistant Political Officer) with the rank of Major (G.S.O. 2).

The journey out to the Holy Land was remarkable in more ways than one, and a fellow-traveller of Waggett's who later signed himself 'T.F.F.' in *The Church of England Newspaper* (11th August 1939) has provided recollections of the voyage. On setting out from Southampton to Havre someone in the crowd on the ship exclaimed: 'There's Waggett' and then 'a general move was made towards him, all anxious to claim acquaintance, or to get to know him.' The overland part of the journey, from Havre to Marseilles, was achieved in the gradual discomfort of a characteristic troop train of that era. Then half way between Marseilles and Malta, early on a Sunday morning, the ship carrying the party was torpedoed. T.F.F. continues:

'Dazed and almost stunned by the shock we scrambled on deck, to find nearly all the boats already gone. Fortunately the torpedo had exploded in the sandbag ballast of the bow or we should not have been left to tell the tale. A rapid scramble down a rope ladder and we were in the last boat to leave. Tossed about for two hours whilst the one Japanese destroyer told off to help us went round and round like a terrier with a rat, letting down depth charges. At last we were hauled aboard. There I recognized Waggett, no longer spick and span, his auburn hair all ruffled, his slacks drawn on quickly over a blue shirt, one side of his braces buttoned, the other hanging down his back. Still, there he was, safe and sound, ready to undertake the great work which lay before him. After a night in Malta, where the people showed us no little kindness, we were off once more for Alexandria, and after passing safely through the mine-field it was suggested that Waggett should give us a service of thanks-giving. In a few minutes his cabin and the corridor outside were packed with young officers—it was an officers' boat which had been torpedoed—and many a heartfelt thanksgiving went up that so many young lives had been spared.'

The situation in which Waggett was going to have to work, on his arrival in Jerusalem, was one which was to need more than ordinarily delicate and firm handling. The Turks had been expelled from the city late in 1917 and with the removal of their oppressions many latent grievances and hostilities came to the surface; supplies were short and the habitual rivalries of the various ecclesiastical bodies had been exacerbated by war con-ditions. On 28th December 1917 Sir Ronald Storrs [1] was appointed Military Governor of Jerusalem under General Sir Arthur Money, Chief Administrator of O.E.T.A. (Occupied Enemy Territory Administration), who in his turn came under the supreme com-mand of General Allenby. This regime lasted until 30th June 1920 when Sir Herbert Samuel entered the city as the first British High Commissioner of the Civil Government of Palestine.

The military administration set to work to maintain, so far as possible, a peaceful *status quo*. [2] How difficult that was going to be can be seen from the following short description of the political and ecclesiastical situation in which this administration had to function. The French Protectorate of Latin Christianity in the Ottoman Empire was a basic factor in the background. This had been recognized since the reign of Francis I who in 1528 obtained rights under a treaty with the then Sultan and it was connected by tradition with Godfrey de Bouillon and the First Crusade; and a consequence of this was that the French Consul General had it well established that the Latin Patriarch might approach the Gover-

[1] See chapters XII to XVI of his *Orientations* (1937) from which the following account is mainly drawn. A full account of the political events in Palestine at this period is to be found in *The Seat of Pilate* by John Marlowe (1959).
[2] This went back to the edict determining the rights of the religious communities issued by the Sultan in 1852.

nor only through him. But the Latin Patriarch at the time, and the Franciscan Custos of the Holy Places—who enjoyed even greater influence in practice than the Patriarch—were thoroughly Italian in their sympathies and were Italian subjects. The Patriarch and the Custos had their differences but they were agreed in this— that they sought the overthrow of the French Protectorate. They saw in the removal of Turkish dominion in 1917 an opportunity for carrying out this design : but any such suggestion of an infringement of the *status quo* was firmly resisted by the British military administration.

This, however, was by no means the end of the complications or of the *odium ecclesiasticum* in Jerusalem. The Turks in their retreat had carried away with them the Orthodox and Armenian patriarchs, and the Moslem Qadi, leaving all three of their communities without a leader. Legions of minor irritations—and worse consequences—were brought about by the fact that both Turks and Germans had requisitioned furniture from various convents. These properties had not been marked and if any inventories had ever been made they were long since lost : the business of ascertaining the rights of competing claimants must have been ticklish and exasperating.

The general tranquillity of the Holy Places was not helped by disedifying scenes which were constantly taking place between the Copts and the Franciscans. The former had managed, in the face of years of opposition, to construct for themselves a very small chapel at the back of the Edicule of the Holy Sepulchre,[3] but the Franciscans had considered it their duty to be guardians of the public right of way and to preserve this right of way by repeatedly passing and repassing with loads of domestic utensils through the Coptic congregation while they were hearing Mass in or near their chapel. This kind of behaviour was always ready to break out also over such questions as the cleaning of the Basilica of the Nativity at Bethlehem. As regards the Sepulchre, the Greeks, Armenians and Latins all squabbled continually over their rights in this, and in the end the use of it had to be the subject of minute regulations issued by the Administration; and

[3] They had been given the right to do this as early as 1573, but it had taken centuries of squabbling before this right was fully exercised.

in order to keep the strife under control the Governor retained in office the hereditary Moslem Guardian [4] of the Church of the Holy Sepulchre. Very special precautions had to be taken about Easter time when disturbances were apt to arise over the coincidence of the Orthodox ceremony of the Holy Fire, the Moslem festival of Nebi Musa and the Jewish Passover.

The Orthodox Church, too, had its own particular internal troubles. In Palestine this church was much more an outpost of Hellenism than the church of the local people, and Orthodox Arabs found themselves excluded from the confraternity and also frequently inadequately provided with pastoral ministrations. Parochial life was not much fostered and the attention of the Church was directed mainly towards the preservation of the Orthodox Holy Places from encroachments by other denominations. The finances of the Orthodox Church, too, were in a very straitened condition. The Russian Church, also, came slightly into the picture. Some time before the war this Church had established itself outside the walls and had built a cathedral and accommodation for large crowds at the Easter pilgrimages. Their buildings included, apart from the cathedral, a large church and hospice next door to the Holy Sepulchre, a convent on the Mount of Olives and a church in the Garden of Gethsemane. The Russian revolution had halted the flow of Russian pilgrims to the Holy Places and during the war the monks and priests who had served this fane had disappeared and the buildings had fallen into decay. By about 1919 the Russian community which had remained in Jerusalem through the troubles began to assert itself afresh.[5]

This, then, was the state of religious institutions in and around Jerusalem when the British took over. Sir Ronald Storrs, in his book *Orientations* (p. 376) describes himself moving at the end of 1917 into a house formerly occupied by the German Protestant Pastor: he says that he had with him Ernest Richmond and 'Father Waggett of Cowley, then a Political (or perhaps a Politico-Religious) Officer and invaluable in his maintenance of close and sympathetic relationship with the three Patriarchates.'

[4] The privileges of this office had been limited to one or two families since the time of Saladin!
[5] See pp. 153ff. *infra*.

'T.F.F.' who had travelled out with Waggett, and whose reminiscences have been quoted above (p. 141) wrote in the same article of Waggett's activities in the midst of this welter of animosities : 'the amount of diplomatic tact used by him to settle the numerous questions which arose in the various sections of the Greek Church will never be known.' The same writer continues in his article with a delightful description of Waggett giving lectures to the troops in Palestine :

'It was my privilege to introduce him to some four or five hundred "Tommies," as one who was as well known in Oxford for his theology as he was in Cambridge for his science. His lecture on the differences between the various sections of the Greek Church kept them enthralled as none but Waggett could have done for over an hour. He had an apt way of illustrating what he had to say by means of the blackboard. First he rapidly sketched a long line of the head-dresses worn by the various Patriarchs and Archimandrites to be seen in Jerusalem, which had become the Mecca of almost every soldier in Palestine. Then, having said something of the different countries to which they belonged, Assyrian, Armenian, Coptic, Abyssinian and all the others who looked upon Jerusalem as their Mother Church, with one sweep of the duster all were gone; and in their place arose a series of mountain peaks with deep valleys between. Next, by means of one long line, the sea had come in between; each peak had become an island, to all outward appearances separated from all the other islands. But going down below the level of the sea we found they all were founded on the one solid rock foundation —"and that rock was Christ." So the great truth of the Incarnation was taught as the Rock on which the Church is built.'

'We realized,' he continued, 'that we were in the presence of a great teacher, one who could accommodate himself to those who knew very little either of the theology or history of the Church, as he could to those who could argue with him on questions of philosophy or science.'

Some jottings from two notebooks of this period survive from which it can be seen how thorough Father Waggett's exploration of his surroundings—both mental and physical—was. He studied most carefully the religious history and economic conditions of Palestine, and took pains to meet and have discussions and exchanges of ideas with leading personalities representative of every interest. He was aware that a considerable time would have to be spent in just looking round before recognition could come and support be forthcoming for useful work. So we see him, according to these notes, immediately after his arrival, visiting Bethlehem—

where he notes the natural cave formation—Jericho and the Dead Sea. Walks in and around Jerusalem itself took him by way of the Kedron valley, the Mount of Olives, the Via Dolorosa, Calvary, the Holy Sepulchre, the tomb of Mary, the Pools of Solomon—where he was interested by the large number of frogs —Bethesda, the Pool of Hezekiah, the Tower of David (then inhabited by refugees from Es Salt), the tomb of Absalom, the Coenaculum on Mount Zion (being used as a Moslem mosque), the Abyssinian and Coptic churches, the Armenian convent and the Convent of St. John the Baptist.

On 18th June 1918 he attended a congress, which he found intensely absorbing, of Zionists at Jaffa and during the congress he dined with Dr. Weizmann (chairman of the Zionist Commission in Palestine), whose views on the question of a University at Jerusalem formed the chief subject of their conversation. At about this time Waggett also had discussions with Major W. G. A. Ormsby-Gore (later to be Colonial Secretary, at this time attached to the Zionist Commission in Palestine as Liaison Officer on behalf of the British Government) on the economic possibilities of the country, its mineral resources and the need for the draining of marshes. He was frequently in touch with the Red Cross organization and with a prominent group of Swedish-American adventists and he attended Arab club meetings and Arab dinners. On 6th July he had an interview with the Grand Mufti whom he found 'very gracious.' About the same time he received visits from the Vicaire of the Greek Catholic Patriarchate, Père Alexius Aquel, accompanied by Père Ayoub, also from the Orthodox priest of Es Salt and from the official administering Canadian relief and the 'Chef du Dispensaire Grec-Catholique' at Jerusalem and many others. He learnt that among the Es Salt refugees there were about 640 Greek Catholics and 1,800 Greek Orthodox. He called on the Anglican Bishop in Jerusalem (Dr. Rennie MacInnes) and on General Chetwode; he had regular interviews with General Money, on whose staff he was, and he dined frequently with the Military Governor in Jerusalem.

On Holy Cross Day (14th September) 1918 Waggett is writing a letter to the *Cowley Evangelist* (*C.E.*, 1918, p. 233) about the water supply of Jerusalem, about the tombs and his lectures and sermons and about the convent of the Dominican Fathers—the 'delightful Frenchmen' of whom the Military Governor wrote that they were so 'entirely detached from the scrimmage of the Communities' (*Orientations*, p. 472) and whose hospitality he (Sir Ronald Storrs) enjoyed so much :

'. . . I went to see Père Abel of the Dominicans, at St. Stephen's, one of the two very learned authors of great books on Jerusalem and on Bethlehem and the Church of the Nativity.

'The Dominican Church and Convent of St. Stephen is on the rise of the Nablus (Shechem) Road which leads on from the Damascus Gate, beyond the Governor's office, as you leave behind that great Saracenic Gate with the ever-changing picturesque groups.

'It was at the Damascus Gate that I met the Armenian Priest who poured out the speech about the water—the fresh running water—which the military power has lately brought all the way from Hebron to run in public taps in Jerusalem. Perhaps I did not tell you about him. He said, "The Turks had this place for 800 years and never gave us a cup of water. The English have been in charge eight months and already fresh water is brought to the people; *Vive l'Angleterre, Vivent les Anglais. Non Angli sed Angeli."* I thought the remark rather well put together, to commemorate a gift brought with no *éclat* and no *réclame* by the R.E. For too long Jerusalem the Blessed has been dependent on the water stored in cisterns from the winter rains, and too often freely modified by the dirt of the house roofs. One recalls the prophetic rebuke—"they have left Me the fountain of living waters and made for themselves cisterns, broken cisterns which can hold no water" . . .

'I had been to the Convent and Church Library before with Father Felix Couturier, O.P., one of our chiefs in the Chaplains' Department and to-day I had an hour of unmixed satisfaction with Père Abel, whose marvellous volumes—made with Père Vincent—on Jerusalem we must somehow acquire for the Library . . .

'To the South end of the Nave there is a wonderful and clear group of old Hebrew graves. The ground about Jerusalem is, of course, one vast Necropolis. Everywhere almost in the rock you will find sepulchres . . . But there's a reason for studying these tombs. I once thought of writing you a letter about the Ancient Tombs around Jerusalem—there were and are of course no tombs in the city; but I have a difficulty. How could one write about the tombs and leave out that Tomb which is incomparably the greatest—the Tomb which we revere not only as the scene of the Burial but much more as the place in time and space of the Resurrection of our Lord? Well *that* tomb I have never yet dared to enter, though I find myself before it on more days than not of those I spend in Jerusalem.

'I don't think I shall ever go in and so I shall never live to write a letter about the tombs around Jerusalem.[6]

[6] Mrs. A. S. Duncan Jones recalls a visit of Waggett to address a parish gathering at St. Mary's, Primrose Hill, in later years. At this gathering he gave a lecture on the Holy Places with special reference to the sepulchre and spoke of visitors going inside. He, Waggett, did not enter—'I did not feel that I was the sort of person who ought to go in.'

'The tombs at the Dominicans' place almost satisfy me . . . passing out by a door of the Church near the East end, on the Epistle side, you enter through a door in masonry a small court. From the court open six rocky chambers, and in each chamber, with an exception I shall come to, are four tombs. The "tombs" are shallow depressions in the stone. The end of one of these is double, made for two persons lying side by side, head to feet. The other two are single. In these shallow depressions lay the bodies until natural process reduced them to bones, which were then removed from the "burying" slab and put into a chamber below which, I should think, is called the ossorium. The depression above was then ready for another deposition.

'Seeing this arrangement makes one understand the "new tomb wherein never man lay." An old tomb would have received a succession, probably a long succession, of tenants . . .

'When I am a little less *affairé* with a whole quantity of small duties I will try to write again about some minor interests in the Holy City. Meanwhile I wish I could telegraph my letter so that you might charitably wish me well for a lecture to Arabs on Plant Life and Agriculture to-night and a sermon to English soldiers to-morrow.'

His notebook reveals that among other studies at this time he went most carefully into the Armenian question. He kept as complete a record as he could of places where Armenian refugees and others were living and of the societies concerned with relief work, also of the hospitals and schools and other organizations for Armenians for which some Government help was pledged. As well as giving details about these immediate practical concerns this notebook of Waggett's is a mine of information about his general reading, books on the history of Palestine, the Crusades, his opinions on Seebohm's *Oxford Reformers,* Schopenhauer, Sanday on the predominance of Saracen influences in Jerusalem, topographical details in the identification of places named in the Bible, the contrasts between Buddhist cardinal vices and Chinese cardinal virtues, the place of courage in the Christian ethic, his meditations on the Psalms and his refutations of criticisms being levelled at the time against Greek Orthodox priests and monks—all showing the immense agility of Waggett's mind in the midst of the pressing demands of an executive office held in a crisis situation.

On 28th September 1918 an article which Father Waggett had written on the administration of occupied territory was sent to the Foreign Office for consideration from the General Headquarters of the Egyptian Expeditionary Force. Later the Foreign Office sent this article to the *Manchester Guardian* with permission to publish in full and to attach Waggett's name. It appeared in the *Manchester Guardian* on 27th November 1918.

The article began with an assessment, as a result of visits to towns and villages, of the value of the British occupation after the withdrawal of German and Turkish forces and of the extent to which the new occupation was welcomed by the inhabitants :

'The impression before the advance (to Tiberias, Semakh, Semra and Amman over Jordan) was certainly one of general contentment and gratitude mixed with some reasonable and some unreasonable disappointments; the impression to-day is of unmixed and universal enthusiasm.'

The author also pointed out that 'the country profited in some directions by the Turkish and German preparations for war. The profit has been enormously overbalanced by enemy operations and by the course of war as such. But it has not all been obliterated. Something remains as record of an unusual interest of Constantinople in Palestine and Syria.' Waggett speaks particularly of buildings, roads, water installations, etc. : 'briefly, you may put your finger on Beersheba on the map and say "here Turkey has done good." ' And he continues, 'Perhaps the most extended advantage arose from the new roads linking Jerusalem with Hebron and Beersheba, and with Amman beyond Jordan . . . An important new road joined Akka with Damascus. Here were benefits of German and Turkish origin, benefits of military preparations.'

Waggett then went on to describe vividly the sufferings of the local populace when the war came, however. The afflictions to which he drew particular attention were starvation, typhus and de-afforestation—including the cutting down of olive trees to provide fuel for trains run by the Germano-Turkish authorities. He then proceeds to comment in the most glowing terms on the way in which the British did not delay one moment to begin alleviation of these miseries after they came into the country. He paid a great tribute to the Military Governor (Storrs) and particularly to the way in which he respected religious feelings wherever he went : actions like the suspension of government work on the fast days had an immensely beneficial effect on the attitude of the people.

'For the first time in a century the ceremony of the Holy Fire at the Holy Sepulchre was conducted, under the wonderfully sympathetic influence of the Military Governor, in order and without any armed force . . . The relations of the different Christian bodies are peaceful, sometimes cordial. The Moslems have had unusual facilities for religious observance, greater facilities than they had under a Moslem Government.'

Waggett added to all this some important paragraphs on the religious divisions in Palestine as he found them and on other matters affecting the lives of the inhabitants at that time :

'I think myself that the visitor is over deeply impressed by the *scandal* of religious divisions, that he thinks too seriously of issues which take a small place in the minds of the charitable Franciscans, the learned Dominicans, and the [Benedictine] monks of Mount Sion. He is unaware of the enormous weight of history that lies behind the whole complication—a history of costly sacrifices, and thousands of martyrdoms—he does not allow enough for an accretion of alien matter upon the real treasures of so venerable a tradition as we are here in face of. But there is something to be said for him; and something again for the more critical observer who finds in religious animosity a childish pose or a calculated business move. The truth is in neither of these judgments. They lack sympathy and do not allow for the facts—here often great and heroic facts—of human life.'

But he adds :

'In effect all the dissatisfied bear witness to an actual state of things; and that state of things is precisely that Jerusalem is not spiritually powerful, and that the spiritual force is diminished by the particular mode of concentration on sites and traditions that we have here.'

Then he continued on the material side of the people's wellbeing—'The foundation of a remedy for the scarcity and misery spoken of earlier must be laid not, as the poor people are naturally apt to think, in a distribution of money or even of food, but in the restoration of order and confidence and, through these, of industry and exchange.' Relief, he says, of course must be given, 'but all this is not a foundation for the future. It is a measure of rescue to make a real beginning possible.' The people's confidence in the paper money that was being issued was growing. The Military Administration was making great advances in the distribution of kerosene—so essential for the well-pumps, necessary for agriculture and fruit growing, and Waggett added : 'Water is there for the getting in what seems the most powdery desert.' Then followed some observations on the administration of justice, so necessary for the restoration of stability in a country which had been through all the vicissitudes which Palestine had experienced. The judges and other legal officers had, in many cases, been carried away by the retreating armies—a step quite contrary to the principles of civilized warfare. He ends with the following reflections on the tasks which lay before the new administration :

'But for sanitation, medical work, education, the Churches and the voluntary agencies will need increased support. There must be great arrears in respect of one thing alone, the scourge of ophthalmia, and one sees still too many sickly women and neglected ill-nourished children. In presence of the needs, insistent still in Jerusalem, is it not one of our first duties to make immediate help contribute to the permanent invigoration of society and of the people, to the restoration of the arts and crafts once native here, and—to turn for a moment to the grimmer aspect of things—to secure through education in the widest sense that self-respect in every class, the lack of which, joined to an unfair strain of poverty, produces darker tragedies than the loss of life or limb.
'In this matter of the revival of industry under the law of beauty, the great case of Jerusalem stands apart and is being studied by the best minds.'

It cannot be always that papers passing through official government channels are couched in language like this with a philosophy of this kind behind them !

By the end of 1918 his mastery of the Armenian situation was becoming recognized and it was being proposed by the authorities of the Administration that he should be the representative of the Armenian religious community at G.H.Q. and also that he should have an official status in the central religious organization which was then being formed. An amusing bureaucratic *contretemps* occurred at this time : a Treasury official in England ordered the issue of instructions for Waggett's recall on the technical ground that no vacancy existed in the post to which he was being appointed ! However this difficulty was soon overcome as a result of urgent representations from the authorities at Jerusalem, perhaps from the Military Governor himself.

In December 1918 Father Waggett supplied to the authorities of the Military Administration of Palestine a long memorandum on the properties of the various religious communities in Jerusalem and on the history of their inter-relations. All the historical details can be found in other authoritative works on Palestine and so will not be reproduced here. But Waggett's observations on the protectorates are worth noting :

'. . . there will be nothing but gain, both politically and religiously, in the disappearance of the protectorates, which have their *raison d'être* in the existence of an Ottoman Power, and will cease to have any meaning when a new Government is created for Palestine . . .

'I do not say, as the Papal Secretary of State (Gaspari) said in March 1918, that the French protectorate has already died a natural death, but I do say that it will do its last useful piece of work in the discussions of Peace settlement, and that as soon as a new Government of Palestine is set up, the Protectorate ought to be explicitly abolished.' [7]

In February 1919 the British Government was considering measures for the safeguarding of the Holy Shrines in Palestine and a number of different recommendations had been made in reports from experts on the spot. Col. Sir Mark Sykes and Father Waggett collaborated in sending memoranda on this subject and General Money, Father Waggett and Col. Storrs had all taken part in earlier discussions on the matter. Broadly speaking Waggett's proposals were as follows :

(i) That the existing Protectorates should be abolished.
(ii) That an official called 'The Commissioner for sacred places in Palestine' should be nominated at first and at each vacancy by the Tutelary Power and approved by England, France, America, Italy, and Russia or Greece—but not nominated by these Powers in turn.

Waggett pointed out that a single official responsible to the tutelary Power would be better than a joint committee of the Religions because such a committee would seldom succeed in face of real difficulties, and would have frequent recourse to the Government of Palestine. The Commissioner could secure all the necessary counsel from the Religions. If, six months after the nominations, the responsible powers have not agreed on the name proposed, the Tutelary Power would make an appointment for that turn. 'Majority would be a bad test. If the responsible powers don't agree the Tutelary Power will of course seek for the man best likely to give satisfaction to the responsible powers taken generally.'

One or two details of Father Waggett's proposals are worth observing :

'All the traditional ceremonial privileges are to be protected by the Commissioner (schedule of flags, salutes, etc., to be made by him). But he shall have no power to secure material civil privileges like exemption from duties; with two important exceptions :
(a) Rights of Education should be defined before the Government of Palestine is set up and secured for various recognized Communities and these Rights the Commissioner would protect.

[7] This and other extracts from Waggett's memoranda, etc., during his time in Palestine have been communicated privately to the author.

(b) Questions of Personal Status (marriage, divorce, possibly succession) should be decided as formerly (up to the first year of war) by the authorities of the different recognized societies, but now under the general supervision of the Commissioner who *alone* shall be entitled to apply for the coactive support of the Government, and for that purpose he may examine the procedure and even the findings of the separate courts . . .'

Then he had important proposals to make on the question of Rights of Access to the Holy Places :

'There should be two sorts of access : (1) the right of a *Church* to hold services in a Building or at a Holy Place, and (2) the rights of individuals or groups of individuals to repair to the Places for Devotion.
'This latter right should be secured to all individuals.
'It is not proposed to increase the number of *Churches* possessing rights of ceremonial observance. But it will rest with the Commissioner to decide whether the number of individuals repairing at any one time to a shrine amounts to a meeting for ceremonial purposes.
'The Commissioner shall control the collection of fees, guides, hours of closing, etc.'

On internal ecclesiastical questions Waggett observed as follows :

'The Churches must learn to settle their own affairs—maintaining touch with their own symbolisers as the Romans do—and only when driven by extreme urgency apply to the Government . . . The discipline of the clergy shall rest entirely with their constitutional rulers : but these rulers must dispense with any coactive enforcement of their decrees.'

Finally Father Waggett adds this after-thought to his suggestions :

'In view of the still recurrent, and too probable future difficulties inside *some* religious organizations, I think I have said too much . . . in favour of excluding the Commissioner from such matters. It might be a good thing for him to be the person to communicate with the Supreme Government of the Tutelary Power when he is convinced that intervention is necessary in the interests of a given organization or even of the Public.
'. . . At this moment a responsible Armenian Ecclesiastic assures O.E.T.A. SOUTH that only the intervention of the administration can secure a good Patriarch or any Patriarch at all.
'This may be quite untrue. The Commissioner would test such a statement.' [8]

At the end of 1918 the Russian community in Palestine had been complaining of Greek encroachments upon their rights.

[8] A glance at Article 13 of the Palestine Mandate will reveal how far attempts were made by authority to implement Waggett's recommendations on the Holy Places. This article tried to solve the problem by setting up a Holy Places Commission but, owing partly to Latin intransigence it became impossible to form this Commission. In the end the High Commissioner was empowered to give *ad hoc* decisions on the basis of the *status quo* : this was the position all through the mandatory period which ended in 1947.

Waggett was again called in to supply information and advice towards the settling of this dispute. The conclusion to which he came was that the Russians never had any rights in the Holy Places :

'If there were a Russian priest in Jerusalem, he would have to get the leave of the Greek Ecclesiastics to say Mass in the Church of the Holy Sepulchre.

'The case is not one of the loss of rights secured, but of disappointment of the hope to secure rights, a hope which seemed perhaps nearer fulfilment just before the war than at some other periods.'

With the fall of the Russian throne, Russian government support for Russian missions in Palestine dwindled away and the Russians saw their influence dwindling also by comparison with the Greeks. But they only really had rights of property and these had been adequately safeguarded. The rise of Athens both as state formerly held by Constantinople also added strength to the Greeks *vis-à-vis* the Russians. On more than one occasion the Chief Political Officer was instructed by the British Government to con- and Church as an Orthodox Centre and towards the position vey their thanks to Father Waggett for his expert advice on all these questions and for his invaluable help in the solution of the problems arising between the different religious communities in Palestine in the early days of the British occupation.

On 24th May 1919 Waggett was writing, again in the *Cowley Evangelist,* about a visit to Amman (the Rabbah which Joab besieged in 2 Sam. 11), about 'long and exhausting walks in the hills' amongst the jumble of Græco-Roman remains. This letter is full of interesting observations on the countryside and its inhabitants. He says that he is, within the next few days, to visit Es Salt, but before that :

'I shall wait here till Monday or Sunday afternoon, so as to "make Sunday" here for the two political officers and the medical officer, and the few Englishmen with the patrolling squadron, who have not, I think, seen a chaplain since they came here.'

Then he says that as soon as possible after that he must start for a 'little tour' of Jewish colonies in Palestine.[9]

Another long chronicle of his journeyings appears in the

[9] About this time he wrote, in Jerusalem, an introduction to *Letters from Ludd,* a small devotional manual written by a fellow officer under the pseudonym 'Captain R.A.M.C.'

Cowley Evangelist written at Jerusalem on 18th June 1919. He begins by telling of a slight earthquake which took place at Jerusalem that morning. This tour was chiefly in the Jordan valley and in the 'hill country of Judæa' where he visited Ain Karim, the birthplace of John the Baptist. He thus describes a visit to the Abyssinian monastery:

'Right down in the Jordan valley below high water mark, and quite hidden in the bush, is a wonderful little, utterly humble, monastery of Abyssinians. They live in grass and wattle huts, round a church of the same materials. The gentle monk who entertained me was in the simplest rags; but carried rather a fine manuscript volume of prayers under his arm. I hope that a photograph of him and the Church may come out.

'Above the perfectly plain chamber, where the little square altar stood, was a rough platform of planks, which we reached by a most irregular ladder with rungs going at all slants. And on this roof platform was the Holy Sacrament lying flat and covered with embroidered cloths which the dear monk kissed with great devotion. "Christos," he explained to me. Partly in dumb show he told us how some of his brethren had been killed by the Turks, and thrown into "Jordan water," these last words in English. I have no doubt because English pilgrims as well as many thousand others come for the water and ask for it in English. "But me," he said, "Christ saved, finishing off all that danger." (He made the gesture of washing his hands.) I was more touched than I can say in this humble home of prayer. The raised platform above the altar is partly for secrecy and also partly to make a holy place out of reach of the winter floods. There is also a pretty substantial round platform in the compound, like a bandstand, for the brethren to go when the river rises.'

In the same letter he speaks of the Russian pilgrims who had been stranded in Jerusalem by the war, and he expresses his affection and admiration for their pleasant manners, their hard work and the intonation of their voices, adding a comment which is of interest in connection with our dealings with their compatriots of forty years later:

'It passes my comprehension how a people so orderly, so gentle, so intelligent and so brave, have allowed themselves to be browbeaten and harried and led into violence by the leaders of a single "school of thought," however respectable that school appears in the eyes of some of our writers.'

Waggett's account, in the same letter, of his presence on Whitsunday 8th June 1919 at the first mass in the reopened Russian Cathedral lights up vividly the almost incongruous nature of his position as priest, soldier and government official all in one:

'On Whitsunday, 8th June, the first Mass was sung in the reopened Cathedral. The place was orderly, bright and clean as a new pin. All the

Russians were there, with calm and happy faces. The singing was lovely. Much of the preliminary ceremonies, litanies, readings, were done by nuns, in hats like the priests', but smaller, with veils and black robes. These also attended to the censer and candles. I was first, as a person connected with the restoration, put on a dais in state with a bouquet. But I beckoned a lay official and asked leave to go into the Sanctuary as a priest, and that was kindly granted; and I had a much happier Mass than I should have enjoyed in my boots and spurs on a platform.'

The rest of this letter is well worth quoting for its interest in the Russian Liturgy and for its description of Father Waggett's position and of his immensely varied services in these days :

'Nothing could exceed the reverence and solemnity of the celebration—such an air and temper of expectation in the long preliminaries—the spreading of the figured corporal, the careful cleansings with a flat sponge which is kept in the corporal, and the quiet prayers. Culminating in the extension of the trembling veil by the three priests engaged in the consecration—but you know all the rite. One thing struck me afresh which I must have seen several times before. When each of the three priests has taken into his hands the Corpus Domini, he holds it there, and they all wait and give each other the Kiss of Peace while holding the Sacrament, and then go to their places at the altar (in front and at the two sides) and very slowly communicate. The deacon, like the priests, receives the two kinds separately, but at the hands of the second priest. And then the two species are mingled, and the people are communicated with both together. Standing as I did inside the Iconostasis by the presiding priest and turning towards the Sacrament, I could not avoid seeing the devout faces of the people as they came up to Communion, and a little infant in its mother's arms.

'I have kept, and hope to bring you, a little loaf from which a piece was taken "for the priest Philip" to be built into the oblation, the "one loaf."

'I must now break off, for a Russian bishop, who is here on a visit or pilgrimage, has come to see me. I very seldom have a moment for writing; and only have to-day opportunity because I ought to be, and am supposed to be, in Cairo, but the train last night failed to start on account of an obstruction on the line. I hope to get off to-night.'

Waggett's advice was also sought in June 1919 by the Chief Political Officer (General Clayton) of the E.E.F. in his attempts to settle a nationalistic squabble between Maltese and Italians within the Franciscan Order. In the same month he was also consulted about correspondence from the Spanish Ambassador in London (Alfonso Merry del Val) concerning Spanish rights in the Holy Places. On this last Waggett commented :

'These papers are full of interest and instruction. The ancient Spanish Rights in the Holy Places are often overlooked because of the prominence of the French Protectorate and because of the Italian relations of the Custodia of the Latin Patriarchate.

'The history of former Spanish services and influence, fully recognized both by the Pope and the Franciscan Order, would show if demonstration were needed how important it is not to act upon reasons drawn from the history of one Catholic Power without considering the history of the rest . . .'

Also in 1919 the King of Italy had been making a claim to possession of the 'Coenaculum' on Mount Sion—the well authenticated traditional place of the Last Supper and of the tomb of David which, since 1552, had been in Moslem hands. Father Waggett was called in once again to give his advice on what answer should be given to this demand. In June of that year he drew up a memorandum on the subject which was eventually sent in as an official report to the authorities :

'. . . I cannot but think that it is "fitting" the "Coenaculum" should be again in Christian keeping if and when the change could be made without giving the Moslems a sense of injury, and I do not think they set much store by the Tomb of David. The place of the Last Supper, wherever it is, is the oldest Holy Place of Christendom, older even than Calvary and the Tomb. It is possibly, even probably, the place of the two appearances to the Apostles and of the Pentecost, the house of Mary and John, and the first Church of the Apostles. As to its being the same place as this "Coenaculum" of ours on Mount Sion, identification is at least as old as the fourth century, or Sanday thinks it much older.

'Then as to its Moslem associations, I don't myself think so lightly as some people of the tradition of the Tomb of David, although, of course, you and I are not quite ready to admit that the Moslems have more part in David than we have ourselves. Still, I don't dismiss as absurd the Moslem Davidic tradition. St. Peter says in the Acts that the Patriarch's "Tomb is with us to this day" and "with us" may quite well mean in "Jerusalem" or even in "Mount Sion" where the Apostle was speaking.

'But whether or no the Apostle was speaking of David's Tomb, it is certain that on David's account the Franciscans were turned out in 1552 in a cavalier manner, after a possession of some 200 years, secured as they supposed by the donation of that great man Robert of Anjou, whom they still venerate as Founder. And it is certain that the Franciscan Order, which maintained the Western tradition of Christianity during the ages after the failure of the Crusades, deserves well of all Christians; for that Order not only kept alive a Western share in the devout keeping of the sanctuaries—a share once so gloriously maintained by the Crusaders, but their justice also, if sometimes only by way of rivalry, helped to maintain the life of the Eastern Churches otherwise entirely cut off from Europe and enfolded in a rather unwholesome Moslem world.

'In veneration, then, of those old Franciscans and of that continuous Order I would, were I the man, look sympathetically upon their some-what fidgety modern representatives, but, as I end by saying . . . I think that sympathy of that sort would best be shown, if and when it is possible to make any change, by entrusting the place in dispute, certainly not to the King of Italy, and not to the Franciscan Order, but to the Pope (as represented by the Patriarch), who can then appoint whom he chooses as guardian. It is a good thing to improve the position of the Hierarchy a little *vis-à-vis* the Custodia.

'But no doubt the perfect thing, from the Christian point of view, would be to keep the Coenaculum and the Ascension Church also free from all sectional occupation, an open place of individual prayer surrounded by the churches of whatever special Christian bodies desire to gather round it. There is a growing feeling in the Latin Communion that this is the proper way to deal with the Church of the Holy Sepulchre itself, and therefore, supposing the Sultan's interrupted correspondence with the Quirinal opens the way later for a transference of the Coenaculum, the time would be ill-chosen for creating a new, or reviving an old, sectional possession of a sanctuary so widely venerated.'

Waggett then, in his notes, goes into intricate historical details, covering four pages of closely written foolscap, which lead him to deny the present claim of the King of Italy.

'To conclude therefore this part of the subject, I cannot find foundation either in history or in modern treaty for the claim of the Italian Kingdom. Romantic claims, drawn from the splendid record of ancient valour and generosity, appeal to me more than any other; but romantic claims are met by a romantic satisfaction, and all the more so as they are coincident with the equally romantic and splendid claims of other successors in the new world to the ancient worthies whose names, like that of Robert of Anjou—the friend of Petrarch, the head of the Guelphs, the refuge of popes like Martin IV and the not too severely treated subject of Dante's verse—many successors, French, Spanish, Hungarian and Austrian, look back to with pride. You can, as I said before, with perfect propriety seek a new legal right under the impulse of tradition—as Clive bought with earnings the home of his ancestors—but you cannot make ancient glory a substitute for legal right. The two things move on different planes . . .

'I come to the "justice" of a claim put forward by the Religious Order called by Count Sforza—whose own famous name has a place in the tangled story of the Sicilies—"the Italian Franciscans."

'. . . The word "justice" is a difficult one to use in Jerusalem, where so much is known of the past. By choosing a particular moment for examination almost any existing set of persons tracing racial or institutional descent from earlier occupiers of the Holy City may be shown to have an historical right to any given spot.

'We shall presently meet a school of thought claiming the whole scene for England on the ground that Constantine was the ruler of Great Britain, and King George V is his legitimate heir; and the plea might appeal to those who remember that the first Christian Emperor could, like George III, have gloried in the name of Briton, by right of his place of birth and his mother's descent . . .

'And further, with respect to different Christian bodies, it belongs to the nature of a religious claim that each party should believe itself to represent, or to be represented in, the original Christian body. It is easy to frame pleas, easier still to destroy them by rival pleas; and I believe we ought to be as slow to reject as to admit a claim like that of the Franciscans.'

Waggett then goes on to argue that the Franciscans held the place from 1333 to 1552 as representatives of the Roman Communion 'not only *in partibus infidelium,* but in a land of persecution. But now (1) that august Communion is represented by a regular Hierarchy, and (2) its cult and life will in future be carried on not precariously under a Moslem tyranny with the assistance of European power and diplomacy, but in a free country.' And so he submits that the 'Coenaculum' should, if it be thought fit that the Latins, who held it after the separation of East and West, should hold it again, be handed over to the Latin Patriarch of Jerusalem under the protection of such commission for the securing of religious rights as might be set up. But Waggett himself supported the view that the best plan was 'not the succession of different rites on the same ground, nor the partition of the ground among different forms of worship, but the exclusion of all rites from the places venerated by all Christians' and allowing each 'Church' to build its own place of worship near the outer wall of the old church. He advocated working towards this as a solution and in the meantime not assigning the 'Coenaculum' to any one for the present.

On 14th June 1919 the Commission appointed by the Peace Conference to investigate the affairs of the Palestine Administration arrived in Jerusalem, and this was the beginning of a very busy time, chiefly of clerical work, for Waggett and his colleagues.

Waggett's knowledge of all these matters and his understanding of the local conditions were regarded as so unrivalled that the Hon. W. G. A. Ormsby Gore [10] recommended that he should be consulted on many points of detail before the Mandate for the Government of Palestine finally went before the League of Nations.[11] In order that Sir Herbert Samuel might have the benefit of consultations with Father Waggett on taking up his work, Waggett was asked to postpone his departure from Palestine until after the former's arrival.

[10] Who was an A.P.O. with Waggett in Palestine 1918–22, and Under-Secretary of State for the Colonies at the time the Mandate was being drawn up; later Colonial Secretary (1936–8).

[11] The mandate was signed in July 1922.

Indeed it might well have saved a great deal of trouble if Father Waggett had been able to stay a few months longer. At just the time when he was making his final preparations to leave —with his promise to deliver the Hulsean Lectures at Cambridge in mind—a new difficulty loomed up for the Palestine authorities. Archbishop Damianos, the Greek Orthodox Patriarch in Jerusalem, requested the intervention of the High Commissioner to support him against the Metropolitans and Archbishops who had recently revolted against his authority. He was nearly 80 years old and was alleged to be illiterate and responsible for all the financial, moral and religious misfortunes of his Church; the bishops under him had been trying to get rid of him for twenty-three years. All this happened at the end of August 1920 and Father Waggett had to leave for England before the official inquiries into the matter had reached a stage at which anything definite could be done. However, although he was back in England by the time the dispute had been fully investigated, Waggett's advice was again sought on several aspects of the case. He expressed the opinion that the tutelary power must accept the invitation—though in many ways they would have preferred not to do so—of the Orthodox community to intervene in this dispute. The different Churches in Palestine had been so long accustomed to seeking outside help of this kind that they should not be refused at short notice : though we should train them gradually to look to us as little as possible. He added that in his judgment this trouble was really a quarrel between local Arabophobe interests and the foreign Hellenistic influence in the Greek Orthodox Church which had been going on for a long time. Father Waggett held that if Archbishop Damianos could be induced to resign it might be all to the good, but that this would have to be done, and probably could only be done, after an investigation of the whole matter by an independent Commission.

On 29th September 1920 Father Waggett, back in England, wrote a letter to certain officials, who were pressing him to return to Palestine early in 1921 to give his much needed help in the settlement of this dispute, that he could not go until March at the earliest in view of his commitments at Cambridge. He added :

'I hope the Patrarch's critics may be disposed to wait until, say, April.

If they will not wait, I hope it may appear wise to Sir H. Samuel to support the Patriarch's authority and position for the present, since it is not proved that a competent Church authority has been found to depose him. Even when and if a canonical deposition comes to be made, I conjecture that . . . action of the Sovereign Power will be found technically necessary for its completion.'

The rest of the tale cannot be told here, but His Beatitude remained on his throne until his death in 1931.

Even though Sir Herbert Samuel had obtained eventually a promise of the services of a distinguished colonial law officer to judge the case it was urged from London in October that the matter should be held over until March 1921 when Father Waggett would be available to return to Palestine. However in the event a commission was set up in that year; it had to do its work without Waggett's assistance.[12]

The question of whether Waggett at any period acted, even for a short time, as Military Governor of Jerusalem—perhaps during an enforced absence for a few days of Sir Ronald Storrs— it seems impossible at this distance of time to answer. His surviving relatives deny any knowledge of his having acted, even for a day, in this high office. On the other hand there is the following Waggett story, written by a correspondent to the *Church Times* (14th July 1939) which one would like to believe has its foundation in fact :

'An Oxford friend recalls to my remembrance the remarkable fact that, during Waggett's war-time service in Palestine, he acted for a short period as Military Governor of Jerusalem. In after years at dinner parties, Waggett's voice could sometimes be heard during a lull in the conversation, speaking of "my predecessor Pontius Pilate." ' [13]

At the beginning of September 1920 Father Waggett returned to England for leave and also so that he might deliver his Hulsean Lectures at Cambridge. He had been appointed to this lectureship in 1914, but his war service and duties in Palestine had by now involved a postponement of six years in the delivery of the lectures. Having once come home for several months like

---

[12] See *Report of the Commission . . . on the Orthodox Patriarchate of Jerusalem* by Bertram and Luke (O.U.P., 1921).

[13] Sir Arthur Cust assures me that the story is apocryphal and that Waggett at no time acted for Storrs as deputy. Sir Arthur adds that from his knowledge of Waggett he thinks that the Pilate remark is out of character.

this it was inevitable that the problem of whether to return to Palestine or not would be a difficult one to solve. Father Cary, S.S.J.E., writing in the *Cowley Evangelist* (1939, p. 170) says that Father Waggett's services in Jerusalem were recognized as so valuable that 'pressure was brought to bear on him to remain in Palestine and to devote himself to the work of pacification.' On 30th December 1920 he wrote to Katharine from Oxford and expressed his feelings on the question thus :

'I am not considering the Palestine question on any simply conventional grounds : or asking what people would think. I should certainly do whatever the society wishes : but I am not going even to *ask* them until I am clearer in my own mind that I *ought* to go. It is not easy. The claims of the Palestine work are manifest—at the same time there will be work to do in England we know not what : but certainly plenty of opportunities to teach if one can first learn. And also I have real need of rest, as you, I think, know. And there's a limit to the extent one is at liberty to wear oneself out *if* wearing out means the neglect of good work in the future. My life does not appear a very exacting one because there is not a great deal of machinery or large premises or plant about it. But it has for many years been one of constant effort, and though I don't in the least want to work less, I want, if I may lawfully have it so, to work with fewer calls of travel and so forth. And before settling down to that sober work I *should* like, if it turned out right, to get a *real* rest of body and mind and soul.'

On 24th January 1921 he wrote from Cambridge, 'They urgently repeat their proposals to me.' But it must have been quite soon after that the decision was made not to return to Palestine.

Waggett's Hulsean Lectures, published in 1924 under the title *Knowledge and Virtue* contain many reflections on the experiences he gained both in Palestine and in France during the war. He speaks at length of the churches of the East and of his belief that a solution of their internal difficulties can make a great contribution towards resolving the conflicts of the whole of the old world :

'To us the Orthodox Church as a whole is the Eastern Church, the Greek Church. To all Syria Greece is Western, European. Constantinople is Rome. What old Rome is to the North, new Rome is in many respects to the Near East. It is the Imperial, the European power overseas. It is contrasted with Syria, with Arabia, even with Egypt, in spite of Egypt's long association with Greece and Rome.

'And the Churches of Jerusalem and Antioch have been in their government for a long time Greek, Western corporations in an Eastern land. Their adherents are the Romans. There are indeed Westerners still more Western, the Latins, who have their own strong missions and faithful adherents . . .

'The danger is that the Church itself should be Greek. There was once a strong Syrian Christianity as there was a strong Egyptian; and they helped one another . . .

'In the fourth and fifth centuries Syria played an important part in the western world. Syrian merchants were everywhere. Syrian priests were bishops in Ravenna and (later) in Paris and even in Rome.

'And so long as the Roman world embraced that nearer East there was, I conjecture, little conscious difference between its Eastern and its European elements. When the Empire fell back before the Persians, before the Arabs (though Syrian Christians were still of influence in Europe) that Syrian Christianity was submerged. But Rome, Byzantium remained. And Christianity remained in consequence a Byzantine force, looking to the sacred Emperor and the only Rome the Christian East was conscious of, the Rome upon the Bosporous.

'Later, as has been said, came people from the far West; Franks, Italians, Englishmen. These were Latins, and there came to be Eastern Latins as well as Eastern Romans. But the Church of the land held to the nearer centre . . .

'In Jerusalem . . . you have within the Arab-speaking country interests which are not Arabian, not Palestinian, but world-wide; and which in their world-wide significance have been the special care of Greeks, speaking the language of St. Paul and St. John.

'Only one type of man could, humanly speaking, solve this problem. He must be heartily and faithfully Greek. He must be heartily and faithfully Apostolic. That is, he must be a great Christian, with the mind of Him in whom is neither Greek nor Barbarian . . .

'A living unity within the orthodox communion will promote more than anything else a real power of conciliation with other communions; for the practice of fellowship within—the fruit of light and the channel for more light—increases the temper of peace and justice for use towards those that are without. St. James says that a man makes war with other men because he is at war with himself. The inward peace should be the first repaired . . .

'If we, by prayer and study, do our part to help what we call the Eastern Church in her own anxieties, setting aside altogether the wish to decorate by her recognition our own great and deeply burdened Church, we may yet see the incumbents of those venerable Thrones come to our fellowship wearing their crowns with a new lustre because they represent every Christian heart within their pastoral charge' (*Knowledge and Virtue*, pp. 120–30).

In 1921 the University of Oxford conferred upon Father Waggett the degree of Doctor of Divinity *honoris causa* in recognition of his varied services in so many fields of both learning and action.[14] Although his decision not to return to the Holy

---

[14] The resolution of Convocation to confer a D.D. on him was passed on 17th May 1921. See introduction, pp. 13 and 14 *supra*.

Land may be regretted, his achievement there was not forgotten. Father Cary (in *C.E.,* 1939, p. 170) records that :

'. . . after the lapse of twenty years a recent visitor to the Holy Land has found his memory cherished by a distinguished leader of the Jewish community and by an eminent and brilliant educationalist who had encountered him in Jerusalem.'

CHAPTER X

In England, India and America 1920–5

FATHER WAGGETT'S main preoccupation in the winter of 1920–1 was the delivery of his Hulsean Lectures at Cambridge. As he says in the introduction to his book containing the lectures, their preparation had to take place 'under abnormal conditions' while

'I was completing in Jerusalem six years of detachment from books and from the atmosphere of a University; and my time had been entirely occupied, earlier by the work of a chaplain in France, and later by duties of an absorbing kind connected with different religious and civil interests in Palestine, while the Holy Land was under a strictly military administration' (*Knowledge and Virtue,* Introduction, p. 11).

These lectures, the most weighty of his published works, were in substance profound reflections on his war-time experiences and on his mission in Palestine. When he had finished delivering the course he wrote somewhat jubilantly to Katharine, in a letter dated 24th January 1921 :

'With inexpressible thankfulness to Heaven I have finished giving the lectures. It is a delightful feeling to be able to write a letter without the fear of losing irreplaceable moments. It has been very hard work. Of course I have not read out nearly all I wrote : and the work of preparing the book will be difficult; but it will not be under a sense of a threatening *date's* looming and a railway journey to make. I have been extra thankful —among the smaller mercies—to have been so punctually ready—always in the Senate-house to meet the Vice-Chancellor a quarter of an hour before the time with bands round my neck and an immense manuscript under my arm. All the old big wigs *very pleased.* They were afraid I was going to do my well-known "brilliant" act.' [1]

[1] There is no doubt that this last remark is significant. On more than one occasion at Cambridge he had, perhaps owing to pressure upon his time, relied upon his native wit rather than on his scholarly competence. Among the 'practical' men, such as an assembly of doctors at Liverpool— as Bishop John How recalls from his time as Rector of that city—the former was enough to produce a contribution of real inspiration to his hearers; but he disappointed a Cambridge audience—expecting a learned discourse with the *minutiae* of references and close analysis—in 1910 when he gave an almost unprepared set of Lent lectures in a series organized under the presidency of the Master of Magdalene following Dr. Rashdall's of the previous year published as *Philosophy and Religion.* Waggett's were not published.

The fame of Waggett's return to England soon spread, and we begin again to hear of a crowded engagement book such as we saw before he went to St. Anselm's House in 1909. After the last Hulsean Lecture he preached at Selwyn College, and in the letter just quoted he says :

'I am giving there a science lecture to-night: and to-morrow at Queen's. Then a lecture at St. Edward's, Westminster, and a meeting next day. In fact, with Lent, there now lies before me a vista of lectures and sermons —including Oxford for the Sundays in Lent.'

but he adds :

'Nevertheless what I hope for is a great deal of quiet reading and note making . . . I have had a great rest here from *travelling*: haven't stirred and Mr. and Mrs. Clark have been most kind.'

And he mentions in the same letter having renewed his friendship with Arthur Benson whose not uncritical remarks on Waggett have been noted above. He had dined alone with Benson who had evidently, after dinner, produced his voluminous diary from which Percy Lubbock provides some morsels. Waggett remarks that Benson 'pulled out after dinner a most interesting book of extracts and scraps. I must begin to keep one.' It would have been highly amusing to have had Father Waggett's comments on people and affairs done after the Benson method; but this resolution must either have been unfulfilled or else the product of it must have been destroyed in the holocaust of his papers in 1940. However here, in the same letter of 24th January 1921, is a piece of the same genre of literature describing the reactions of a group to whom he had given a scientific lecture—and it is kinder to the clergy than Benson was wont to be :

'I did a piece yesterday to say "It's nonsense to say that Heredity is *everything* because it is something. Such exaggeration is criminal, and the scientific gents ought not to leave it to *us* to expose the nonsense" . . . upon which a kind and *intelligent* friend says (1) "my doctor-friend was so amused by your reference to science" as if it was a joke that I knew about it and (2) "I was so glad to hear your enthusiasm for Heredity." Quite intelligent people though. The clergy are much better—much wider awake. This is a dark secret not commonly known. Except for a barrister here and there very few but the clergy can attend to a sentence from the beginning to the end.'

At about this time he was obliged to enter King's College Hospital, London, for treatment to his right arm which had caused him some trouble in France during the war. He came out with the pain quite removed and it was found to have originated in the shoulder and not to be neuritis, as he had supposed, but a splintered bone. He had no knowledge of how the damage had been done.

Among the friendships revived in this post-war period was that with Gilbert Chesterton. Waggett used to see him before the war at meetings of the Synthetic Society and the two men had a great affection and respect for each other. The Chestertons had been in Palestine in 1919–20 and they had seen a little of Waggett there, but there is no evidence of any close collaboration at this period.[2] However it is recorded in Chesterton's biography (*Gilbert Keith Chesterton* by Maisie Ward, 1944, p. 389) that Waggett and Gore were the two Anglican friends whom Chesterton consulted about his religious position between 1920 and 1923 when he finally decided to join the Church of Rome.

In the *Cowley Evangelist*, April 1921 there appears a sermon by Father Waggett in which he returns to a theme we have seen before and expresses it with renewed emphasis and clarity:

'The old lesson of Easter, so often given us by the Father Founder, is the lesson always freshly necessary and welcome. It is the lesson that the Risen Life of our Lord is a new life, and not the resumption of the mortal life; that the happiness of the penitent, after pardon, is a new happiness, not the resumption of the old satisfaction before the penitent began to be sorry; that our Easter must bring something very different from a resumption of the ways that the call of Lent disturbed and the discipline of Lent suspended.

'Of course there is no need to say this of *sin*. No one thinks he is free to sin again after pardon. We are quite sound in opinion on this point. In practice there are life-long difficulties unknown only to people who know nothing about themselves.

'But of lawful ease we must say something of the same kind. The special practices of self-denial are carried in Lent beyond the measure at which they can be permanently maintained. At Easter there is a right relaxation of some Lenten restrictions; but the *spirit* of discipline ought to be maintained at Easter . . .

'This old lesson is always freshly needed . . . its burden is that last year's knowledge will not serve for *this* year; that this Easter must have an original happiness, fresh as a new day, in which rays of light that never before fell upon this earth sparkle in dew-drops never before formed . . .

'. . . Now it is possible to conceive the Risen Life of our Divine Saviour as if it were only the suffering and mortal life restored. But by

[2] Sir Arthur Cust recalls a dinner in Palestine at which Waggett and Chesterton were deliberately put next to each other with the object of producing 'fireworks,' but they hardly spoke to each other.

such a conception we miss an important part of the truth. Lazarus came back from the grave and the state of the departed. He was recalled into the state he had left. Truly he must have taken up the earthly life again with a new spirit. But he was brought back again into the old. We can hardly avoid a sense of great sadness as we conceive a soul which had passed the river of death and was now again on this side, with the stream again in front, the parting again to make . . . For the glory of God, that man whom Jesus loved and for whom He wept, doubtless bore in great thankfulness the office of an example of the resurrection power: doubtless the Recalled, the *revenant* lived once more a mortal life in grateful reverence. But may we not conjecture that he went softly [3] all his days having this world's death before him once again? Lazarus took up again the life once left.

'Not thus was it when the Lord of Life, made man for us, broke the bonds of death. He died for our sins *once* . . . He returned to the earth, to the scene from which He made His exodus. But He returned not to the life laid down. He went forth through the grave and gate of death to a life quite new for man, the life immortal, eternal. We may say—how often we have said—that Christ left the grave as if by another portal from the portal of entrance. The tomb became *in effect* a corridor. Entering earthwards, He rose heavenwards . . . He came, in a mode how different, on earth, leaving empty the garments of the tomb . . .

'Yes, this victory does not reverse the former defeat and the word 'vindicated' ought not to have been written. For indeed the splendour of the Lord in His Easter is not the recovery of what He surrendered on Good Friday. His wealth is not in recapturing the plunder made by worldly violence. His honour is not the vindication of His name by refuting in confusion the scorn of worldly malice. Such a refutation was never made, that violence was never crushed. The surrender of the Cross remains for the world final, unreversed . . . Now the Spirit, moving in hearts humbled to receive Him, convinces their worldliness of sin, translates them . . . teaches them to honour what they despised, to worship the Life persecuted by the world. But in this state the world as such is not converted by external power; nor is its assent captured by earthly miracle. Remember, the world has not seen the risen Lord. The end of the story of the Cross for the world is death. The last the world has ever seen of Jesus was His dead Body carried to the tomb.

'When He rose He showed Himself alive, not to all the people, but to witnesses chosen before of God.

'. . . No reversal, then, of the defeat; no refutation of the scorn; no vindication before the world; but a victory passing on, passing up; a new state entered and occupied.

'So our Jesus passed on, leaving behind not a worldly victory, but a heavenly influence . . .'

Father Waggett took part in the First Anglo-Catholic Priests' Convention in 1921. The general subject of the Convention was 'Priestly Efficiency.' H. F. B. Mackay had delivered a paper on the Holy Eucharist and Waggett, in the discussion which followed, said that Father Mackay's paper had set him thinking of :

[3] Cf. p. 121 *supra.*

'. . . that inner spiritual development, which the old Protestant people called the spiritual manducation of the gift of the Lord in the Eucharist, which carries us by mental prayer throughout the day and throughout the week—stretching from one Mass to another and from one communion to another, like a wonderful curtain hung upon golden pillars with crystal sockets to make a great tabernacle with God of the whole life.'

Waggett then went on to say that he noted with delight in Mackay's paper what was to him the magic name of the Abbé Huvelin whom he had known intimately. He recalled how on one memorable visit :

'as I glanced from the bed where the Abbé lay in pain, I saw the little domestic altar to which he just managed to stagger, morning by morning, to make his offering, and I felt how all this inward and deep knowledge of the soul of man and of the life of Christ sprang from that place and that action, and fulfilled it.'

Waggett is reported as continuing :

'The Priest's retreat might well be the subject—as it might be the foundation and origin—of all his communions; and on the other hand as he descends from the altar let him resolve that the rest of his life shall be a retreat with God upon the great secret there folded up and given into our breasts like a choice crystal still veiled but waiting to be un-veiled and adored and understood more and more in the secret place of prayer' (*Report* published by the Society of SS. Peter and Paul, London, 1921, p. 87).

In 1922 Father Waggett was chosen by the clergy of the diocese of Oxford to be one of their Proctors in Convocation. In the autumn of that year he was sent as one of the missioners on the Mission of Help to India for six months, returning in April 1923. This was a similar campaign to the General Mission to South Africa in which Waggett took part in 1904. Information about the Mission, list of those taking part, programme, etc., is to be found in *C.E.,* 1922, pp. 241ff. He sailed for India in the S.S. *Nevasa* in October and wrote to Katharine during the voyage of :

'a dancing, gay sea, still cold, with blue waves and white horses. Port-land Bill in the early morning. Either come aboard there, or domiciled in the ship, quite a little flight of chaffinches, two young thrushes, a jackdaw, and two water wagtails. In the dining saloon there was some little warbler—perhaps a willow-wren : but it soon disappeared, probably going on its way.'

Later in the same letter he tells how the small birds soon dis-appeared when a hawk came on board; he mentions the 'perfectly fascinating' children and babies who were his fellow passengers and the 'marvellous coastline' of Africa. A meeting on board to explain the purpose of the mission was well attended as were the Sunday services.

His first letter, which survives, from India is written from Belgaum on 4th November 1922 :

'The mission begins here this evening. At Bombay our hours were entirely filled, the Metropolitan having come over to see the Mission. He gave us two wonderful meetings of instruction on Saturday and Tuesday and spent all of Monday with us too. On Tuesday evening—this is besides the morning conference—there was a service in the Cathedral at which the Metropolitan made a great address and gave his blessing to each missioner separately.'

From Neemuch on 2nd December he wrote :

'This is a most wonderful change from Bombay. I was very glad of my winter habit on arriving, and it is cold now at eleven, except in the sun. The almost absence of crows makes the garden full of various birds, and the air is deliciously silent . . .

'The great thing is not to let the clergy be discouraged, I mean the seculars, the Establishment people. They have a disconcerting task, and deserve every possible support, and all our prayers.

'I dined last night at the R.A. Mess, all eager to help; and I am hoping later to have an evening with the Railway guards and clerks at Rutlam.'

The next comes from Cawnpore on 19th December 1922 and speaks for itself of Waggett's crowded time-table and of the tantalizing position in which he was—being in India for the first time and yet being able to see so little of the wonderful country and its natural history, the latter being of such particular interest to him :

'It is uphill work all the time. But out of the small "congregations" individuals want long talks, so the days are extremely full. This is the first day-time I have had alone and indoors for several weeks. I went to Lucknow and back yesterday and go from here to Calcutta and then back to Allahabad. So I am far from the brethren in Bombay and Poona, and can seldom write.

'Missions up to now have been at Belgaum, a capital little school for officers and a nice Anglo-Indian church: Malabar Hill, a small church in Bombay where there was hard work and real fruits; Neemuch, the soldiers welcoming, and also the railway people; Rutlam, a tiny railway community; Indore, very good, quite small and an old C.M.S., but the Church-let "filled" every morning at Mass for instruction as well as evening. Here also I saw the Presbyterian establishment and gave an address: Cawnpore, Memorial Church, now going on, up-hill, people friendly but do not have the practice of "Coming to Church." There has been no interval except in the train, and I came third class from Agra (for want of room) and that was hard work, no sitting down.

'But now I get a brief interval before the Free School, Calcutta, and shall not feel quite so like a waiter who, having just handed one set of diners the finger bowl, has to fetch instantly the *hors d'oeuvres* for the next set.

'I have seldom had time to look at India; but did see an elephant yesterday and a monkey, and am all the time (when out of doors) enthralled by the birds. I am keeping well, thank God.'

On 28th December 1922 he wrote from Lucknow :

'My last minutes at Cawnpore were very full, and I just caught the train here. The motor broke down on the way to the station. Here I hope for a few days' rest, with only a sermon to troops and a "few wordses." In fact I believe there will be three days without any utterance—the first pause since we landed. I have got a tribe of letters to write to approaching missions—Calcutta, Allahabad, Bangalore, Coimbatore.

'I baptized the babe of my host yesterday—otherwise was free, but that meant an endless visit to an iron and steel foundry, quite good. Poor dear India is becoming "industrial." Such a mistake! Far better for them to grow food and import fenders.'

From Madras on 22nd February 1923 he wrote of a visit to Coimbatore in the course of the Mission :

'I left Coimbatore last night and arrived here just now. Coimbatore is a small place but quite alive; and all that is done there is real. The Church is occupied by devout Eurasians with a few Indian Christians. The small European community, composed of a few Civil Servants and the directors and so on of the Agricultural and Forestry Colleges, kindly allowed me to address them twice in the Club, and also invited me, in the most gracious possible way, to a kind of argument party at the Agricultural College. I am afraid my mental position is rather disconcerting to them; but we parted friends, and I was myself immensely interested, refreshed and helped.'

With that his part in the mission was finished, but he still had to go to Calcutta and give six addresses there—'two Religion and Science Lectures, an address to the clergy, a speech at the Bible Society's annual meeting, and an address to the Rotary Club, a body of enlightened business men' (same letter as above). Then he went to Bombay to give some more lectures and back again to Calcutta for Palm Sunday, Holy Week and Easter—presumably to give Holy Week addresses and to assist at services in churches there. He had a berth booked in S.S. *Malwa* to sail for England on 7th April. This was the ship which had taken him on to Alexandria after the torpedoing of May 1918. His last words written from India say : 'I have kept, thank God, wonderfully well, with incessant work, not less exacting because all on a small scale. The relief to-day of having twenty-four hours without an address is quite beyond words' (to K.B.W.).

Soon after his return to England Father Waggett delivered a paper, in July 1923, to the second Anglo-Catholic Congress on 'The Creation and End of Man.' He became an immensely popular speaker at gatherings of this kind during these years, and at these meetings, as at the Cowley Fathers' church and at other churches, when he was going to speak or preach the assembly was nearly always crowded to the doors. This is how he began his discourse on this occasion [4] :

'Your purpose is the greatest and clearest possible. It is, first, to recall the Holy Name of God, to make that Name sound clearly in England, to set all our interests under its protection, to make all serve the glory of God.

'And secondly, you intend to serve the cause of the multitude of our own and of every land. Like the Patriarch you are indignant that of the Heavenly Bread, you should *eat your morsel alone* (Job 31 : 17). You desire that what is known and loved by the few should be known and loved by all.

'. . . My effort in response is not to offer a proof of God or even a description of the doctrine of God. I only try to state the place due to the thought about God in all Christian reflection, purpose, practice. That place is easily stated, not easily preserved.'

He then continues :

'Of many things that should be added, let me secure one of great practical value. It is that this knowledge begins to be lost as soon as it ceases to grow; and that it can only grow in a life of prayer. Those that *seek* God shall find Him, and not those who, without seeking only talk or only think about God. A true thought of God is really the gift and presence of God, the operation of the Holy Spirit in our minds as we are joined together in the Church "with all the saints," that is with the general body of Christians, the most part of whom are poor and undistinguished.

'In the constancy of this belief in God and thought about God, our thoughts and words, our purposes and actions, attain reverence, wisdom, tenderness, patience. It is for lack of such constancy that our actions are sometimes feeble and violent, our accents shrill and unconvincing, even our religious worship cold and earthly. In all life "Reality" will be our watchword, and this reality is attained in the ever carefully cherished knowledge and awareness of the presence of God.

'It is not easy to preserve thus a sense of the eternal. "We do not," said one who knew very well what he was speaking of, "we do not lift up our hearts by accident or casually." It needs courage and much sacrifice of curiosity and self-will to escape from the *Dream* of this world, with its bewildering detail, its thorny maze, to the *Business,* which is the worship of God in spirit and in reality.

'But it is only when it is believed to be independently real, self-subsistent and self-sufficing, that the world is a dream, a fascinating

4 *Report of the Anglo-Catholic Congress 1923,* pp. 14ff.

vision or a terrifying nightmare. Escaped to God and looking on the world from the presence of God, a man sees the world also to be real, —real in a second sense, for it is the object of God's love and prepared as the scene and opportunity of our loving service. It is no longer then an impending grandeur, but now a real jewel, made by God, depending on God, preserved by God.'

He then passes on to consider Man as a being who has been given his being by God :

'If we welcome the Divine Name at the head of our thoughts, so we welcome the division that is proposed for those thoughts,—I mean the division of the subject into two parts; first God, the Divine Glory and Being, and secondly God, the Creator of all and of us who worship Him, and who now "have boldness" to speak to one another of Him.

'. . . And now give me leave to pass on directly from the thought of Creation in general to the thought of the creation of moral beings, which for our purpose means the creation of man.

'. . . in a perfect unfallen creature, there would be that dependence and that reception of power and light to which the fallen creature is recalled by an act of mercy, lifted by a rescue and a translation into the Kingdom of Grace.

'Dare I say that the natural power of the unfallen creature would be what we now know as Grace; that his natural knowledge would be inspiration, his natural science revelation, the knowledge and the love of God? Not quite. For such words might carry a meaning precisely opposed to mine. We must remember that in an unfallen man, there would still be a distinction between natural innocence and the supernatural bestowal of righteousness; between the gifts of ordinary reason that constitute in the man normal reaction to the world, and the gifts of wisdom that receives the vision of Divine Glory. Both the natural excellence and the supernatural endowment are constantly given by God and are ours only as gifts. And the true purpose of man unfallen, the end of creation, was such a welcome of the Divine Glory as now we know as Grace.

'I beg you to consider this as carrying with it two consequences. First, our present state of *real* dependence upon God and our present wisdom of *conscious* dependence upon God do not indicate a fall from perfection in the creature. Secondly, the sovereignty of God and our recognition of that sovereignty do not mean that our attitude,—rightly altogether subject and dependent,—is rightly altogether abject and self-contemptuous.

'Let us take the second first. It is when confronted by a tyrant that man is nothing. Confronted by a king he is noble. And certainly man is not humanly, morally, religiously nothing over against God. We are the creatures of His hand, the sheep of His pasture. We hold from His loving purpose, being, hope, reason, the soul's life. We hold from His pardon everything that belongs to peace. His mercy is not an occasional resource. It is the sole and ever necessary condition of our smallest tendency towards spiritual wealth. If we buy of Him, we must buy with His own coin, like children of a father. His mercy is not required in rare crises. It embraceth us on every side. But on the other hand it does on every side so embrace us. We are compassed about with songs of deliverance, and these are the ordinary, the normal, the regular music of our march.'

And then follows a passage in which Father Waggett's own particular contribution to the understanding of holiness shows itself :

'The nature God has called into being is not only real, it is significant and significant of God. He speaks to us through it; and it is to our own grave loss that we neglect to hear the message. Let us encourage one another to conceive that this humanity, this human nature from which we sometimes wish to withdraw ourselves, may be, more than we think, a revelation of the Eternal, the Incomprehensible.

'Do you think it is for nothing that the Almighty has called the creature man into existence, and made him, or allowed him to become, so convincing, so interesting, so noble, so base, so humorous and so tragic? Do you say only tragic, humorous, base, noble, interesting, *to us* His fellow-dust? Very well, since He is all this to us, did God mean this significance to us to be misleading, this thrill that man gives to us to be utterly uninspiring; this message that man brings to *us* the fellow-men, to be utterly empty, a tale told by an idiot, all sound and fury, signifying nothing? I cannot believe it. I find it hard to conceive how any believer in the Incarnation can believe it. If Mary's soul and Mary's voice could magnify the Lord, I find it impossible to believe that my hard-featured, hard-handed neighbour gives no evidence of His glory. If Jesus is the Word of the Father, I find it hard to believe that His brethren,—so entitled, you know, in Scripture,—give us no token of what the Father really is.

'No. This human nature is not nothingness, and it is not machinery. It is not machinery, and it is not dead, *perinde ac cadaver*. It is alive and has a future; and I may learn something of God in its trials, its sorrows and joys, its efforts, failures, and partial successes. I must believe that if there are in many lives,—the lives of the saints,—shining proofs of the Divine Goodness and Power, some there are in *every* life some great lights of revelation; some "forgiven injuries, conquered temptations (now and then), and difficulties conquered by endurance" ' (Thackeray, *Esmond*).

'The life of the most ordinary poor man is a course of such victories over circumstances as many of us would think to be remarkable and memorable if they occurred in one week or one day of our lives. Remember this, and then ask,—or rather, ask no more,—whether human life is indeed nothing, whether it yields no evidence of the glory of God. What we learn by the sincere watching of human lives—especially of the "rougher" or more "natural" kinds—is more certain and more important than some consequences drawn by tortured thought from documents or from tradition . . .'

And he ends with the following magnificent song in praise of Dependence (such a rebuke to much modern educational theory whose chief aim seems to be the acquiring of Independence) :

'I said the condition and the knowledge of dependence are not marks of an inferiority to our own better selves or more honourable possibilities. They are the mark and the condition of our essential perfection, the guide to our only conceivable advance. What do I mean? I mean that the perfection of man cannot have been and never can be a solitary and self-subsistent perfection. That would be *another* perfection, a perfection additional to the perfection of God: that is to say it would be another *God,* which is impossible and unthinkable. The perfection that alone can come to be the creature's perfection is God Himself, no other, no less. He gives not His glory to a Second, but He giveth *Himself* to the creature whom He has called into being, not so that the creature may contain and measure his incomprehensible Majesty, but in order that the creature may become a partaker with many others, in Christ, of the gift of the Divine Nature, the advent not once for all achieved, but incessantly renewed, of the Divine Presence.

'Is not dependence then great? Is not the fall of man the fall from dependence to a fancied and most unreal independence,—from a real wealth that is all made up of receiving to a frozen poverty that is imagined private wealth?

'And will not such a thought as this, so undeniable, so inevitable, guide us when we are inclined to forget God, and be a help to us when we come to consider . . . the meaning of sin, and the character of that rescue which Christ has accomplished for us by His most Precious Blood, —that is to say not by a sentence of indulgence, not by a brief act of authority, as when a king enlarges prisoners at his accession, but by the laborious victory of a moral renewal and a moral re-establishment of that created nature, whose ruin is to live apart from God, and whose glory is an entire welcome of the majestic generosity of God's self-bestowal . . .'

At the end of September 1923 Waggett went to Newcastle on Tyne to lead a ten days' parochial mission. On 6th October he wrote to his niece, Mrs. Robert Aitken:

'My opinion and my feeling about religion are expressed in Hymn 190 (or thereabouts) *Hymns Ancient and Modern, Jesu dulcedo cordium:* I have had great works and great worries ecclesiastically these last months: but am not at all daunted.'

On Armistice Day, 11th November 1923, he preached a remarkable sermon on 'Silence, Sorrow and Hope' at High Mass in the Cowley Fathers' church in Oxford:

'Silence was prescribed to us as our mark of reverence to the Dead, and of thanksgiving for release from a war that seemed unending . . . So, if we break silence at all, it must be with large obliteration of some things which might naturally rise to our lips. The manuscript of a sermon to-day would have many black bands, blocking out all words of pride, or fierceness, or vanity, or worldly anxiety, regret or resentment; all reflections upon the things that might have been, the lives that might have been spared, the peace that might have been wrought. From all that we keep silence with our lips; and we must try to keep silence from them in our thoughts as well; to put quite away all thoughts of the wisdom of individuals, and the particular plans of progress now set before us; so that we may come in the silence back to the presence of God, through forgetting whom it is that men fall into wars, and cannot build themselves a peace. Yes, in silence we may return to God, and think the higher, greater, truer, nobler thoughts that belong to His sanctuary . . .

'Surely we are helped towards this quiet prayer by the thought of the heroic dead who, under God, won us the peace, and by whose unhesitating, silent, uneloquent, uncomplaining, unconscious sacrifice it has come to pass that we are to-day living in freedom. To those who remember the war, or who have outgrown the passing, rather vulgar fashion of forgetting it, I would say this. I do not ask you to recall your share in heroic passages of arms, but rather some scene as homely as this—the sight of heavy, stalwart, burdened men, with shaggy jackets of goats' hair, hung round with all the utensils of a moving home, bound together with the strap of the rifle, plodding wearily, after an exhausting leave, to the station, just to go back once more to their duty and, if need be, to die: just a homely, humble, common sight, which was seen every day in London during those anxious years; just these men, plodding back through mud to death, quite uncomplaining.

'If you can get over for the moment the false refinement of oblivion, just remember that the average unwounded life of a second lieutenant was about three weeks from the time he landed in France in 1914 . . .

> "Nothing is here for tears, nothing to wail
> Or knock the breast, no weakness, no contempt,
> Dispraise, or blame, nothing but well and fair
> And what may quiet us, in a death so noble"
>
> (Milton, *Samson Agonistes*).

'. . . But this high mood will not last very long. Our hearts are too tender, too warm to retain it. These were men like ourselves, not heroes of romances or figures of an imagined past—these were our companions. I always think as I walk through Westminster Abbey that the Unknown Warrior may be the man who picked me out of the sunk-hole, where I should have drowned in mud unless he had dragged me out by the collar of my coat, and who passed on before I could thank him. He may be the man who kept me waiting for my horse when I was trying to get away from "Harley Street," and whom I ungraciously scolded and could not catch up to make friends with again. He may be one of those thousands of men to whom I ought to have spoken the word of salvation but failed to speak it. Anyhow, he is one of the men with whom we walked and talked, whose rations we shared, whose broad shoulders bore our burdens, and who, when we grumbled at a little cold, or small quarters, or insufficient sleeping space for the pony, had only a short night, an hour or two, to rest before they went back again to fight and to die. For I am thinking of the ones who died. We cannot be simply heroic when we think of them, they are too near to us. There *is* something here for tears, something to wail for and to knock the breast, because we failed them in their hour of need. Better than a vain attempt to maintain a stout hearted stoicism is it to follow them into the blessedness which is theirs now. "They are all gone into a world of light." "I see them walking in an air of glory"; and it would surely be more comforting still, more true, more sound and in the end more brave, to think of them with Jesus, to see them as John saw his own sorely-tried, ordinary, weather-beaten, half-frozen, scourged companions of the persecution in Asia. He saw in Heaven, standing before the Throne and the Lamb, a multitude no man could number, clothed in white robes and with palms in their hands. And there was an unspoken question in his heart. And when one of the elders in the vision said to him, "What and who are these arrayed in white robes, and whence came they?" St. John, not daring to utter his wild guess of affection, said "Sir, thou knowest." "And he said to me, These are they which came out of the great tribulation and they have washed their robes,"—the blood of their own sacrifice being transfigured by mingling with the Blood of the Lamb, so as to receive the merit of that stream which issued from the Saviour's side. They were the common people whom John knew well—his flock, faulty, inconsistent, sometimes good and sometimes not quite so good. Some burdened mother whose work was so constant and so hard that time and again she missed the gathering together of the faithful on the Lord's Day, and was not at Mass, and must be reproved by her pastor. Yet she endured to the end, and sealed her faith with her blood . . .

'That is how it is with those who were true and selfless and died for us. And we are left behind to do a strange and small work . . . We lament because the promise of that day, which we older folk remember in the dim past of 1918, seems to have come to nothing. The light of peace was but a flash, and has faded away into darkness. "The summer is past, the harvest is gathered and we are not saved." We are still lost, still in disunion, in anxiety and fear; we know not when the trembling balance of warring selfishness will topple over into the old abyss of madness and destruction. We are not saved, and we must set to work to do the building of the peace.

'If we are disappointed, it is for two reasons; first because we thought peace would come easily, and secondly because we looked to rebuild our lives out of the relics of the past alone.

'It is partly because we supposed that peace would come when war should cease; that to stop firing is to begin loving; that to refrain from destruction is the same as building the city. Those who had any sense warned us all through the conflict that it would not be so; but we obstinately believed that we had only to leave off wasting and there would be wealth, forgetting that wealth comes not only from ceasing to throw the bread into the fire, but from beginning to stoke the oven for the baking. We have sat with folded hands; we have left off shouting; and we expected that if we ceased to shout there would be beauty; that if we left off fighting the brother there would be the kingdom of the Redeemer. And we have to learn though so late that peace is not a negative but a positive thing, not the absence of strife, but the careful and patient building up of a vast harmony: it is the glorious fabric of a music strangely ordered by a delicate and strong art. For peace is nothing less than the whole life of the peoples in civility. It is learning, medicine, commerce brotherhood. It is ruled and ordered freedom in joy and happiness . . .

'And, in the second place, we were disappointed because we thought that we had only to pick up the bits that were left over from our former state; to collect again the old possessions. But the life God gives us is a newness of life, even as the Saviour when He had tasted death for every man resumed not simply the life He had lived, but a life reborn after the original purpose of the Father. He went on to an undying life, immortal. He did not simply gather together the life that had been

177

scourged, stripped, crucified and buried, but, to use a figure, left the sepulchre by another door . . .

'So we, if we are to live for God, if we are to find in God this new life of real peace and real joy, must seek it in a spirit of abandonment of all that is past, accounting these things but loss for the knowledge of God and the communion of Jesus; and we must come in the spirit of a deep humility longing for pardon and restoration; not lifting up hearts vainly satisfied by what we have managed to keep or regain of ancient honour, but hearts bowed down with the sense of an irreparable fault recorded by the graves of a million men,—come in penitence, that we may receive the only joy, the only peace that men can ever find, the peace of reconciliation with God through the precious blood of Jesus Christ, in a new life . . .' (*C.E.,* 1923, p. 267).

Father Waggett seems, on a reading of his sermons belonging to this period, to have been at the very zenith of his powers of expression in these years. Physical strength seems to have been his in abundance, too, and gone seem to be all references in his letters to periods of exhaustion, headaches and so forth and the need for rest. The spring of 1924 found him in New York, lecturing at the General Theological Seminary and giving a course of sermons at St. Paul's Chapel. Three of these sermons were published in the *Cowley Evangelist*. The first, delivered on 31st March 1924, was on the subject 'What is man that thou art mindful of him?'—What does God see in human nature to make Him approach it with salvation? :

'Jesus, what didst Thou see in me that Thou hast dealt so lovingly? We all know it (this question) in our own lives and we have the answer; we have the answer in the terms of the question: "It is in love that He hath dealt with me." And though there are times when I can hardly believe that I have really found Him and that He has really found me, yet, thank God, many of us have the complete assurance of this and we can only wonder at the mercy and the grace which hath quite certainly and without all wonder found us.

'Many a sinner has cried, "How great the joy that Thou hast brought, so far exceeding hope or thought!" And we are wise when we approach the world problem of God's coming into the world by His incarnation in the spirit of tenderness and gratefulness that is born of our own experience.'

And there follows one of the very few rebukes which are to be found amongst the recollections of Father Waggett or among his writings. He must have had some unfortunate experience just before this course of addresses began to bring forth the following well-considered remonstrance :

'I don't know, indeed, that we can make any serious progress in Divine studies excepting in this temper of humility and gratefulness and tenderness. And that is what makes one sometimes regret the kind of sharp rebuke one receives in this land of vivid intelligence and continually active thought; it isn't the criticism that the preacher minds, but the disclosure of a mood, apparently neutral, purely judicial, not hesitating to hurt—not that spirit of tenderness and friendliness in which alone, so far as I can guess, Christians may hope to make progress by taking counsel with one another, either in theological criticism or in the knowledge of our Lord and Saviour, Jesus Christ.'

And then this glowing expression of his own patient and loving experience of the perversity and ingratitude of men worked out in terms of our Lord's knowledge of the shortcomings of His own :

'So then it is with the grateful feeling that we all of us have, of how God has been good to us severally, has made good what was lost and washed away what was unclean, and above all, come to us and disclosed Himself to us in the most intimate possible knowledge. Though we have forgotten Him and been independent of Him in spirit, it is in the remembrance of all this that we must approach the great question, Why is God incarnate? Can I believe in this gospel that God has really come into this world and lived for it and died for it?

'And remember, the question becomes all the more tremendous when we reflect that through the Divine, timeless knowledge which, in the terms of our infirmity, we call His foreknowledge, the failure of Christians to make use of grace, that is to make use of Jesus, must always have been (to use the language of our time) as manifest to Him as was the failure of man to love his Creator, or the failure of Israel to go on trying to serve Him who had delivered them from Egypt and brought them into the land of rest.

'And we wonder still more wonderingly that Jesus was born for us, when we reflect that He must have known that many would not receive Him; that of those who received Him, many would be inconstant, inconsistent, and starting aside like a broken bow, and that the history of His own church, His own newly recovered flock of sheep, grown out of the wilderness where they were lost, would be as perverse, as ungrateful, as uncertain, as greedy, as much longing for the honour of men, as those others whom He had tried to shepherd before.

'The whole history of the failure of the church must have been present to the Lord's timeless mind, only I think we may add for our comfort, that to the same timeless, Divine mind, there must also have been present those good things that are to come. There is a Church to come, that we cannot dream of, without spot or blemish, or any such thing, without narrowness or uncharity; with wide knowledge, with ever deeper familiarity, through experience, with the amazing power of God's grace, the abundance of His grace, the overflowing power which is His, to usward who believe.'

And this is how Waggett expresses what God in Christ saw in the human race, to make Him become incarnate and know that patience with us would have its perfect work :

'So then all that is present to him; so we must judge this question of why God saves the world, by our own secret knowledge that God really saves us and is good to us. Though we in no way deserve His goodness and in no way show any promise of a return for it, he deals with us for the sake of what shall be; he deals with men for the sake of what shall be . . .

'. . . Always look, then, on your neighbours, and look into your own heart and say of yourself and of them, This nature, so disordered; these spirits, so selfish and so loveless, are energies and persons that God hath made for Himself, and He still loveth them and means to recover them . . .'

Waggett's second address in St. Paul's Chapel, New York City, on 1st April 1924 was on God's mercy in keeping, preserving and restoring His whole creation in spite of all that looks like failure and moral ruin. He begins by emphasizing that the great word in the New Testament on this subject is *restoration* : not replacement but restoration :

'. . . God is thus contrasted, in his mercy, with man in his ameliorating efforts, for man very often—not always, but often—especially in a swiftly progressive society, is apt to proceed by destroying and replacing. I have heard it said that in your more vigorous and wealthy societies, the English are sometimes looked upon with a certain amount of pity because we make our things too strong and keep them too long. Our railway engines, our locomotives, are built as if they ought to be monuments, and they last so long that they become monuments; some are put on pedestals and used in the stations, and so forth, but others remain monumentally obsolete and yet strong and not worn out, upon the track, getting slower and slower.

'I want to avoid the word in common use. How shall we find a substitute for the word "scrap"? Our habit, in swiftly progressing societies, is to do away with and cast upon the rubbish heap what has stood long enough, and replace it by something else to a better model or out of better stuff. That is not God's way. God's wonderful way is that He respects and loves all things that He has made; as we say in our Lenten collect, "Who hatest nothing that thou hast made." There are no cast-off robes in God's treasury, no persons whom He can spurn, no utterances of His which are withdrawn from circulation. The covenants, the promises and the blessings of God are without repentance; that is to say, without His repentance—He does not change His mind about them.'

He then passes on to a most important brief study of the contrast between the words καινος and νεος in the New Testament :

'. . . Let me, because of that truth, choose the place in Scripture, in the New Testament, which may seem to you at first sight most contradictory. In the Apocalypse St. John, being in the spirit, saw a vision of the things to come, and he says, "I saw a new heaven and a new earth: for the first heaven and the first earth were passed away and there was no more sea. And I John saw the holy city, new Jerusalem, coming down from God out of heaven." This looks at first sight as if we were to believe that this frame of things we see was finally to cease to be—this universe—and be replaced by something better. "I saw a new heaven and a new earth," for the old sky and the old earth had passed away.

'And so, let me, as I have this unusual opportunity of taking counsel with thoughtful people—I don't mean any disrespect to any congregations, but still it is an unrivalled opportunity—let me invite you to a little New Testament study this morning upon this word that is translated "new." There are in the New Testament two words which are equally translated "new" in English—"neos" and "kainos." "Neos" means, for the most part, a separate and different individual of the class which takes the place of an old one done away with. So a man might speak of his new coat, and he means then that the old coat is done with, parted with, and that he has got another coat instead. That is the meaning of "neos" —another thing in the place of what has become old. So a new man, a young man, is a freshly born specimen of the race, with a clear skin and an unshaken nervous system, who takes his place in our ranks, instead of one who, having done his duty, has gone to his rest.

'Then there is another word, "kainos," and "kainos" means fresh and is applied to things which were once not fresh and are made fresh again without losing their identity. "Anakainosis" means the refreshing and making new once more of what had become old and worn, and the Holy Writer in this Book of Revelation says in this place, "I saw a new heaven and a fresh earth," and then the sentence that follows seems very difficult at first for me, when I am sustaining this view of "kainos," for he says, the first heaven and the first earth had departed, but in this place "first" refers only to earliness—the earth in its early state had gone away, but it was the same universe that he saw in his prophecy; he saw fresh, young heavens and a young earth, and he missed something which belonged to the familiar feature of the part of the universe he knew. He did not see a fresh sea. It was just because the sea was not renewed, that there was no more sea, no more separation.

'. . . I beg you to remember this distinction between those two words. It is a clue which guides us through many apparently contradictory teachings in the New Testament, and on the whole, though there are exceptions, the teaching of the New Testament is that God is going to make all things as they were at the beginning—not the beginning that we know, the beginning of history when the creation has already shown its perversity toward the will of Him from whom it springs, but its first beginning, which is in the heart of God; that original, unspoiled, wholly beautiful, lovely and eternal purpose of making an unperishing universe and an unperishing mankind . . .

'I am quite sure that this is the part of the message that we need. I think that in our recoil from an absorbing care for the things that are seen and an absorbing service rendered to the things that are less than ourselves, we have been apt to find our escape by thinking that we should belong to something which lies wholly in *notion,* and we call this notional world heavenly. We call this unreal interest spiritual, we think that if we could but disentangle ourselves from all that is actual, we should, in leaving the actual, leave the evil, and in finding the imaginary, find God. Whatever else this be, it is not the Christian religion, it is not the historic Christian religion.

'. . . But this notion of escaping from the world to find God, of escaping from the seen to find God in the invisible, is the real materialism; for what does it mean? It means that we regard some things as outside God. The strength of numbers, the thighs and sinews, the brains of our people, the thickness and elasticity of our steel, the power and expansive energy of the forces we have harnessed; all this great world of activity and actuality around us, where is it going to? What is it for? Is it to go ringing down the grooves of change for ever without God? This exclusiveness is the true materialism, and we must learn of Christ, that all this also must be reclaimed with whatever sacrifice of pride and wealth; it too must be redeemed . . .'

Father Waggett's third address on this visit to New York was given on 4th April 1924 and was remarkably his own contribution to the understanding of the place of prayer in the Christian life :

'. . . in all our prayers we have not begun to have the Christian motive while it is a prayer for our own consolation and strengthening and glorifying and beautifying, for our own victory over sin, for our own detachment from the miseries and vulgarities of the world, for our own translation to a higher plane, or even for our own transformation into a higher life—none of this is of Christ. Those who went before Him knew this. Job said, "Woe be to me if I have so much as eaten my morsel alone." And yet sometimes there are Christians who are content to enjoy the unspeakable blessing of the Holy Communion itself, whose very name might teach them better, as if it were to be a treasure of a selfish life and an ornament of private gain . . .

'And we also, in our very beginning of the life of prayer, must begin in the spirit of sacrifice from the start; not hoping first to be nourished, that afterwards we may be strong enough to fight, nor first to be cleansed, that afterwards we may be worthy to die; but we are cleansed by dying, and we are strengthened in fighting, and we are found of God, and find Him, in being lost ourselves, and in losing the whole world . . .

'It is a slow thing—moral progress; it is a slow thing—ecclesiastical perfection; it is a very, very slow growth—the growth of Christian knowledge, but every man can at once determine to choose death and not life, can he not? Did you not see tens of thousands die for their country, under your eyes? I have seen hundreds and hundreds of men fall; I have seen thousands of them die, each one in the swift instant of trial choosing death instead of life. Here you have death and truth and not life and falseness ! Every man is capable of this at once, long before he has become perfect, while he yet has to retrace the whole maze of accepted sins and to find his way out of a whole complexity of false positions, and at once he says, "Christ is mine, and He is a die-er, and I will be a die-er too. I choose the life, not of self-preservation, but of self-sacrifice; I choose, in fact, here and now, at once, not myself, but God, who out of this world must draw us to Himself through the narrow and dark gate of death."

'Even the very feeble Christian can begin to be a real Christian; that is to say, a sacrifice-Christian, a man of the Cross, a man of the others, a man of God; and in the first, faint stirrings of that prayer I spoke to you about, he may already exhibit the stirrings of a truly unselfish devotion.

'But you say, "Unselfish—isn't that the hardest thing of all?" It is hard as a temper; it is hard as a moral accomplishment, but it is not hard as an intention. There are, thank God, in this world now to-day, many millions of men who have accepted this intention and made it their own. Though their selfish flesh quakes and their fierce temper revolts, and their tired frame binds them down in sloth, yet their shot is sped, their lot is cast, and in the day of trial they turn out too . . .'

And then this on the Church which is really praying in the way in which he has defined prayer above :

'In the Church there should be no life for the Church. A Church which is busy surviving is of no kind of consequence to God. A Church that is busy is self-protection has not begun to murmur or to stutter the first accent of the real gospel, for she knows not the name of Christ—Christ is crucified, Christ is given! She can have no life but the life of Christ. He is all her life. There is no other contribution of vitality upon which she may draw. Christ is all her life and Christ is all. Christ, God in man, is all for man in whom God dwells not yet. Christ, the eternal Word, having in himself the plenitude of the infinite knowledge, is altogether, to the last ray of that light, for the world which is still in darkness, separated from God, alienated from the life of God, and buried in the infirmities of its own nothingness. We are for each other, that Christ may reign in all, and the whole of us, as one body, in so far as we rightly bear the name of Christ, are for the world.

'It is a terrible thing—a Church that is not worldly in that sense. There is no use in a religion which only attracts the pious. The pious are for the impious; the religious are for the irreligious; the members of Christ are wholly—not partly, but wholly—for those that have not yet come into His saving grace, and their life from start to finish is thus of sacrifice . . .'

During the same visit to America in 1924 Father Waggett gave an address on Prayer and Meditation to a Church Convention. This address was published in the *Cowley Evangelist* (1931), but it has not been found possible to trace exactly the place and composition of the assembly before which it was originally delivered :

'. . . For prayer—in view of the fact of Creation and God's purpose—appears as something more than an expedient for obtaining succour in temptation, comfort in trouble, strength in labour, light in darkness, or security in doubt.

'By prayer we obtain all these particular blessings. But prayer itself is the entirely indispensable attitude, experience, and activity of the life that is being saved. It is more than a means to another end which is holiness. For since holiness is the communication of God, prayer which is the welcome of God is holiness itself in its initial stage, and already, in the most imperfect worshipper, is the unspeakable gift of God, and the real life of Christ in the believer.

'. . . We shall not be fair and we shall not be safe if we do not hasten to add that the description that indicates larger lines for the opportunity of prayer also sets before us in the most convincing way the immeasurable *difficulties* of prayer. We must not forget or obscure these, and the man who does not know them has not long persevered in prayer. There is an ease and a peace in prayer. It is the ease of an accepted duty, the peace of a settled loyalty, of a simplified desire. St. Teresa says somewhere that he who prays is delivered from the toil of the journey and is borne as in a boat with sails. But the man who sails far meets both toil and crisis enough, and St. Teresa's own book is a record of difficulty valorously confronted . . .

'. . . Let us be sure we are on the wrong path—a path not truly ours, not truly human,—if our prayer, like our external task, is not every day, or at least every year, more difficult. Let us look at least with caution and hesitation upon promised short-cuts. The utmost succour of the corporate devotion is not doing its true work when it seems to relieve the soul of effort. It does that true work only when it releases the soul from solitary ease to Churchwide endurance. It is only in the Church, in the Spirit-bearing fellowship, that we can do the appointed work. But in the Church, in the Spirit-bearing fellowship of love, it is work and a full tale of work that each is appointed to do . . .

'. . . But it is in the very toil of muscle and brain and heart that his (Man's) spirit rises to welcome the empowering love of God. As we see the creative Word in the flood of existence, so we see the *redeeming* Word in the tasks of human life,—we see the Cross. All the road of perplexity, of sacrifice, of suffering, of death belongs to God. It is the very road of Christ. Nothing hinders our prayer in the demand of toil. What hinders us is the rejection of toil, the abandonment of problems, the choice of easy answers, of a path of least resistance, the pursuit of a personal and self-centred peace. The fullest share in the agony of society, in the ever fresh and now, as it seems to us, nearly overwhelming, demand of human corporate needs, will give to faith the strongest, the most incessant prayer; and the *Ascensiones in Corde,* the flight of the soul to the sources of strength, the heavenly conversation itself, will be most secure in those who, through unwearied sharing of man's burden, are most conformed to the rule of Christ.

'The habit of effort becomes one with the habit of supplication and the very substance of the Soul is changed by the power of God-given habit to the fashion of the redeeming love that bore, and still bears, our burdened nature. Thus our difficulties become our supports. The believer drinks of the brook in the way, therefore shall he lift up his head. And the way is the Way of Sorrows. We have not to escape from this scene of struggle in order to find God . . .'

Back in Oxford in these years Father Waggett was much sought after by the undergraduates, as many who attended the Cowley Fathers' Church in the Iffley Road at that period will testify. Whenever it was known that he was to be the preacher the service was packed to the doors, with a preponderance of junior members of the University. Apart from this Waggett used opportunities he had for being a father and counsellor to individual undergraduates. Naturally he felt particularly able to be on friendly terms with the sons of his own social circle and such young men found a rich privilege in associating with his brilliant mind and dedicated personality with all its variety of background, experience and wisdom. A charming letter which the late Viscount Knebworth wrote home in 1924, when he was an undergraduate at Magdalen, illustrates well the manner of Father Waggett's approach and the kind of spell he exercised over a large number of that generation.

'One morning last week, the first this term, I forgot to get up. Eventually I made the supreme effort and struggled along to the bath. It was then too late to get breakfast in Hall, so I collected some eggs here, some butter there, bread somewhere else, and finally a pear from J.C.R. Returning thus laden, and feeling very unshaven, to my room at about 10.15, I find seated in my chair Father Waggett! We fell upon each other's necks, the eggs fell upon the floor, sleep fell out of my eyes and the cigarette fell out of his mouth. We talked all the morning about God knows what, and bit by bit my breakfast got cooked and eaten, and then I went with him to feed the birds in the Botanical Gardens, though he had first to assure me that it "was done." He was too delicious and in such good spirits, I do hope he'll come again.

'Father Waggett took me up to London the other day to hear him speak. Really I took him up, but he made me come. I motored him. He wore twelve coats, four cloaks, eight scarves, nine hats, three handkerchiefs, twelve cassocks and two rugs over his knees, and he was (a) invisible, and (b) unconscious from cold! . . .

'Father Waggett spoke of "England 100 years ago" in theory and in practice—everything. He was quite brilliant, very amusing and very radical. No one dared criticize him at all. They gave us a good dinner, anyway, and I motored back in about an hour and three-quarters.

'He's a perfectly heavenly man, I think, in every way, only I should like him to be stronger. I dare say he is really, and anyway you'll say his frailty is his charm. Perhaps, but to me it's rather ridiculous. What a brain, though. I don't know of any that I like better or think more perfect.' [6]

[6] *Antony (Viscount Knebworth)*, by the Earl of Lytton, London, 1935, p. 216.

The comment on Waggett's fragility in this letter is interesting because it does not seem to square with the general impression of him at this time. There are isolated references, in private papers of this period, to weariness, but little more. It must have been the time in his life when the spirit of the man had become so stabilized that it almost overcame the very gradually increasing frailty of the body and made him practically unconscious of it. He was, after all, 62 by now and the fiercely burning fire of his intellect, the perpetual journeyings, the unremitting hours of intense labour added to the strain of the war years must have been taking their toll. Knebworth himself was not destined to remain in this world for long and perhaps he had an inner consciousness of what was happening to his own frame and an inward eye for the smallest signs of dissolution in others. Nevertheless very few would have seen anything of this in the Waggett of 1924: he still had several years to go during which his radiance was to pour forth unabated.

On 2nd November 1924 Frank Weston, Bishop of Zanzibar, died in Africa. Waggett had known him well and had seen him on his last visit to England. He wrote of Weston as being 'of those who are indeed "set in the Body" as special gifts of Christ to men' and he contributed an appreciation of him to the *Cowley Evangelist* which shows in a particular degree Father Waggett's own spiritual eye for the greatness of another man, another priest. The background introduction is necessary for the understanding of what Waggett had to say about Bishop Weston :

'How splendid if Holland were here to speak of Frank Weston's finished labour in the Church on earth! For no one knew by heart, and in the heart, as Holland and one other man knew the history and meaning of the Universities' Mission to Central Africa and of a bishop of Zanzibar.

'Canon Travers is the lifelong servant of the Mission and the faithful watcher of all its interests, and he must be its historian for he is its living record. Holland and Father Russell have been its poets and its prophets. And no one could like Holland proclaim and make us feel "the height, the depth, the gloom, the glory" of that splendid, so long tragic, always heroic life, the life of the Universities' Mission and of its great bishops. Year after year, Holland's presiding genius made of the great evening Mission meeting in the Holborn Town Hall a glorious demonstration and experience; and to any new attendant, to any new worshipper—for we were worshippers there—it was a revelation, undreamed of before, of what a missionary meeting could be, of the power of the mission cause to lift and carry the soul in the air of the real Gospel life. From the first notes of "Fling wide the banner" to the good-night blessing, that meeting, in Holland's hands, was a great spiritual endeavour, full of joy and sorrow, of the solemnity of bereavement and the unfading hope of conquest; a work of the faith that overcomes the world, a work of the Resurrection and of the Risen Lord.

'You do not waste your time in hearing of those days, for it was the spirit of those days, of that work, that we saw and loved and reverenced in Frank Weston. Nothing more honourable can be said of a man, and especially of a bishop (than), that he was in the true succession of Bishop Steere and of Bishop Smythies, that warrior saint so closely linked with Father Puller. But the happiness of recollection must be restrained, else it would be easy to dwell upon a last visit to the great Bishop where he lay in much pain in Russell's Brooke Street room, worn with long journeys on the rough and narrow paths which then connected station with station, but radiant with courage and an informed faith. He owed, he said, all he knew of theology to "Puller" his chief at Roath.

'The Mission, and in due course the see of Zanzibar, enlisted in Frank Weston a man marked out to take up the work of such men as Smythies, and Maples, and Hine and Richardson.

'To begin at the superficials, he was a man of stature and attractive appearance, of natural dignity, with a full share of the qualities which make it easy for other men to defer to the man who wears those qualities, that "personality," simply, humbly, and unconsciously. His unclouded faith and his love towards God were developed in intelligence and the power of utterance. His books, completed in the short intervals of labour that would have exhausted another man, are so well thought out and constructed that they challenged the attention of exacting scholars, and of an intelligence so critical—but, it must in fairness be added, so enthusiastically generous—as Dr. Sanday's. On more than one occasion, men of more than one kind differed from him in judgment. But I suppose it never occurred to any man that an utterance of the Bishop of Zanzibar was other than an utterance brilliantly sincere, of a judgment fundamentally brave and wise. We exulted, even when we differed, at the sight, glimpsed through the dim air of the world, of that thin spire of smoke, which gave assurance that a man was burning his boats. His activity from first to last, his entirely frank and unargued respect for men of every kind and race, his urgent and unwearied love of souls, his constant and unwearied return to the standard of one living in the Divine Presence, his quite unfaltering devotion to duty and to the search for truth and peace—all these things made of Bishop Weston a force not to be resisted in the restoration to missions of the only dignity a missionary can value, by the manifest persistence, in our time, of the Apostolic work and example.

'For him, and through him for us, the work of Christians to-day is the work of the first witnesses of the Resurrection and founders on the Rock of Christ, of the Universal Church. To any counsels of ours at home he brought a breath—a gale—of larger air, and made the most hesitating servants of the Cross desire to lose all that Christ might find His own . . .

'. . . Surely such an appointed chief, set in the body, for the purpose of the Lord, was this man we knew face to face. He was apostolic, for, though no man can fill again the place of the first witnesses, he carried safely and faithfully their proclamation to men who had not heard it, and by hearing were added to the Lord. He was a prophet and evangelist to the Gentiles and to us. He was a pastor of unwearied zeal inspired by the Chief Shepherd, and found strength and time in a life of pastoral care to be a teacher of learned and unlearned. In the measure bestowed upon him for his special place, he gave his life for the increase of the Body and its building in Divine Love . . .'

At the end of this year (1924) Father Waggett's Hulsean Lectures were published by the Cambridge University Press as *Knowledge and Virtue*. In the introduction he laments that more revision of the text had not been possible and explains that the finishing touches had perforce been carried out either in India or at sea. Nevertheless these lectures are a really scholarly work and in weight and thoroughness entirely deserving of their place in the series and worthy of comparison with the collection of Bampton Lectures at Oxford—though they are a shorter course than the latter. Waggett sent a copy to Archbishop Davidson, who had been his diocesan bishop in his later days at Tabard Street. Dr. Davidson wrote a letter of acknowledgment on 10th December 1924, rather characteristic in manner though containing a not insignificant testimonial :

'I have not yet had more than time to glance into its pages. They appear to give one, as yours always do, abundant food for thought.'

An introduction to the thought of *Knowledge and Virtue* must wait until a more thorough study of Father Waggett's writings can be published. This would also include a summary of *The Industry of Faith,* a volume of sermons which was published in the following year (1925). In the introduction to the latter Waggett explains his purpose :

'. . . many are despondent at this time about Christian efficiency. Together with much movement there is also much languor. Some do not know how to find work and others despair of being able to do it. It is, in point of fact, in response to the definite request of people who in various degrees share this despondency . . . that the following very rough sermons are put into print . . . the sermons are an attempt to point out not by any means all of the conditions of advance and of usefulness in the life of faith, but still some of those conditions.'

In 1925 there appeared also a translation of St. Robert Bellarmine's *The Mind's Ascent to God* containing a preface by Waggett.

In August 1925 the missioner at Charterhouse in Southwark

was transferred to a new post; the Committee said that they could not make a new appointment during the holiday period and there was eventually a vacancy of three months. Waggett was asked if he could step into the breach and he agreed; so to his intense surprise and interest he found himself in his old post from August to October that year. In a letter published with the Special Report of the Committee for 1925 Father Waggett thus endorses the appeal for a new Missioner:

'. . . such work as an older man can supply is inadequate to the many opportunities and demands of the Mission. No sensitiveness is too quick for the varied appeal of the place; no energy steady enough for its unending work . . . you need the high spirit, the elastic sympathy of a young man, and his inexperience of failure.'

At the same time he gave his impressions of the Mission as he now found it, forty years after its foundation and more than thirty years since his relinquishment of the post of Missioner:

'In many ways the affair seems to me strangely unchanged. Perhaps this is because I am older, and Tabard Street is to me now what Tabard Street was to me then. One forgets. *Tempora mutantur* but we change with the changing times; and the years bring—a doubtful gift—the philosophic mind. Still, unless I am deceived, a great deal here is exactly the same as of old.'

There were—not always among the churchgoers—the faces of old friends and exactly the same *kind* of neighbours as before. But the opening of the street had made a great difference from the earlier conditions when:

'. . . we were nearly shut in, and our street, then an unbroken curve of small houses, was like a college quad., and was lined of a summer evening by stationary groups; for when the Public House shut in those days at midnight we had beer on the pavement, to pass the hours when it was hard to breathe indoors.'

The second great change was that:

'in the place of ramshackle cottages we have in great part of the streets well-designed and comely blocks of tenements, where, by the way, the rents are too high for old Tabard Street people.'

Old trades had gone and there was now insurance against sickness, accidents and unemployment. But there were still:

'too many men and women, ill-fed, defaced, pallid and miserably clad. The economic revolution has not gone so far as we hoped to wipe out the all but desperate degrees of poverty.'

Housing was still scarce and rents were high. On the other

hand there was a real improvement in the health of the children and splendid schools had been provided for them. And :

'. . . oh! the advance in our songs since I was a young man here; the decency, the kindliness; the infrequency of outcries, of fights, and screams of anguish . . . I need not now ask the Bishop of Southwark, as I asked the present Primate when he was our Diocesan, to be president of a society—quite successful in its time—for substituting the handsome old English swear-words for exclamations much more distressing.'

On the side of worship there was a great improvement in many ways :

'The Church is beautifully ordered and cared for; and the services and worshippers very reverent indeed. There is much prayer; not slight and passing, but persevering, ardent, generous, hopeful; and the foundations of the Mission are still found in narrow homes of the people.'

But, as Waggett well knew, the workers were too few to reap the great harvest of souls awaiting them, and :

'. . . the Mission must more than ever be understood, not as an affair between the minister on one side and the congregation on the other, but as a common enterprise for the Divine Kingdom. Everybody in the Mission, Church, club, meeting, association, must be a worker; not a passenger; not a hearer of the Missioner nor even his emissary; but a worker for God. So only can Charterhouse contribute anything considerable to the improvement of this great South London—perhaps the largest equally "poor" city-population in the world—or even make much difference to our corner of the Borough and Bermondsey, by St. George's Church, a corner that still—just as it did forty years ago—bears marks of its long association with the Marshalsea, the Mint and Horsemonger Lane; of its nearness to the old sanctuaries of the Bishop of Winchester —the Bank Side, the Bear Garden—the refuges of actors—like Shakespeare and Cyril Maude—and other excommunicate persons. There is a flood of life about us, much of it heavily burdened life. If every church was full, the people in them would be but a drop in this tide.'

CHAPTER XI

A Characteristic Year—1926

FATHER WAGGETT appears never to have kept the resolution, made after dining one evening with Arthur Benson in 1921, to keep a full diary. But he has left behind some disconnected jottings—very intermittently entered—in a journal for 1926. The diary does not begin until 12th February, but thereafter it does give a fair idea of the kind of life Waggett was living at the age of 64.

On the day of the first entry—12th February—Father Waggett went to St. Mary's Hospital, Paddington, to see a microscope which had been ordered for the Cowley Fathers' mission at Poona by Sir Almroth Wright. He afterwards dined with Sir Almroth [1] and his brother General Wright. The next day, Saturday, he went for the week-end to University College, Southampton, staying in the 'fine William and Mary house' which had formerly been the home of Lord Swaythling and which now had been converted into a residential hall for the college. He comments, 'House marred by half hexagonal juttings front and back.' At the station he was met by Professor Cock, then Principal of the College on whom he makes a comment worth noting : 'a most friendly and interesting man, *rather* like Pass, but not ugly.' On the Sunday (Quinquagesima) he celebrated the Communion at 7.30 and preached at 9.30, both in Stoneham Parish Church.

All through Lent this year Waggett preached at the Cowley Fathers' Church in the Iffley Road on Sunday mornings, and in the afternoons he dashed up to London to preach at Evensong at St. John's, Holland Road. The third Sunday in Lent was particularly busy because in addition to these regular engagements

[1] It will be remembered that Sir Almroth Wright was a scientist of international repute, that he was the original of 'Sir Colenso Ridgeon' in Shaw's *The Doctor's Dilemma* and that one of his many distinguished pupils was A. Fleming (afterwards Sir Alexander) the discoverer of penicillin.

he had Canon Ottley and another to lunch and a long talk with Ottley afterwards; then after the service at Holland Road in the evening he visited the Magdalen Mission at Somers Town and there met Basil Jellicoe and others.

On a number of successive Tuesdays in the early spring of this year Waggett was giving a course of lectures, probably on Religion and Science, at Sion College. While he was in London on these occasions he once or twice dined with his brother Ernest in Wimpole Street; and the diary also contains notes of several flying visits to Bournemouth to see his sisters. On a return journey from Bournemouth to Oxford on Saturday, 13th March, when he had the usual busy Sunday to follow, the journal says: 'Made wrong connection at Basingstoke,'—but it does not reveal where this landed him!

In the same month, March, there was an extra sermon at All Saints', Margaret Street, an English Church Union Council Meeting, a long talk with Lord Halifax followed by lunch with his son Lord Irwin and further long conversations with the latter about Church Union matters. He was attending meetings of the Palestine Exploration Society about this time and in the train to Hastings on 15th March, on the way to address some Sisters there, he had a 'great talk' about Palestine people with Sir Arthur Money who happened to get into his carriage. All this shows that Waggett's connections with the Holy Land were by no means severed.

Then Palm Sunday, 28th March, saw him staying at the Deanery at Worcester. For the first time for many a long month we then come across a note of fatigue—'I was overtired and stayed in bed until near luncheon.' In the afternoon he addressed some species of nonconformist gathering on which he comments: 'Made a sermon at a sort of undenom. welfare Brotherhood. Kind, friendly, earnest people but their meeting quite unnecessary.' This adventure seems to have given rise to some discussions among the brethren at Cowley, for there is mention in the diary some weeks earlier of talks with Fathers Conran and Trenholme on the subject, and it is evident that some of them were opposed to Waggett's addressing such a meeting.

On the Monday in Holy Week he went to stay with the Dean

(Burn) of Salisbury and he carried out a number of preaching engagements in that neighbourhood. While there he had discussions with Archdeacon Dundas on the 'unbeneficed Clergy Committee' in preparation for a forthcoming debate on that subject in Convocation. 'To Old Manor House Asylum to see a sick priest' occurs in the diary under the Wednesday in this week. He returned to Cowley for Easter Day. After Easter he went to stay with the Bishop of Exeter.

The journal then contains notes about the General Strike of May 1926 and of some of Waggett's activities in connection with that. He had to abandon a projected journey to Portsmouth to give addresses on account of the crisis. He was in consultation with the Master of Balliol and others about the possibility of holding a conciliation meeting in Oxford at the height of the strike. Apparently nothing came of this, but Waggett was asked to appeal to the Bishops of Liverpool and Exeter and to the Archdeacon of Leicester to give their help in this direction. The General Strike came to an end on 12th May. In Father Waggett's diary for 11th May when, presumably, a settlement was not far away, he entered the following :

'We must ingeminate peace in a peaceful manner. When the Lord Protector beat the Scots at Musselburgh a Scots Lord prisoner asked how he now liked the marriage of the king, Edward VI, to their queen. "I always," quoth he, "did like the marriage, but I do not like the wooing." "God's own work must be done in God's own ways." '

On the Sunday after Ascension Day (16th May) he preached at Cowley and later in the day saw various friends, including Brightman. On the next day he went via Cambridge to Bury St. Edmunds where he was the guest of Archdeacon Farmiloe. On the 18th he conducted a Quiet Day at Newton Green and on the 19th he went to London for a meeting of the Cowley, Wantage and All Saints' Missionary Association. Back in Oxford on 20th he was present at a 'theological dinner' at Christ Church with the Canons and others after which a paper was read by Dr. Prestige. The Whitsun week-end, which immediately followed, he spent at Saighton Grange near Chester at the invitation of Lady Grosvenor to whom he ministered. While he was there he paid several visits to Chester and called on the Bishop (H. L.

Paget) his old friend and chief. He also visited Hawarden where he saw some friends who were in distress. In the midst of all this travelling and visiting he was reading N. H. Baynes's volume on the Byzantine Empire in the Home University Library.

On 17th June 1926 (though this is not mentioned in the diary) Father Waggett preached in Westminster Abbey at the Festival Service of the Gregorian Society. The following extract is a very good example of the lyrical quality of his sermons at this period. It also shows his power to express an important, yet still amusing, pathetic and painful process such as the revival of plainchant in the Church of England :

'. . . When religion was, in many respects, and certainly as an effort of worship, at a low ebb, there came first a movement of power and thrust and courage. Our helpers and forbears in the Faith broke down many strongholds by a dour resolution, suffering many things at the hands of those who were content with worship as it was. That work of power has been maintained until, if I may dare to say so standing in this venerable place, this ancient church has become the settled leader of everything that is august and fine in worship, and will hold that place by the constant devotion, not only of its priests, but of the whole college of those who serve in this famous Abbey.

'After the work of power came the work of beauty. After Mackonochie, Palmer—whose name I name to-night because, as you probably know, he lies a-dying. When I left Oxford, he was thought near the end : he may have passed over the border now and entered into what will surely be a wonderful peace, for he has been a faithful servant of Christ and His Church, especially along this fair road of musical joy and beauty. The change which we rejoice in is not limited to the fields in which the ancient Plainsong of the Church is loved, but has had its influence everywhere, just as all through the ages the real character of ecclesiastical music has had its roots in this ancient music of yours. The recovery of its practice has not been easily accomplished. How wonderful that we should hear to-night so exquisite a psalmody, in which all the ancient forms are rendered with the full power of magnificent choirs and of a highly accomplished technique in voice and accompaniment ! It was not always so. When first this ancient chant was revived, it was revived in some places by earnest men who thought that in the service of God sincerity would serve instead of art. I shall never forget the thrill, almost of terror, when first in trumpet tones and in the massive gait of a runaway herd of oxen, the Eighth Tone Fourth Ending burst upon our frightened ears at St. Alban's, recalling even then still earlier childish terrors. I had been once or twice in childhood to the opera, and was reminded of Meyerbeer's *Prophete*. It was a song of defiance, loud, harsh, heavy, tremendous, awful, though always religious; a thing apart from all we had known of the delicacies of musical art. At first we were invited to believe that what was ancient, religious, Catholic and devout might dispense either with properly produced vocal tones or with any precise art in the instrumental accompaniment. I hope I do not speak ungratefully of those early heroes of the fight in which you are the accomplished conquerors. But I assure you, boys and younger men, the revived Plainchant was impressive and alarming rather than entrancing and soul-uplifting, because the revival was in its origin an antiquarian revival, and like some other antiquarian revivals it was effected by men who knew very little of antiquity. Our restorers stopped far short of the real origins of this music. They were far, I think, from connecting the music of Ambrose and Gregory with the melodies of Christian but still classical Greece. They gave us something recalling the romantic forest-life of the Middle Ages rather than the exquisite art of the calm and stately world of Greek antiquity. It was an antiquarian revival; it was effected as part of a reaction, and must, therefore, if it was to be real, be long and difficult. An almost hasty revival, on grounds only indirectly musical, brought fresh and unnecessary difficulties. For the great tradition had to be saved from an imperfect study that set before the chant, not the obstacles of prejudice or ignorance, but the obstacle of a false presentation, a presentation almost as different as possible from the true manner of the song of the Church.

'For the song of the Church, if it is accompanied, must be accompanied upon a flexible silver flute; and whenever it is sung, it must be sung, not with the shout in which hoarse men demand less bread and more taxes, but in the tones of persons who have used the throat, the voice, the tongue, the larynx, as a sacred gift, and warble as blackbirds warble with fresh pipes in the fresh day, and the thrushes discourse one another from grove to grove in the golden light of a summer evening. That is what Plainsong is; it is an utterance, exquisite, flexible, changeable, sympathetic—various with the varying moods of faith, lifted by every wave of true devotion, and able to lift the heart as on ever new wings, to sing with grace in the heart praises to God.'

And then this on the qualities which he believed Plainsong alone to have :

'. . . I am not one of those who welcome Plainsong in such a way as to become ungrateful for the wonderful achievements of polyphonic music in Italy, or of that great and special school of music which, right down to our own times, is one of the treasures and the graces of our own English Church . . .

'. . . We are not traditionalists in such wise that we are content to say words because they were once said. We are traditionalists only in this sense—that we accept from outside ourselves the disclosure of the love of God in Christ . . .

'. . . Suppose you were engaged in your meditation; suppose, through silence and patience and the abandonment of busy curiosity and of selfish anxieties and ambitions, you reached that central chamber of calm that is within the storm of life, and entered the temple where God hides you with Himself and which He Himself visits—the sanctuary of your soul. Suppose that by some great blessing of God—a blessing that is always ready for us, but seldom comes because we seldom wait for it—you knelt before the altar, seeing with the eyes of the understanding the adorable sacrifice of the Lamb of God, marking by faith the very approach of His silver feet, gladdened by the beams from His eyes, and waiting, with a heart at rest and yet on fire, for the coming of the Saviour in His Body and in His Blood; and suppose, after your Communion, you were plunged into an even deeper silence, and began, with an experience to which no words can point, and for which you can find no words, to feed upon Him in the heart by faith. Now what music could break upon your ears in such an hour, in such a moment, without distracting, disturbing, bewildering you? I yield to none in love for the exciting and romantic strains of Wagner. They come upon me like a breath from beyond the seas; but I should be disturbed in my mental prayer by the songs from the "Meistersingers" or even by the Dresden *Amen,* because I cannot but connect it with all the elaboration of the heroic operas. At the sound of that orchestration I should be obliged to rise from my knees. But should there come upon me the sound of the ancient song of the Church, if I were invaded by such Psalms as you to-night have sung, I should be as undisturbed as on the day when my body lies before the altar and they sing the ancient melody of the *Asperges.* I should be undisturbed because such music, wedded to such words, would simply flood the soul, carrying it on to ever greater joy and peace. Here would be something better than silence, safer than solitude, deeper than any sensation or absence of sensation, a wave to lift the soul into the heart of peace, which is God Himself, our Redeemer.'

(*Church Times,* 25th June 1926)

Then the first week of July found him much occupied with the Church Assembly and with the Inter-Communion Committee. From the 12th to 16th he was attending Convocation and immediately after that he returned to Oxford for the summer retreat and chapter of his order at Cowley. Father Waggett was present at sessions of the British Association which met in Oxford in early August that year, and there he had conversations with Sir Oliver Lodge and many others. On Sunday 8th August he preached to the Association at the Church of SS. Philip and James. On the next day he went to Knebworth for a short visit in the course of which he preached at the parish church. On the 16th he left Knebworth for London where he lectured again at Sion College; thence the same day to Bournemouth where he saw his sisters and spent several days walking in the neighbourhood and seeing a large number of old friends. On Sunday 22nd August he helped at Mass at St. Osmund's Church at Parkstone at 8 a.m. and preached in the same church at 11 a.m. He notes in the diary here, 'very tired.'

On 28th August he left Bournemouth for Oban, staying at Saighton on the way. From Oban he went for a short steamer cruise with some friends to Port Appin. He notes in his diary that the water was like glass and 'never saw so many and different birds on the water'—guillemot, razorbill, merganser, ducks, gannets, gulls : 'porpoises also and seals and a whale.' On Sunday 5th September he notes : 'Held a service at Glenkinglass the Lodge. Stalkers, gillies, servants and children. Fourteen I think in all. Metrical Psalms, Lessons, Prayers, Discourse.' On 11th September he moved on to Inveraray to stay with the Duke of Argyll, and on the next day he preached at Inveraray Church. On the southward journey he visited the Glasgow Art Gallery and stayed again at Saighton, preaching on Sunday 19th in the neighbourhood. A few more days then in Bournemouth and on Sunday 26th he was preaching again at Cowley. Thursday 30th September saw him again in London in the morning for 'Jerusalem advisory meeting'; then in the afternoon he took the train for Charlbury whence he was taken to Chadlington to preach at the Harvest Festival. He notes : 'Mr. Ponsonby and the Ch. Ch. choir. Fine. Very pleasant people. Large supper party.'

On 1st October Waggett went from Charlbury to Hoar Cross, the home of the Meynell family between Lichfield and Stoke on Trent. Lord Halifax joined the party the same evening. On Sunday 3rd October he preached in the magnificent Church designed by Bodley at Hoar Cross and visited the Boys' Orphanage. By the 5th he was back in London once again lecturing at Sion College on 'Gen. view of the effect of scientific movements on Religion.' Later in the day he attended, still in London, the annual meeting of the Jerusalem and the East Mission. He caught a bad cold the next day and was obliged to stay in bed with it on the 8th, presumably in London—for on 9th he notes 'to Oxford, grumbling much.' But all the same he was preaching in Oxford on Sunday 10th. On the 11th he was in London again for a meeting of the Cleaver Trust and he notes 'got Alan Leslie chosen for new Trustee.' [2] He then stayed a few days at 7 Margaret Street, Father Mackay's house. On the 12th he lectured again at Sion College, this time on Psycho-analysis. On 14th Waggett was present at the session of Convocation at which the

[2] A distinguished young ecclesiastical lawyer, and expert on the law of transport, who was killed in a fall from a cliff in Devon in 1928 at the age of 38.

Catechism was discussed: he notes, 'Sat with Stone and Kidd (just back from Malines). Bishop Harry Southwell seeming better and talking more freely than in C. Ass. He has been very ill and resigns his Bishop work and goes back to Provost of Lancing. Keeping Canonry of Chichester.' The 15th also was taken up with Catechism discussions at Convocation and Waggett notes: 'Did all we could . . . Put in Sin and Repentance to our report to Primate.' He notes that he had a very pleasant dinner that evening with Mackay alone. On the 16th October he travelled back to Oxford having conversations with Professor Peters, Professor of Biochemistry, whom he chanced to meet in the train. On Sunday 17th he preached for the hospitals and then spent most of the rest of the week at St. Edward's House, Westminster, transacting business connected with the house. The following Sunday (24th) he was back in Oxford preaching at Cowley in the morning. Two dons from Oriel lunched with him that day at Cowley and the same afternoon he had talks with two Radley boys. The 4.35 train took him to London to preach the evening sermon at the Magdalen Mission, St. Mary's, Somers Town. After supper he had long talks with Percy Maryon Wilson and Jellicoe, and he spent the night at the Mission.

Waggett returned to Oxford on 25th to make a speech at the English Church Union annual meeting there on the needs of the Union. The next day back to London to give a lecture on Ellison and Boyd at Sion College. On 27th he was present at a meeting of the Association for the Promotion of Retreats and he also looked in at St. Stephen's, Gloucester Road and 'saw Victor and his merry men' (Lord Victor Seymour). The next day he had a series of consultations and interviews at St. Edward's House, and managed to get away from the house for a bare hour and a half to the South Kensington Museum where he notes: 'the immense subway remarkable.'

On the last Sunday in October (31st) Father Waggett preached at University College, Oxford in the evening and afterwards dined in hall with the Master, Sir Michael Sadler. Later the same evening he went to part of a meeting held in the Examination Schools for the Universities' Mission to Central Africa at which the Archbishop of York and the Bishops of Masasi and Nyasaland spoke. The next day he went, at the invitation of P. V. M. Benecke, to hear the Bishop of Masasi speak at Magdalen about tribal initiation under Christian control. He also had talks with Brightman about this time.

At the beginning of November the diary shows several notes of Waggett's great grief at the death of his friend Clement Henry Howard. He took part in his funeral on 2nd November. From 2nd November to the 18th the diary is completely blank—signifying almost certainly not a break in activity but intense preparation of one kind and another for a very busy period at the end of the month. On the 18th he began conducting a short retreat at King's College Hostel, London. On the following day, after giving the first address in the morning, he went over to the Church Assembly and took part in a discussion on Ethics. Later in the day he also made his voice heard in a debate in the Assembly on assistance for Armenian refugees. Back at the hostel he was occupied with interviews until dinner time. After dinner that evening he went to the theatre with his brother Ernest and his wife. On Sunday 21st November he heard his friend Mackay preach at Westminster Abbey in the morning and he himself preached at St. Giles's, Reading, on his way back to Oxford, where he arrived late and, not surprisingly, 'cold and tired.' Much business awaited him at home. Amongst other things he 'consented reluctantly to speak at E.C.U. against exchange of pulpits' on the following 13th January. He signed Professor Turner's printed letter to the Primate about Origen and with Turner went to visit Brightman and discuss this subject. He seems to have been having trouble at this time with a review he had been asked to write of Bishop Weston's *Life*.

On 13th December he was at the Censor's dinner at Christ Church and he caught a bad gastric chill on the way back to Cowley. But after a brief spell in bed he arose undeterred to fulfil an engagement at Crowstone School, Westcliff. After a short visit to Lord Shaftesbury at Wimborne St. Giles, Waggett returned to Oxford once more to wrestle again with his review of the life of Frank Weston. On 20th December, according to the same diary, he seems to have come very close indeed to achieving the impossible. He was at Kingston Lacy in Dorset for a meet of the local hunt in the morning; then he went to Parkstone for a brief glimpse of Marian and Katharine and then on to Cambridge to be present at a Feast at Jesus College in the evening.

On Christmas Day he preached at the Society's church at Cowley on 'the Appeal of the Presence to Loyalty.' His notes in his diary under this heading read :

'3 exhibitions— (i) irresistible force.
(ii) moral compulsion or attraction.
(iii) the appeal of personality.
the presence recognized by the throbbing of the heart—welcomed by the racing of the pulse.'

On Sunday 26th December he enters, 'still wrestling with review.' There must be some story—long since lost—to explain Waggett's otherwise quite unaccountable difficulty with this review of the Life of Bishop Frank Weston. So the diary ends.

This seems a very full year in itself. But in addition to the work observed above, and the preparations which it involved, Father Waggett found time this year to translate, and to have published, *Lectures on the Holy Eucharist* by Jean Landriot, Archbishop of Rheims. Also not noted in the diary was his presence at Sunday evening At Homes for art students held by Dr. Percy Dearmer and his wife at Chelsea. Waggett was one of the several distinguished speakers who were invited to open debates at these gatherings, and he was 'a general favourite' and he went to the At Homes again in the following year. (*The Life of Percy Dearmer* by Nan Dearmer, pp. 275–6.)

CHAPTER XII

The Last Active Years 1927–30; Illness 1930–9

IN the summer of 1927 Father Waggett took an active part in the Third Anglo-Catholic Congress. He read a paper once again on this occasion and he also presided at the session in the Queen's Hall on the last evening of the congress. The general subject of the deliberations at this year's meetings was The Holy Eucharist, and Waggett's paper came in the section of the proceedings devoted to 'The Background of Sacramental Belief,' the title of his own paper being 'The Christian View of the World':

'If I quite understand what is expected of me, we are now, in preparation for devout reflection upon the Eucharist, to mark some of the characteristics of Christian thought about the world, that is to say, the scene of our mortal life. Such a study of Christian thought might lead us a long way, in respect both of the range of facts thought about, and the modes of thought about the facts. Indeed, I suppose that in one sense there are as many Christian views of the world as there are Christians. At present the Christian view would for many be the Evolutionary View. To others a Christian view would have regard to the *relative* character of sense perceptions. But there are, perhaps, some features of thought which are, in a special degree, characteristic of all Christian thought.

'There is one, indeed, that is universal and regulative. There is no Christian thought about anything that has not for its entirely constant and perpetually fruitful centre an absorbing belief in God. The fear of God, the knowledge and love of God is the foundation of all the Christian's science and of all his wisdom. It is because this fact is thoroughly familiar to every one here, and made the law of life and thought, that we have been given no paper about the adoring search for the knowledge of God, without which all attempt to contemplate the particular revelation given us in the Eucharist must be entirely vain and even dangerous.

'. . . The Church credited—and it is a matter of credit—with an unlimited transcendentalism is the champion of reverence for the phenomenal world; and in every repetition of the Creed cries with exultant confidence that God is the maker, not of heaven only but of earth as well, that the Father created and holds in existence by the Word and the Holy Spirit, all things not only invisible but visible. The Church has always by a divine instinct condemned the supposed spirituality that found a moral exaltation in the inward and the psychical. Like a wise mother she knows that if bodies consecrated to be temples of the Holy Spirit can be corrupted and ruined by sin, certainly tempers and wishes and spirits—creations invisible, but possibly not unphysical—are at least as much open to perversion, to misuse and to destruction.

'Give me leave to add a few words on each of these heads, and then to point to their connection with Eucharistic worship and belief.

'. . . The Christian regard for the actual, the particular, the material. There is nothing securely divine in the contempt of earthly experience: there is no valid contrast between the actual and the spiritual. The non-material is at least as actual as the most enduring or the most rapidly perishing of the things of sense. And the actual, however material, however brief its tenure of the stage of existence, however narrow its range or short its orbit of reality, is capable of being, by the power of the Creator Spirit and by the ministry of the spirit of man, as truly, though not as grandly, spiritual as the unimagined powers and splendours of the Divine Presence. The clouds also, though they change and vanish while we admire them, are his messengers, and he maketh ministers of the instantaneous rise and fall of the fire.

'The neglect or contempt of the material, and of the regular successions of our "outward" life, whether personal or social, takes on the air of a specially spiritual mood. But it leads to practical atheism in the conduct of life. In the mid-current of the immense wealth, power, and grand organization of life in America there is evident a strong and humble spirit of detachment. Many of the heroic Christians in that wonderful land incline to regard exclusively what are called the things of the soul. In this way they do a real Christian service. But if such an effort of detachment remained without counterpoise, it would lead in less enlightened spirits to the conclusion that what happens to the man's *mind* is of consequence, while what happens to the man's money is not of consequence, or has less consequence, in the high measures of morality and faith. It would lead to the abandonment of the material resources to a godless management, unrelated in purpose to the salvation of man and the kingdom and glory of God.

'Do not mistake me. The transcendental thought, the way to truth by *escape* from the visible and the changing, is a real mode of human thought too; and it does not exist for nothing. In it, indeed, and by it, we find the convincing witness of the eternal; it is in contrast with the unchangeable thus, perhaps unconsciously, discovered that we are aware of time and process. But when it is thorough-faced and persevering this metaphysical perception becomes much more than tolerant of the particular. It finds the infinite *in* the contingent. For, indeed, it is not the particular, it is the abstract and the abstraction that confines the spirit and the mind of man. As in virtue he that would do good must do it in particular actions, so in thought, he that would find truth must find it if not in particular objects yet through particular efforts of subjection to the eternal truth.

'The infinite significance of the Particular shines once for all in our Lord; He is the principle of all health; but He is not content to abide in His world as the unshaken promise of restoration. In the fullness of time He also appears in it by Incarnation, bears our burden and our sickness, and that not for mankind only, but for men and women and children.

'. . . There is hardly need of words to remind you of the Christian reverence for human life; but sometimes even here error has crept in.

Distrust the spirituality that flings about the word "man-made" as an unanswerable accusation. There is, indeed, a "man-made" that is not divine, that is "human-all-too-human" in its pride and ignorance and moral weakness. But those who adore the Incarnate Word dare not say that what enlists the faculties of man and uses the pathetic endeavours and affections of man is therefore, and to that extent, not of God.

'Finally, we may, very simply, point to the Eucharistic bearing of these common characters of Christian thought, this actualism, this scientific temper, this humanism.

'. . . "We are not ashamed of the Gospel" of Christ's power in the Eucharist, because the gift has a material side. We do not believe that our Communion by the Spirit in this world with the Exalted Saviour, our King in heaven, whose coming from heaven we look for, would be purer or more secure if that Communion were always free from all implications of occasion and place, of "earthly" counterpart and visible instrument.

'. . . And, I add, do not be afraid of the doctrine because the Eucharist has a human side, a share even for our striving, the grievously backward and variable effort of our humanity.

'We shall not think to exalt the mystery by supposing it lifted above the level of human fortunes, out of the tangle of human infirmities, human generosity, human abasements of penitence, human exaltations of desire . . .

'We know we cannot measure the heavenly powers and actions contained in this gift from the crucified and risen Saviour. Do not be sure that we know the limitations of our mortal share in it and that not only in response. For we know not the measure in which the Almighty uses the human spirit and human spirits to compose the instrument of his mercy and build the road of his august approach.' [1]

In this year Father Waggett was appointed by Trinity College to the living of Great St. Mary's, the University Church, at Cambridge. The consent of his Society, the Cowley Fathers, had to be obtained and this, when he was now 65, was the first time Waggett had been a beneficed priest. He was instituted by the Bishop of Ely on Sunday, 29th May 1927, having been delayed some months by illness from taking up his new work. In many ways it seemed an excellent choice and appointment—many in Cambridge at the time thought it so—because Father Waggett's teaching powers and his skill in approach to much younger men were acknowledged with gratitude throughout England and in many other parts of the world as well by this time; also because of his competence to deal with questions arising in the debate between religion and science. But it was too late in more ways than one. Those who knew him well in these last years realized that in

[1] *Report of the Anglo-Catholic Congress 1927,* pp. 1ff.

a manner they could not quite define the eleventh hour had struck. He was no longer really abreast of undergraduate thought, and he was apt to quote as stars or produce at meetings distinguished men who were just receding on the stage and not quite known to the young men of that generation. In addition to this the debate between science and religion had reached a stage at which he was no longer quite master of it. His hard-driven frame and mind, also, were no longer capable of the quick response and many-sided mental alertness which were needed in a position of that kind in a University city. This is not to say that this period of just under three years, his second time of resident work in Cambridge, was a complete failure: but the high hopes which were entertained of his having another great spell of influence with an entirely new generation could not be fulfilled. The present Dean of Worcester has described Waggett as 'undoubtedly one of the Cambridge figures of my undergraduate days,' but it would have been difficult to describe exactly wherein his greatness lay at that time. His ministry had become rather like that of the elder statesman or the wise and holy man slightly remote from the main stream of affairs. His sermons at Great St. Mary's certainly drew large crowds of undergraduates, but when they came they heard the wisdom of a man with a deservedly great reputation for sanctity and oratory and not a message in quite the right idiom to take *them* over into the fourth decade of the twentieth century.

Professor Austin Duncan-Jones of Birmingham University, also an undergraduate of those days, writes the following which gives an impression of Waggett's position *vis-à-vis* the junior members of the University:

'. . . He still had some connections with Trinity—dining rights perhaps —and he used to be allowed to hold meetings in the Old Combination Room. I don't think there were many of these meetings; in fact I only have a distinct memory of one or two. Father Waggett sent us—I mean undergraduates at large—a beautifully engraved card, inviting us to come and hear "Father Douglass of Calcutta, the best missionary." There was a large attendance. Introducing Father Douglass, Father Waggett said their first acquaintance had been when he called on Douglass, a freshman at Christ Church, to canvass him about some college society: "I wasn't a clergyman then, I was a spark." Of Father Douglass I remember little but his appearance: he was handsome, quiet, and ascetic. Father Waggett stole the show. It must surely have been at another meeting that Father Waggett talked about mechanism and vitalism in biology, and described experiments he had done himself—I suppose forty years before. A biologist friend of mine was scornful of it all, as hopelessly out of date. That illustrates the sad failure of communication between Father Waggett and the undergraduates of my time. I don't know how much he was aware of it himself. He enjoyed those Old Combination Room meetings, and said at one of them that if we were good he would, one of these days, bring us "Gilbert Chesterton or Hilary Belloc"— names which, I suppose, he could have conjured with twenty years earlier. At one of these meetings, he contrasted the lively social doings of the Cambridge Christian societies as they were then—"shows of cocker spaniels organized by the C.I.C.C.U. etc."—with their apostolic simplicity when he had known Cambridge before—"young men on their knees round green baize tables" . . .'

The Revd. A. G. Kayll, now Vicar of St. Leonard's, near Tring, who was Waggett's assistant priest at Great St. Mary's from 1927 to 1930 recalls that the congregations in those days were very mixed. The evening congregation consisted of a few college servants and perhaps some shopkeepers living in the parish, but in the morning the attendance would be made up chiefly of dons who lived outside the parish boundaries but whose custom was to worship at the University Church, with the addition of a number of other distinguished persons from the residential parts of Cambridge. At either service there might be a sprinkling of undergraduates who were drawn by some well known preacher, frequently by Father Waggett himself when it was known for certain that he was going to preach. But Waggett had no idea of publicizing himself.[2] People often came to the Church hoping to hear him preach and were deterred from making the effort again by finding that another preacher, unannounced, was to deliver the sermon. He little realized how much publicizing had been done to draw the crowds to hear him when he visited some distant church, and when his assistant remonstrated on these lines he murmured : 'People ought to come to church to worship God, not to hear me preach.' There was frequently confusion until the last minute before a service about who was to be the preacher. Mr. Kayll recalls more than one occasion when there was a heated argument between the Vicar and his curate in the procession from the vestry to the chancel about which of them was to deliver the sermon at the service just beginning.

[2] For this and much of the information in this chapter I am indebted to the Revd. A. G. Kayll who took great trouble in sending me his recollections.

Father Waggett had not been a beneficed priest before and so, in spite of his immensely varied experience in many directions, he had not been through the pressures and frictions of an incumbent in the day to day dealings with his people and the parochial machinery. He avoided, however, many of the obvious mistakes. For instance, being a Cowley Father, one would have expected him to think it right to introduce a Sung Eucharist as the principal act of worship on a Sunday morning; but he thought it best not to disturb the evangelical tradition of the parish and continued the old-fashioned Matins and sermon. There were almost no troubles of a ritualistic nature and it is significant that when his successor suggested moving the large crucifix which Waggett placed on the pillar behind the pulpit Dr. Roderick— a churchwarden in the fine old evangelical tradition—resisted the proposal most stoutly. The crucifix remains in position to this day.

But Waggett was not at his best in dealing with Parochial Church Councils and with the intricacies of parish finances. He had that strong sense of humour which frequently produces outrageous remarks for fun, and this had the result of profoundly puzzling some of his church councillors and causing many embarrassing situations. He several times sent his curate to speak to some member of the congregation whom he thought that he had offended by giving them insufficient attention at a time when his mind was occupied with some quite different matter. He hurt the feelings of his simpler parishioners occasionally, quite unintentionally, and was very sorry indeed when he learned that he had done so.

At the beginning of his incumbency of Great St. Mary's Father Waggett lived at 15 Trinity Street, there being no official benefice residence. About September 1927 he moved to 33 Millington Road where he stayed until March 1928; then for the rest of his time he rented a house in Park Street. At this last house the Revd. A. G. Kayll recalls that Waggett used to receive many distinguished and interesting visitors : among them T. E. Shaw (Lawrence of Arabia) to whom Waggett was able to give advice from his experience of the Middle East, and Father Vernon of the Society of the Divine Compassion who had many long discussions with Waggett before deciding to join the Church of Rome—very much to Waggett's disappointment.

Waggett was suffering from ill health at this period probably a great deal more than either he or his friends realized. He was frequently in moods of depression and suffering from high blood pressure which at times made him irascible and difficult to live with. It has already been noted that his institution to the living had to be postponed because of his being unwell; and later the same thing happened when he was pledged to deliver a University Sermon. His inability to find a real *rapport* with the undergraduate mind of that era may also be rightly traced to this cause. The strongest religious movement in Cambridge at this time was the Inter-Collegiate Christian Union—an undenominational organization—and Waggett appeared to make little effort to sympathize with its aims. Another thing was that he felt that he was an Oxford man finding difficulty in adapting himself to the Cambridge way of looking at things. He is reported to have said on one occasion : 'The difference between Oxford and Cambridge is this—whereas an Oxford man deals lightly and interestingly with seven or eight subjects in one sermon, a Cambridge man will take one subject alone and deal with it from every possible angle until it and his congregation are exhausted.' Cambridge, perhaps partly because of its penchant towards science, was not tolerant of cranks at this period. Waggett was not a crank, but he was a genius whom Cambridge perhaps suspected of being a crank. The unfamiliarity of the sight of a religious habit in the streets of Cambridge probably did not help.

In spite of all these difficulties Waggett at this time retained the power of making those who worked with him to be devoted to him. Mr. Kayll remarks : 'He had a real gift of making those who worked with him love him, though at times they might be terrified of him.' And he adds—'To see him striding along a crowded Petty Cury holding an animated conversation with two or three people separated from him by some distance because of the crowd was a sight never to be forgotten.'

The following letter to his niece (Mrs. Robert Aitken), dated 30th July 1927, apart from the impression of days as busy as ever, gives some idea of the demands which parish work and organizations were making upon him :

'Though it is now Saturday night and almost Sunday morning I had better *not* wait for a more favourable time to thank you for your *lovely* poem. This last week or more has been a lost week in letter writing except for the innumerable letters my dear Miss Pate opposite has taken down for me . . . But your dear gift came more than a week ago. I have been putting it by, because I wished to write in this disgraceful hand instead of "dictating." I think I must put a notice in the paper to say that "typing" means *no* lessening of love and joy. Otherwise—as things are—the more I love people, the longer they wait for an answer to their prized communications. As for the great of the Earth, they never get any answer at all . . .

'This place, which was proposed to me as a rest, is the most exacting parish in the world with more treats, mothers' meetings, trustees' meetings and confabulations than I could have supposed possible. "I have been in Savoy," as my papa used to say, but "Journeys end in mothers' meetings." Oh! for the academic repose of Tabard Street.

'But we shall yet some day, after this changing life is ended, take root downward and bear fruit upward. *Not* here and now. Meanwhile you, my dear, must see to it that the Waggetteian genius for *not* playing the cards does not prevent *you* from setting on paper and sending to the world what you have stored up. Our Waggetteian idea when we have a good hand is to put it in our pockets and resign. Far from an extra ace up our sleeves to be *produced* for gain, we conceal the aces fate has actually dealt us; I think *you* should do better than this . . .'

The reader must deduce for himself whether, or not, this talk of aces not played was meant to have any reference to his present position and opportunities at Cambridge. His powers, though, had gone beyond their zenith and parish priests and others in Cambridge at that time tell sad stories of his forgetting appointments to give addresses, conduct Quiet Afternoons and so forth; hosts and hostesses recall his failure to appear when he had accepted invitations to luncheon. It is significant that the first reference to him in *The Granta*—the best known undergraduate magazine—after his return to Cambridge was the following in the 'Motley Notes':

'WHY DIDN'T FATHER WAGGETT . . .

a bit faster? And who was late with his manuscript of his 'Varsity Sermon for the *Cambridge Review*? Naughty! (*The Granta*, 17th February 1928).

This does not mean that he was unable sometimes, perhaps frequently, still to show remarkable flashes of brilliance and to draw forth responses from his audiences in the most adverse circumstances. The Revd. Leslie Arnold O.G.S., now Vicar of Cowley St. John, Oxford, recalls a remarkable instance of this at the end of this year, 1927. The scene was in Brighton on a sleepy December afternoon of that year when one of Waggett's Advent exercises was to give some addresses to young men from Cambridge who had volunteered to take part in the 'World Call Campaign.' A group of these undergraduates was being commissioned to preach in the churches of Brighton on missionary work abroad, and the team included Gilbert Harding (the late famous B.B.C. entertainer), Douglas Horsley (later Bishop of Colombo and Gibraltar), Gilbert Jessop, Kenneth Macbeth (later of the Oxford Mission to Calcutta) and Leslie Arnold; and these young men were assembled in the choir stalls of the church of St. John, Preston, Brighton. As his address, intended to inspire them to interest in—if not committal to—apostolic labour abroad, proceeded, Father Waggett perceived that his auditory were becoming slightly somnolent. Thereupon he changed the pace and tone of his discourse and interjected briskly—'Of course as you go round to these churches preaching to the people about missions you will find that the best way to set about it is not to try to *teach* them anything but to *draw them out*: just like that machine we used to use in the "labs"—the WIMSHURST Machine—from which we used to draw out sparks—CRACKLE! CRACKLE!' He left his chair on the sanctuary step saying this word 'Crackle' sharply right into the face of each member of his congregation, snapping his fingers under their noses as he did so—thus jerking them back into consciousness from the slumbers into which they were involuntarily subsiding—and then resumed. Waggett was still Waggett even though at Cambridge, apparently, his sparks did not now fly so well.

He was booked to preach the University Sermon on 6th May 1928, but was not well enough when the day came to carry out the task. His sermons during his tenure of office as Vicar of the University Church did not, apparently, find their way into the *Cambridge Review* and it is remarkable how rarely his name appears in the annals of the University at this time.[3]

The Revd. H. S. Hutchinson, Rector of Cranham, Gloucestershire, recalls that in October 1929 he attended a retreat at Ely Theological College conducted by Waggett, who 'entered the

---

[3] Mr. Kayll attributes this to Waggett's unwillingness to send in notes of his speeches, etc. See pp. 205–8 *supra*.

chapel for the first address, wearing the "Mona Lisa" smile which he reserved for his less regenerate occasions and began the retreat by remarking : "I have just conducted a retreat for a lot of diocesan bishops. One of the poor darlings said to me, 'I think we shall save the Church of England, but only just!' I said to him, 'My Lord, I have no use for a Church which I have got to save, I expect it to save me and you.' " '

Mr. Hutchinson also records that some time later Waggett went to Nottingham at his request and addressed a meeting of the Mechanics Institute on 'Church and State.' The audience was disappointing in the extreme, though the address was humorous and profound with a good deal of side play in twitting the reporters at the Press Table. Next morning there was little or nothing about the meeting in the local papers, but Father Waggett scanned the *Nottingham Guardian* eagerly and his eye fell on the chance headline 'Sleeping Woman Gassed.' 'What a gorgeous description of the Church of England!' he remarked, 'I bet that is a report of my speech!'

But Mr. Hutchinson also remembers more valuable utterances by the conductor of the retreat at Ely. In his notebook he finds the following written down during one of Father Waggett's addresses :

'A few years ago I was dining with Armitage Robinson when he was Dean of Westminster. After dinner Armitage said, "We will now go and see the Abbey." I don't know if there were such things as electric torches in those days, but if there were deans did not have them. We crept along the dark cloister and, reaching the door, the dean fumbled with his keys and we went inside. There he pulled a candle out of his pocket and, lighting a match, lit the candle. At first we could see nothing, but as our eyes grew accustomed to the light we saw the Abbey as I have never seen it before or since—the grace of the pillars, the vast masses of moving shadow. Our Lord is the Light of the World, not a glaring light which destroys all mystery : His light is like the light of a candle, and first our eyes must grow accustomed to the darkness. A sense of darkness must always both precede and accompany a sense of light. It was worthwhile for the Children of Israel to be lost in the wilderness when they had a Pillar of Fire to lead them out; it was worthwhile for the Wise Men to cross the desert at night when they had the star to lead them to the Incarnate Lord. If you have not a sense of God's presence thank Heaven you have got a sense of His absence : the only desperate people are those who have no sense of darkness at all— they are so blind that they don't even know that they can't see.'

Another dictum of Waggett's on this subject of light which

Mr. Hutchinson sends was repeated years later by Bishop Blunt of Bradford in a speech in the Convocation of York:

'The Unity of the Church is like the unity of the light of a candle. The nearer you are to its centre the more you can see; but you can never draw a circumference round it and say "Inside this circumference is light and outside it is darkness." '

Bishop Blunt repeated this in a critique of a Church Union pamphlet on Unity which regarded the unity of the Church as being like the unity of a closed box. Modern ecclesiology, even that of several Roman Catholic scholars, has brought out again the wisdom in Father Waggett's illustration for this matter. Father Waggett added in his Ely retreat address:

'No amount of darkness can put out the feeblest light, darkness is powerless against it. That is what St. John meant in his prologue, and when I say the Last Gospel at Mass I always read the words "The darkness *overwhelmed* it not." '

One more note from the Revd. H. S. Hutchinson's retreat note-book must be preserved as a memorial of Waggett's Catholic Evangelicalism. It is a note on the Sacrifice of the Mass:

'The greatest need of the Church to-day is for old-fashioned Evangelicals who will talk to us about the Atonement. In the Mass we tell God what Jesus did, and there is no better expression of exactly what we mean by the sacrifice of the Mass than the hymn "Rock of Ages":

> "Nothing in my hand I bring,
> Simply to Thy Cross I cling;
> Naked, come to Thee for dress;
> Helpless, look to Thee for grace;
> Foul, I to the Fountain fly;
> Wash me, Saviour, or I die." '

As his years advanced Father Waggett was increasingly given to the habit of 'thinking aloud' in public, occasionally to the embarrassment of the company in which he was; but more often this foible charmed and delighted his neighbours as a characteristic of his brilliant personality which remained in their memories for years. On one occasion he was reading during a meal in the refectory at Cowley and one of the guests present was taking a great time to finish his repast, so that Waggett was obliged to continue reading at a time when he felt particularly in need of his lunch. He muttered in clearly audible tones as he had to embark upon yet another chapter of the book, 'I do wish that guest would hurry up' and then resumed the narrative completely unconscious of what he had done. A present member of the Society recalls. 'We were all quite shattered!'

Father Pridham, s.s.j.e., remembers that on another occasion —probably at about this period—it was his (Father Pridham's) lot to be reading from the *Imitation of Christ* aloud at breakfast one Sunday morning when Father Waggett was to preach later at High Mass in the Society's church. As the reader came to the lines, 'A certain one hath said "As oft as I have been among men, I returned home less a man than I was before," ' [4] he observed a twinkle of acute observation on Waggett's face—which, of course, could not find further expression at that moment. However, in the pulpit an hour or so later came the first chance to speak his comment and out it came : Father Waggett first said, 'Darling Thomas, didn't you know that you were quoting a heathen philosopher?' and then he spoke his text and proceeded with the usual absorbing sermon.

Father Waggett was particularly fierce at all times of his life with members of a congregation who were ill mannered enough to look at their watches while he was preaching. At a church in the north of England towards the end of his ministry someone did this and Waggett stopped his discourse immediately, the congregation waiting in a heavy silence; then, after a pause, he said, 'In deference to the gentleman with the watch I shall close my sermon'—and he did. The author has received accounts of almost exactly this occurrence from other parts of the country and also from South Africa and India.

In August 1929 Waggett suffered some slight seizure which incapacitated him for a fortnight, but it was hoped this was a mere passing symptom from which he would soon recover. However, two months later, at the end of October when he was preaching at All Saints', Margaret Street, London, he suddenly began to be incoherent in his speech. It was the beginning of a toxic stroke —the immediate cause was thought to be poisoning from a decayed tooth—and he was very soon to be paralysed from the waist downwards. Expression was impossible for a time and for the rest of his life difficult.[5] He was quickly taken to the Mission

[4] *Imitation,* Book I, Ch. XX.
[5] Mrs. Robert Aitken writes this note: 'If eloquence and popularity and distinguished company had been what made him less than saintly, those last years perfected him!'

House at Oxford, where he stayed for some weeks. He returned to Cambridge in January 1930, but it was not long before he had to lay down his work and resign his appointment as Vicar of Great St. Mary's. Yet he was to linger in this world for nearly nine years more. He was at Oxford for the first six years after the stroke: then in 1936 he was taken to Parkstone to be with his sisters Katharine and Marian, and finally he went to a nursing home close at hand.

Still during the last years of his final physical infirmity Father Waggett's brain was active, though it seemed to be working behind a screen. He used to be wheeled in a chair into the Society's church for the Sunday High Mass, and at other times 'a few old friends would come to see him and talk to him of Charterhouse and tell him its most recent news which he loved to hear.' [6] He took great delight in being wheeled into the Iffley Road to see the traffic. Father Adams, s.s.j.e., spent many hours reading aloud to him and has recalled the great gratitude and affection which Father Waggett expressed for these kindnesses.

When he was moved to Parkstone he was chiefly in the devoted hands of his sisters; but both they and his niece, Mrs. Robert Aitken, wished to place on record their undying debt to the skilled nursing of Mrs. Mynors-Wallis under whose care he recovered for a time much of his capacity to speak. Those who remember his last months say that through all the deprivations of his outer life his inner attachment to his vocation seemed to become ever deeper and firmer; those who waited on him were astonished at his thoughtfulness and at the sympathy with which he entered into their concerns. A few days before his death the owners of the nursing home brought to him their newly baptized daughter and Father Waggett gave the babe a wonderful blessing. This was the last outward act of his ministry.

Philip Napier Waggett had been a priest for more than half a century and a religious for forty-four years. He received the Last Sacraments at the hands of the Vicar of St. Peter's, Parkstone, and he died in the closing hours of 4th July 1939. His body was brought to Oxford and was laid in the Cowley Fathers' burial ground in the churchyard of the parish church of Cowley St. John,

[6] Private letter from Father Adams, s.s.j.e.

next to the grave of the Father Founder, Richard Meux Benson.

Soon after his death the Bishop of London, Dr. Winnington Ingram, wrote to Waggett's two sisters :

'So the dear brother has been taken at last. I can't be sorry. He is his own dear self again now. You *have* been good sisters. I am glad he was allowed to die with you. God rest his soul.'

Ernest had died in January of the same year; Katharine nursed Marian to her end in 1940 and she herself also departed in that year.

LIST OF PUBLICATIONS

A—WHOLLY BY P.N.W.

1901

The Age of Decision (five sermons to young men preached in St. Giles' Church, Cambridge, with an introductory essay and a sermon preached at Charterhouse on Founders' Day, 1900). Longmans.

The Holy Eucharist, an address. Oxford (printed for private circulation).

1902

The Heart of Jesus. Addresses given in St. Paul's Cathedral. S.P.C.K.

Is There a Religion of Nature? Lectures in St. Paul's Cathedral. S.P.C.K.

Science and Faith. An address. (Pusey House Occasional Papers No. 3.) Longmans.

Science and Conduct. An address. (Pusey House Occasional Papers No. 4.) Longmans.

1903

About Modern Thought and Christian Belief. An address. (Faith and Freedom Press Pamphlets.) S. C. Brown, Langham & Co., Ltd.

1904

Religion and Science. (Handbooks for the Clergy, ed. A. W. Robinson.) Longmans.

1905

The Scientific Temper in Religion. Addresses, including *About Modern Thought and Christian Belief* (above). Longmans.

1906

The Holy Eucharist with other occasional papers, including the paper of the same title (above) and *The Manifold Unity of Christian Life* (*J.T.S.* article in list below.) John Murray.

1907

Hope and Strength. Addresses. Longmans.

1912

Our Profession. Lent and Easter sermons 1912. Longmans.

1924

Knowledge and Virtue. Hulsean Lectures, Cambridge, 1920–1. Clarendon Press.

1925

The Industry of Faith. Mowbray.

B—CONTRIBUTIONS TO JOURNALS AND TO COLLECTIVE
WORKS

1900

'Church Affairs in South Africa' in *Journal of Theological Studies*, Vol. I.
'Evolution and the Fall of Man' (reflections on Bishop Gore's note in his volume on the *Epistle to the Romans*) in *The Pilot*, Vol. I, p. 475.

1902

'The Manifold Unity of Christian Life' in *J.T.S.*, Vol. III.
Review of Mr. Hobhouse's *Diversions*, in *The Pilot*, Vol. V, p. 523.

1903

'Darwin and his readers' (review of *More Letters of Charles Darwin*, ed. F. Darwin and A. C. Seward, 1903) in *The Pilot*, Vol. VIII, p. 414.
'Darwin and his Interpreters,' in *The Pilot*, Vol. VIII, p. 450.

1904

'The Church as Seen from Outside' in *Ideals of Science and Faith*, ed. J. E. Hand. George Allen.

1905

'Henry Parry Liddon' in *The Churchman* (New York), 10th June 1905.

1906

Three sermons in *Churchmanship and Labour*, ed. W. Henry Hunt. Skeffington.

1908

Two sermons in *Mission Preaching for a Year*, Part II, ed. W. Henry Hunt. Skeffington.

1909

'The Influence of Darwin upon Religious Thought' in *Darwin and Modern Science*, ed. A. C. Seward. Cambridge University Press.

1913

Article on 'Heredity' in *Encyclopædia of Religion and Ethics*, ed. James Hastings. T. & T. Clark.

1918

Article on 'The New Palestine' in *The Manchester Guardian*, 27th November.
(Also many unsigned articles and reviews in *The Guardian* during these years and later.)

C—INTRODUCTIONS TO, AND TRANSLATIONS FROM, WORKS
OF OTHER WRITERS

1901

Introductory essay to *The House of Wisdom and Love* by M. E. Dowson. S.P.C.K.

Preface to *Meditations on the Life and Teaching of Jesus Christ* by G. B. Budibent. Mowbray.

Preface to *Pilgrim Songs*—meditations collected chiefly from addresses by H. Montagu Villiers, by Evelyn Villiers. Mowbrays.

Preface to *Ascensiones in Corde,* a translation of Cardinal Bona's *Via Compendii ad Deum.* Mowbray.

Preface to *Guide to True Holiness* by Paul Huguet (Marist Father), trans. Agnes C. Fisher. Mowbrays.

Introduction to *The Mystical Personality of the Church* by R. de Bary. Longmans.

Preface to *Letters from Ludd* by 'Captain R.A.M.C.' S.P.C.K.

Preface to *The Mind's Ascent to God* by St. Robert Bellarmino (trans.). Mowbray.

Translation of *Lectures on the Holy Eucharist* by Jean F. A. T. Landriot, Bishop of La Rochelle and Saintes, later Archbishop of Rheims. Faith Press.

INDEX

Abel, Père, 147
Abyssinian monastery, 155
Acland, Alfred, 138
Adams, Fr. 213
Adderley, Revd. James, 21, 24, 77, 137
Adderley, Revd. R. E., 28
Aitken, Mrs. R., 12, 175, 207, 212
Alexandria, 171
All Hallows' Sisters, 79
All Saints' Sisters, 57, 63, 84, 95, 102, 106
All Saints', Margaret St., 116, 212
Allahabad, 170
Allenby, Gen., 142
Anglo-Catholic Congress, 172, 201
Anglo-Catholic Convention, 168
Anson, Revd. H., 30
Appin, Port, 196
Archer-Hind, R. D., 109
Argyll and the Isles, Bishop of, 75
Argyll, Duke of, 197
Aristotelian Society, 33, 42
Arkle, Miss G., 115
Armenians, 147ff., 199
Armistice Day, 175
Arnold, Revd. Leslie, 12, 208
Aquel, Père Alexius, 146

Balfour, A. J., 105
Balliol College, 86, 105
Balliol College, Master of, 193
Baptism, doctrine of, 94
Baynes, N. H., 194
Beauty, 42
Bechuanaland, 68
Bedford, Duchess of, 82, 102
Bell, Canon C. C., 30
Belloc, H., 204
Benecke, P. V. M., 193
Benson, Dr. A. C., 125f., 134, 166
Benson, Fr. R. M., 11, 49, 83, 87, 214
Bethlehem, 143, 145

Bible Society, 171
Biblical Criticism, 22, 91
Biology, 204
Birrell, Augustine, 102
Bloemfontein, Bishop of, 67, 75
Blomfield, Bishop, 25
Blunt, Bishop, 210
Blythe, Miss, 65
Bodley, 197
Bombay, 170
Bosco, Don, 55
Bouillon, Godfrey de, 142
Brandreth, Revd. H. R. T., 111
'Brethren, The,' 110
Bridges, Robert, 140
Bright, Dr. J. F., 64
Brightman, Dr. F. E., 24, 193, 199
British Association, 196
British Medical Journal, 17
Brocklebank, Edward, 103
Brown, Dr. Haig, 18
Bryan-Brown, Mr. A. N., 14
Bulawayo, 98
Bull, Fr. H. P., 137
Burn, Dean, 193
Burton, Fr. Spence, 11
Burke, 44
Byron, Harriett B., 84

C.I.C.C.U., 204, 207
Calcutta, 170
Callaway, Fr. 64
Cambridge, 79, 103, 108ff.
Cambridge Pastorate, 109
Cambridge Review, 103
Cape Times, 67
Capetown, 57ff.
    mission work in, 66
Capetown, Archbishop of, 68, 74, 85
Carmelite Fathers, 97
Carthusians, Old, 37
Cary, Fr. Lucius, 80, 162, 164
Catechism, 198

Catholic Movement in Cambridge, 109
Cawnpore, 170
Cecil, Lord Hugh, 95, 102
Ceremonial, 114
Chadlington, 197
Champneys, Revd. M., 12, 111
Chaplain, P. N. W. as, 136, 138
Chapman, Abbot J., 30
Charlbury, 197
Charterhouse, 18, 45, 80
Charterhouse Mission, 34ff., 97, 189
Chester, 106
Chesterton, G. K., 105, 126, 167, 204
Chetwode, Gen., 146
Chinnery-Haldane, Bishop, 74
Christ Church, Oxford, 20ff.
Christ Church Mission, 25ff.
Christian, Prince and Princess, 16, 37
Christian Social Union, 23
Church Chronicle, 98
Church Congress, 122
Church of England Newspaper, 141
Church and State, 210
Church Times, 34, 161, 196
Church Union, The, 192
Churchman, 39
Clark, Mr. and Mrs., 166
Clayton, Gen., 156
Cleaver Trust, 197
Clifford, Edward, 101
Cock, Prof., 191
Coenaculum, 157ff.
Commonwealth, 76
Confirmation, 134
Congreve, Fr., 69, 101
Congreve, Gen., 127
Congreve, William, 105
Conran, Fr., 58, 192
Constantine, 158
Convocation, 169, 196
Copts, 143
Couturier, Fr. Felix, 147
Cowley Evangelist, 52, 59 *et passim*
Cowley Fathers, see S.S.J.E.
Cowley, St. Mary and St. John's, 57
Cowley, Wantage and All Saints' Mission, 193
Cross, Dr. F. L., 12, 119

Cuddesdon College, 23, 79, 102
Cust, Col. Sir A., 12, 161, 167
Custos, Franciscan, 143

Daish, Mr. T., 126
Dalby, Fr., 12
Damianos, Archbishop, 160
Dark, Sidney, 9
Darwin, Charles, 9, 29, 55, 107, 112
Darwinian biology, 22
David, Tomb of, 157
Davidson, Archbishop, 36, 188
Dearmer, Dr. Percy, 200
Death, sermon on, 115
Denys, St., 76f.
Dependance, sermon on, 175
Despatches, P.N.W. mentioned in, 140
Diney, Dr., 95
Dispensary at Capetown, work of, 58f.
Dominicans, 146
Douglass, Revd. F., 30, 204
Dublin, Trinity College, 95
Duncan-Jones, Prof. A., 12, 204
Duncan-Jones, Mrs. A. S., 147
Dundas, Archdeacon, 193
Dutch in South Africa, 71

Easter, P.N.W. on, 167f.
Eastern Churches, problem of, 163
Edinburgh, 96, 102
Edward VI, 193
Egyptian Expeditionary Force, 141
Ely, Bishop of, 203
Ely Theological College, 209
English Church, principles of, 81
English Church Union, 108
Eton, 96, 105
Eucharist, the, 201, 205
Eurasians, 171
Exeter, Bishop of, 193

Farmiloe, Archdeacon, 193
Ferguson, Sir W., 15
Fleming, Sir Alexander, 191
France, 130ff.
Francis I, 142
Franciscans, the, 143, 159
Freire-Marreco, Mr. G., 12
Front, P.N.W. at the, 131
Fulham Palace, 102

G.H.Q. in France, 135
Gaselee, Sir Stephen, 126
Gaspari, Cardinal, 152
George III, 158
George V, 158
Gibson, Bishop, 65
Gladstone, Mr. 39, 42
Glasgow Art Gallery, 197
Godley, Dr. A. D., 11
Goethe, 44
Goodhart, Harry, 109, 125
Goodness of God, P.N.W. on, 179
Gore, Bishop, 22, 23, 49, 84, 95,
    105
Gosse, Edmund, 33
Granta, 208
Gregorian Society, 194
Grosvenor, Countess, 83, 193
Guards, Brigade of, 130
Guardian, 42, 54, 77

Haldane, Lord, 105
Halifax, Lord, 77f., 83, 101, 192,
    197
Harding, Gilbert, 209
Hawarden, 194
Head, Dr. H., 106
Hegelian philosophy, 22
Help, Mission of, 169
Henson, Bishop Hensley, 108
Heredity, 103f., 124, 166
Hicks, Bishop J. W., 75
Hill, Fr., 12
Hill, H. W., 108
Hine, Bishop, 187
Hoar Cross, 197
Holford Exhibition, 20
Holidays, 27, 32, 95, 124
Hollings, Fr., 80
Holy Name Sisters, 86
'Holy Party,' 22
Holy Places, 143, 145f., 153
Horsley, Bishop, 209
Hospitals in France, 130, 134
How, Bishop J. C. H., 12, 109,
    111, 165
How, Bishop Walsham, 25
Howard, C. H., 199
Hulsean Lectures, 24, 124, 161ff.,
    165
Hutchinson, Revd., H. S., 209
Huvelin, Abbé, 169
Huxley, T. H., 55

Illingworth, Dr., 22
Illness (P.N.W.), 32, 45, 74, 97,
    112, 137, 207
Imitation of Christ, The, 212
India
    Metropolitan of, 58, 170
    Mission of Help to, 169ff.
    S.S.J.E. in, 57
Inebriates, Home for, 69
Inverary, 197
Iona, 74, 78, 85
Irwin, Lord, 192
Italy, King of, 157

Jackson, Bishop, 25
Jacobi, 43
James, William, 122
Jellicoe, Fr. Basil, 192, 198
Jenner, Sir William, 15
Jerusalem, 142
    Commission in, 149ff.
    East Mission, and the, 197
Jessop, Gilbert, 209
Jesus College, 200
Johannesburg, 63, 73, 100
Johnston, J. O., 39
Journal of Theological Studies, 70,
    76, 87, 95

Kafirs, baptism of, 61
Kafir conditions, 63, 66f., 125
Kayll, Revd. A. G., 12, 205ff.
Keble College, 78
Key, Bishop, 65
Khartoum, Bishop of, 135
Kidd, Dr. 198
Kimberley, 63, 73, 100
King's College, London, 105, 199
King's College Hospital, 166
King William's Town, 63
Knebworth, 196
Knebworth, Viscount, 185
Knowledge of God, P.N.W. on,
    172ff.
Knox, Revd. W. L., 111

Lambeth Report, 67
Lancing, Provost of, 198
Landriot, Archbishop, 200
Latter, Mr. O. H., 18, 45
Lawrence of Arabia, 206
League of Nations, 159

Lectures to
  Chaplains, 125
  Troops, 145
Leicester, Archdeacon of, 193
Lent, 28
Lent lectures, 114f., 165f.
Lepers, 62
Leslie, Alan, 115, 197
Ley, Fr., 65
Liberal Catholicism, 110
Liddon, Canon H. P., 22, 39
Liston, Robert, 15
Liverpool, 165
  Bishop of, 193
Lodge, Sir Oliver, 105, 196
London, Bishop of, 80, 83, 134
London Docks, 31
Longridge, Fr., 114
Longworth, 22
Lord's Prayer, P.N.W. on, 137
Lothian, Lord, 75
Lovell, Prof., 89
Lubbock, Percy, 125, 134, 166
Lux Mundi, 23, 42
Lyall, Sir K., 106
Lyttleton, Hon. Alfred, 105
Lytton, Earl of, 185

Macbeth, Kenneth, 209
McInnes, Bishop Rennie, 146
Mackay, Preb., 168, 197
Mackonochie, Fr., 194
Madras, 171
Magdalene Mission, 192
Malays in South Africa, 60f.
Man, doctrine of, P.N.W. on, 173ff.
Manchester, 103
Manchester Guardian, 148
Manning, Cardinal, 37
Maples, Bishop Chauncey, 187
Marlowe, John, 142
Marriott bequest, 68
Maryon-Wilson, Revd. Sir Percy, 198
Masasi, Bishop of, 198
Mason, Dr. A. J., 79, 103, 108
Mass, the, P.N.W. on, 211
Maturin, Fr., 53
Maurice, F. D., 39
Maxwell, Fr., 136
Medical Society, U.S., 16
Medicine, Royal College of, 18
Merry del Val, Alphonso, 156

Meyerbeer, 194
Meynell family, 197
Missions, P.N.W. on, 72ff.
Mohammedans, 60
Money, Gen. Sir Arthur, 12, 192
Moore, Aubrey, 22, 38
Moseley, Prof., 20
Mufti, Grand, 146
Museum, South Kensington, 198
Music, P.N.W. on, 194
Mynors-Wallis, Mrs., 213
Mystics, the, 76, 92ff.

National Society, 102
Nativity, Basilica of, 143
Nebi Musa (Moslem feast), 144
New York, 178
Newcastle-on-Tyne, 175
Newman, Cardinal, article on, 117
Newton Green, 193
Non-jurors, 16
Nottingham Guardian, 210
Nyasaland, Bishop of, 198

Oban, 196
O'Brien, Fr., 11, 12, 47
Oratory of the Good Shepherd, 111
Oriel College, 198
Ormsby-Gore, Major W. G. A., 146
Orphanage, Boys', 197
Orthodox Church, 144, 162ff.
Osborne, Fr., 57
Otley, Canon, 192
Ottoman Empire, 142
Oxford
  Doctorate, 163
  Movement, 22
  P.N.W. at, 20ff.

Page, Fr., 50, 57ff., 74, 116
Paget, Mrs. E. K., 25
Paget, Bishop Francis, 22, 54, 84, 115
Paget, Sir James, 25, 33
Paget, Bishop Luke, 25, 29, 30, 38, 102, 194
Paget, Stephen, 21, 24
Pain, P.N.W. on, 75f.
Palestine, 141ff.
  Administration of, 148f.
  Exploration Society, 192
  Mandate, 153, 159

Palmer, Dr., 194
Parkstone, 196, 200
Pass, Canon Leonard, 109, 113
Passover, 144
Pasteur, Louis, 33f.
Pate, Miss 208
Patriarch
  Armenian, 143
  Latin, 143, 159
  Orthodox, 143, 160
Patriarchate
  Greek Catholic, 146
  Jerusalem, Commission on, 161
Pellatt, Miss, 58f.
Peters, Prof., 198
Pilot, 80
Plainsong, 53, 194f.
Poems, 51f.
Ponsonby, 96, 197
Poona, 170
Poor Law, 38
Poplar, Christ Church Mission, 24
Poverello, the, 48
Powell, Canon Hulbert, 127
Prayer, P.N.W. on, 183
Prestige, Dr. G. L., 49, 193
Pretoria, 100
Pridham, Fr. 212
Prince of Wales, 133
Prisoners of War, 139
Proctor in Convocation, P.N.W.,
  169
Progress, P.N.W. on, 98
Protector, the Lord, 193
Protectorate, French, 142f.
Publications of P.N.W. See list,
  page 215
Puller, Fr. 50, 57, 187
Pusey, Dr., 22
Pusey House, 23

Quadi, Moslem, 143
Queen's Hall, 201

Radley, 198
R.A.M.C., 16f.
Rashdall, Dr. Hastings, 102, 105
Red Cross, 146
Renaissance, 48
Restoration, P.N.W. on, 180f.
  Resurrection, Community of the, 49

Retreats, Association for Promoting,
  198
Reynolds, Sir Joshua, 44
Rhodesia, 71, 99
Richardson, Bishop, 187
Richmond, Ernest, 144
Robben Island, 62
Robert of Anjou, 158
Robinson, Dean Armitage, 210
Roderick, Dr., 205
Roman claims, 50
Romanes, George 28ff, 38, 53ff.
Rotary Club, 171
Rowe bequest, 108
Royal Society, tercentenary of, 9
Ruskin, John, 43
Russell, Fr., 186
Russia, 101, 115
Russian
  Church, 144
  Liturgy, 156
Russians in Jerusalem, 153f.

Sadler, Sir Michael, 198
Saighton, 193, 196
St. Alban's
  Duchess of, 105
  Holborn, 119
St. Anselm's House, 109, 112, 166
St. Bartholomew's Hospital, 105f.
St. Columba's Kafir Home, 57
St. Cuthbert, Society of, 64
St. Edward's House, Westminster,
  80ff. *et passim*
St. Francis, 48, 137
St. Frideswide's, Poplar, 24
St. George's Home, Bourdon St., 95
St. Giles'
  Cambridge, 113
  Reading, 199
St. John of the Cross, 123
St. John's
  Bishop of, 64
  Holland Road, 191
  Preston, Brighton, 209
St. Leonard's, 22
St. Mary's
  Great, Cambridge, 103, 203
  Hospital, Paddington, 191
  Primrose Hill, 147
St. Matthew's, Westminster, 79, 83
St. Osmund's, Parkstone, 196
St. Pancras, 30ff.

St. Paul's
  Cathedral, 17, 33, 84
  Chapel, New York, 179f.
St. Peter and St. Paul, Society of, 169
St. Peter's
  Cambridge, 113
  Parkstone, 213
St. Philip and St. James, Oxford, 196
St. Philip's Mission, Capetown, 57, 63
St. Robert Bellarmine, 188
Saladin, 144
Salisbury, Lord, 39
Salisbury, Rhodesia, 100
Samuel, Sir Herbert, 142, 159ff.
Sanday, Dr. William, 86
Sanderson, Dr. 53
Santayana, George, 56
Schopenhauer, 148
Science and Religion, 53, 87ff., 103, 171, 192
Scott, Sir Walter, 136
Scott Holland, Canon, 22ff., 32, 74, 105
Seaton, Dr. E. C., 17
Seebohm, 148
Select Preacher, Oxford and Cambridge, 85
Selwyn College, 166
Selwyn, Dr. E. G., 113
Seminary, General Theological, 178
Sepulchre, Holy, 143, 158
Sermons, 27, 78, 106
Seward, A. C., 55
Seymour, Revd. Lord Victor, 198
Sforza, Count, 158
Simpson, Revd. Mr., 100
Simpson, Revd. F. A., 127
Sion College, 192, 196
Smart, Canon, 100
Smythies, Bishop, 187
Society of Divine Compassion, 206
Society of St. John the Evangelist, 17, 47 et passim
  early history of, 57
South Africa, 56ff.
  Church of, 70f.
  Mission, 95f.
Stanton, Prof. V. H., 137
Steere, Bishop, 187
Stephenson, Gwendolin, 22

Stepney, Bishop of 82f., 101
Stone, Dr. Darwell, 119, 198
Stoneham Park, 191
Storrs, Sir Ronald, 142
Strike, the General, 193
Strong, Bishop T. B., 86
Stubbs, Bishop, 116,
Sultan of Turkey, 142, 158
Summerson, John, 30
Swaythling, Lord, 191
Sykes, Sir Mark, 152
Symbol, 118
Synthetic Society, 105, 167

Talbot, Bishop, 22, 105
Temple, Bishop F., 23, 26
Temple, William, 105
'T.F.F.,' 141, 145
Thomson, Prof. J. J., 103
Thorold, Bishop, 34, 49
Thwaites, William, 64
Tidworth, 140
Tilley, Mr. H., 18
Tractarians, 22
Travers, Canon, 186
Trenholme, Fr., 192
Trinity College, Cambridge, 113, 203
Trinity, doctrine of, 93
Tsolo, St. Cuthbert's, 64
Turks, 143
Turner, Prof., 199
Tyrrell, Fr. George, 110

U.M.C.A., 186, 198
Umtata, 63ff.
Underhill, Evelyn, 93
University
  Church, Cambridge, 106
  College, London, 106
  College, Southampton, 191
  sermon, 103, 209

Vernon, Fr., 206
Vidler, Dr. A. R., 111
Vincent, Revd. G. H., 30
Vyvyan, Bishop, 46

Wadham College, 95

Waggett
  E. B., 16, 30, 38
  Mrs. F. B., 16, 86
  Florence, 17
  Dr. J., 15, 38, 112
  J. F., 16
  Judith, 77
  Katherine, 17, 26 *et passim*
  Marian, 17
  P.N.W., See Cursus Vitae
Wagner, 196
Wallis, Fr., 64
Wantage, Lady, 105
War, P.N.W. on, 127
Ward
  Maisie, 126
  Wilfred, 105, 117
Watkins, Revd. W. U., 62, 100
Webb, Mr. H. F., 100
Weissmann, 53
Weizmann, Dr., 146
Welldon, Bishop, 85
West Jones, Archbishop, 68
Westcliff, 199
Westminster
  Abbey, 86, 210
  Dean of, 106
  Hospital, 85

Weston, Bishop Frank, 186, 199
Whitsun Preface, sermon on, 119
Wilberforce, 39
Winckelman, Abbé, 44
Winnington-Ingram, Bishop, 214
Witton-Davies, Ven. C., 12
Women's Help Society, 37
Wood, Canon E. G., 110
Woodgate, M. V., 49
Woolwich Garrison Church, 97
Worcester, 95, 192
  Dean of, 204
World, Christian view of, 201ff.
Wounded, P.N.W. and the, 132
Wright
  Sir Almroth, 191
  Gen., 191
Wyndham, George, 105

York, Archbishop of, 198
Young, Francis Brett, 140
Younghusband, Sir Francis, 102

Zionists, 146